1

Sun Tzu and the Art of Litigation
Tipping the Scales of Justice in your client's favour

First published in the USA 2012. Protected by US and other copyrights.

ISBN-13: 978-1479136902

ISBN-10: 1479136905

Contact: Nigel Morris-Cotterill : via www.antimoneylaundering.net

All trademarks and copyrights are acknowledged.

CAVEAT:

Nothing in this book is or is intended to be legal advice. All persons are cautioned to take appropriate advice from competent professional advisers in their jurisdiction. No liability shall attach to the author or the publisher for reliance on anything in this work. .

Introduction

Litigation is a blood sport, a gladiatorial contest.

Each side names its champions who are ordered to fight to the death. The champions, outside the case, may be friends or, at least not hostile to each other. In the combat arena, they are bound, by contract, custom and professional etiquette, to use all means - within the bounds of the law, the Rules of Court and professional conduct - to achieve the best result possible for their client.

There are those that argue that the conduct of litigation should be cosy, almost a team effort between opposing champions, that the hard litigator is a dinosaur. True litigators like those that adopt that position. They are easy meat.

Litigation is brutal. But it is also full of finesse and strategy. It is as much a mind game as a fight game.

The successful litigator takes care to understand his opponent, he knows what weapons to use and when. He also knows when to release some of the pressure. A full-on assault takes energy. There are often times when a litigator knows that he has an advantage and offers his opponent the opportunity to surrender.

Litigation is war. It is ridiculous when litigators address their letters to their opponents to "Dear Andrew" or "Dear Steve." Are they litigating or arranging a date? It is essential, right from the outset, to intimidate one's opponent and, because his client will see the correspondence, your client's opponent. Put simply, outside the confines of the case, then be as chummy as you like. In the conduct of litigation, always, always be prepared to attack or defend as the circumstances require. And let your client see that you are his champion.

Litigation is as much, if not more than, an art as it is a skill. While technical ability is important, flair and flexibility and the ability to out-think one's opponent are the true strengths of the great litigator.

Litigation is not always, indeed is often not, a question of the total destruction of one's opponent. Often, a good result is to settle for something less than the maximum possible, to recognise when the cost of victory may be so great that it erodes some or, potentially, all of the benefits.

Many clients do not recognise that: some will claim that only a total win is acceptable, that it is a matter of principle. A good litigator therefore has to be able to negotiate with his own client, to explain the concept of a nett win. And some-times, when the odds are stacked against his client, a litigator must explain the concept of minimising the harm of an inevit-able loss.

Litigation is a battle of wills. Often a litigator's greatest weakness is that which he considers his greatest strength. An over-confident, an arrogant litigator, one who has a belief in his own infallibility will risk failure when a more modest approach would be safer and may result in a better outcome for his client.

Litigation is a test of character. The character of both the litigator and his client. There will be times when surrender seems more attractive than to continue, no matter what the merits of the case.

Litigation is a test of intellect. A litigator needs to out-think his opponent in terms of facts, strategy and law, constantly thinking, questioning, testing hypotheses and alternative stratagems.

Litigation is a test of stamina. For the great litigator, the fact that he is an artist more than a craftsman means that he engages on an emotional level; his client even more so. Like all artists, the good litigator will find reaching his goal to be tiring no matter how rewarding it ultimately proves.

Litigation is a matter of honour for the good litigator. He knows the rules and plays to their edges, sometimes pushing them outside their perceived limits but believing that he is still inside the ultimate boundaries. This is how new law is made: by the reinterpretation of law and the rules by which those laws are enforced.

A litigator is, in this way, a force for change as well as a force for justice. It is his role to identify where there are weaknesses or failures in the law as it is currently applied.

For this reason, he is not only a brutal warrior but adept at working out how best to re-draw the way laws should be applied and a canny exponent of the arts of persuasion.

The litigator is a teacher and a constant student, he is a master chess player and, when needed, a ruthless thug.

But if litigation is war, a brutal contest, then justice has for millennia been portrayed as a lady. The Greeks worshipped Themis, a deity of minor grade but, eventually, one of the

Oracles of Delphi due to her ability to prophesy the results of a decision. Often viewed as blind (hence the phrase "blind justice"), Themis' blindfold has been given many interpretations. My preferred interpretation is that she decides according to the evidence presented before her, without outside influence and the prejudices and inevitable injustice that such bring. In statues she bears a sword, which mythologists say demonstrates her ability to cut a clear line between truth and lies. The Roman equivalent, with a very similar history, is Justitia - hence, through the use of Latin in English, we have the word "Justice."

Like most women, Themis and Justice need to be wooed and persuaded: rarely is a blunt and forceful approach the most effective. The litigator, then, is also - in the purest sense - a seducer.

He has many tools at his disposal. But the most important are his intellect, his ability to communicate and his fearlessness in pursuit of a just result.

He may command an army of assistants and secondary advisers. He is a general. Because litigation is a war. And those that succeed are those that apply themselves to the practice of law as an art and to the practice of litigation as a struggle both to survive and to defeat his opponent by whatever lawful and honourable means are at his disposal.

Nigel Morris-Cotterill,
2012.

I phoned a friend.

"Jane," I moaned. "I've lost it. I have lost three cases in the past three months."

"Everyone loses sometimes."

"I don't."

"When did you lose before these three?"

"I don't remember: probably a year or so."

"And before that?"

"Another year, maybe"

"Nigel, you just don't get it do you? You've lost three cases in a year. The rest of us lose three cases a week. Stop complaining and get back to work"

About the Author

Nigel Morris-Cotterill joined an English law firm in his school and college holidays, starting at just 15 years of age.

From the outset, he demonstrated an aptitude for litigation, within weeks beginning to make - and win - applications in the County Courts of England and Wales. He made his first appearance as an advocate in open court at the age of only 16 years. He won.

Before starting his own firm, he worked as a locum in a variety of firms, from major City of London firms to one-man-bands in tiny towns, gaining exposure to a wide range of cases and techniques.

In his own firm, Morris-Cotterill acted for the UK's largest financial institutions, major international corporations and for individuals, delivering the same standard of service to all.

He retired from full time practice in 1994 to concentrate on developing a money laundering risk management and compliance consultancy which grew into The Anti Money Laundering Network, an international group encompassing consultancy, training, software and publications.

He no longer practises but is available to assist law firms on a non-practising consultancy basis.

Morris-Cotterill is the author of "How Not To Be A Money Launderer: the avoidance of money laundering and fraud in your organisation" (reprinted 2011 and available paperback in e-book: see www.countermoneylaundering.com) and countless articles and papers including published academic research.

Dedication

To Roy and Mary whose support made my extraordinary career possible and to Lump who should not be left out mainly because he never hid in my shadow, but rather I in his. Literally;

To (the late) John Heap, who took me into his firm despite youth, long hair and outrageous clothes and gave me my first opportunities to shine;

To (the late) Michael Manning, John Heap's senior partner, who taught me the single greatest lesson in being a successful litigator - and that dressing right and adopting "the advocate's strut" and way of speaking can create a strategic advantage;

To Mimi and James who suffered the consequences of my dedication to my art;

To all my clients who had faith in my judgement and abilities and the barristers who had the confidence - and often courage - to put my frequently unusual strategies into effect in court;

To Dorothy and all the team in my own firm and to Chris and the others who took me in when to continue as a sole practitioner became impossible;

To Alicia and the team in Kuala Lumpur who have provided global support to a distributed Anti Money Laundering Network group of companies;

To OB, Paul and The Angels who smoothed my move half-way across the world and made me very welcome; and

To Jo, without whom my world would be desolate and my life pointless.

Collectively and individually you made me who I am and helped me achieve beyond my own belief in myself.

Thank you.

Sun Tzu and the Art of Litigation

Notice regarding source material.

This work takes Sun Tzu's *The Art of War* in the form generally regarded as the most authoritative.

Lionel Giles, an Englishman, translated the work in 1912, saying that earlier translations had been both wrong and contained significant omissions.

Following a career in the British Army, Giles (1875–1958) worked at The British Museum where he was an assistant curator and Head of The Department of Oriental Manuscripts and Printed Books.

The Art of War: The Oldest Military Treatise in the World was one of a number of books Giles wrote during a long and highly regarded career.

His interest in translation came from his father, Henry, a diplomat and Sinologist, who was one of the creators of the Wade-Giles approach to translation and Lionel Giles used that approach in his own work.

My work uses only Sun Tzu's original "bullet points." Books with the narratives added later, including Giles' own commentary, are widely available and I recommend them.

The copyright position in relation to Giles' work is complicated: under US copyright law, the work is out of copyright. Under EU/UK law, it remains in copyright until at least 2028 i.e. 70 years after Giles' death. This book is published in the USA.

Notes on The Art of War

Sun Tzu was a Chinese military commander, ultimately a General. That much is known to be so. However, there is uncertainty as to when he lived and when his book, *The Art of War*, was completed.

Historians seem to agree that he was a prominent general during the period of Chinese history known as "The Spring and Autumn Period." That was during the first part of the Eastern Zhou Dynasty. But even the period of that Dynasty is fiercely debated. Most historians agree that it began in about 771BC but the end is argued as any time between 473 BC and 403BC.

It is also a period associated with Confucius.

However, it is also said that The Art of War was not completed until the "Warring States Period," which lasted from 475BC to 221BC when China was, largely, unified under the Qin Dynasty, considered the second part of the Eastern Zhou Dynasty, although, technically, the periods do not fully coincide.

Whatever the precise dates, bamboo scrolls containing the work were discovered in Shangdong Province in 1972 and have been established as having been created in the second century BC.

What is obvious, then, is that the work is probably not the work of one man, although there is common consent that Sun Tzu originated the work and its principles.

The original book is divided into thirteen chapters, each with numerous points. There is no narrative in the original but later editions contain extensive explanatory notes. The original can, perhaps, be seen the ancient equivalent of a seminar slide presentation. Therefore it was open to individual commanders to fill in the gaps, to apply it to specific circumstances.

It follows, then, that the book is not a battle plan but, rather, a manual on how to construct and execute a battle plan. It is not a single system but, rather, a pick-and-mix counter from which the most appropriate strategies are chosen in any given set of circumstances.

There are, of course, areas of conflict inherent in any system designed for interpretation "on the hoof."

But the real strength of *The Art of War* is that it tries to avoid "on the hoof" action and reaction. Thousands of years before the term "proactive" was mistakenly applied instead of "pre-active," Sun Tzu demanded that there be a risk analysis and plans readied for all foreseen eventualities.

It might seem strange to consider the thoughts of a battle commander about 2,500 years ago as the embryo from which the whole idea of risk management grew. But remember that this was a time of great thought. Confucius, often derided at the time but officially adopted later, was developing the core of a system of morality, justice, ethics and a wide range of interpersonal relationships.

Incidentally, Lionel Giles also produced an authoritative translation of much of Confucius' work.

But Sun Tzu's work goes further than ordinary risk management. It covers a wide range of strategies, of man management and business structures and management and, even, commercial negotiation.

This, of course, is in part a result of the lack of narrative - it is possible to read it into almost any situation one can think of.

But it is of most value where there is some form of combative relationship. And that, for our purposes, means litigation.

"Don't only think how you can win.
Also think how you can lose."

Michael Manning,
Solicitor, England.

Sun Tzu and the
Art of Litigation

Tipping the scales of Justice
in your client's favour

孙武

Nigel Morris-Cotterill

Terminology

There are differences in terminology between jurisdictions - and even from time to time within the same jurisdiction - in the terminology used in litigation. In this work, in order to provide consistency, a common approach has been adopted. Inevitably, there is a significant simplification of the meaning of the terms.

Plaintiff: a person who issues an *action* in order to enforce a right in civil proceedings. Sometimes called a "claimant."

Petitioner: a person who issues a *petition* to the Court, for example in matrimonial proceedings. In this work, in general and for the sake of simplicity, the term "plaintiff" includes "petitioner" unless the context specifically refers to one or other.

Prosecutor: a person who, on behalf of the state, issues a *charge* which commences proceedings in a criminal court.

Defendant: a person who must respond to an *action* or to a *charge*

Respondent: a person who must respond to a *matter.*

Third Party: a person who is not a primary defendant but whom either the plaintiff or defendant alleges contributed to the circumstances or has benefited from the circumstances and should be required to contribute to any penalty.

Action: Legal proceedings issued in a common law court. In effect an action is a statement of rights and a request to the

Court, as representative of the Monarch, to examine the evidence, confirm the rights and that they have been breached and to award a suitable remedy. In higher courts, an Action is commenced by writ and in the lower courts by plaint. Actions are also used to enforce statutory rights.

Matter: legal proceedings issued in a court of equity or certain other types of proceedings e.g. matrimonial proceedings

Petition: legal proceedings issued, originally, to the Court as representative of the Monarch who alone had the right to determine certain types of case and the results were in his discretion.

Charge: the first step in bringing proceedings before a criminal court.

Letter Before Action: the first contact between the lawyer for the prospective plaintiff and the prospective defendant. It sets out the grounds of claim, the harm, the required remedy and the consequences for non-compliance.

Injunction: An order that a person does or does not do something. Technically, an injunction is restricted to an order to not do something but over time convoluted orders that, in effect, ordered a person not to do a negative, have been regarded as a pointless device and so orders requiring positive action are widely now also regarded as injunctions. The penalty for breach of an injunction is contempt of court, not a penalty due to the other party.

Undertaking: there are two kinds of undertaking in litigation: one given by an lawyer to his opponent and one given by any person (lawyer or party) to the Court. An inter-lawyer undertaking is enforceable through the rules of professional conduct. An undertaking by a lawyer to the court is enforceable through the rules of professional conduct and, in addition, through the rules relating to contempt of court. An undertaking by a party is enforceable by the court through the rules relating to contempt of court.

Interlocutory application: an application made by one litigator on behalf of his client at any stage in the proceedings after commencement but before the final hearing.

Writ: see "Action"

Plaint: see "Action"

Statement of Claim: that part of the documentation at the time of issue of proceedings that sets out, in formal terms, the *cause of action*, the harm suffered, the remedy sought and other formal terms such as the requirement for *costs* and interest on *damages*.

Cause of Action: in order to bring an *action*, a plaintiff must have cause that is to say a right that has been infringed or must be enforced. If a writ (etc.) does not evidence a cause of action recognised by *law*, the proceedings must be struck out.

Damages: a monetary award ordered by the Court or agreed in negotiation between the parties.

Fees: the amount (in currency) that the lawyer charges his own client for the work done.

Costs: the amount (in currency) that a losing party is ordered to pay to the winning party. These may be determined by a formula (often with reference to *fixed costs*), by agreement or by a court-appointed officer who reviews the case in a process called *taxation* and orders the payment of the amount he considers appropriate.

Fixed costs: certain acts during the conduct of proceedings may have a pre-determined quantum as to the amount that one party will be ordered to pay to the other as part of a costs order. Such fixed costs are set out in the Rules of Court. Fixed costs apply "inter partes" not between the lawyer and his own client.

Taxation: the process by which an officer of the court assesses the amount of costs that the losing party is liable to pay to the winning party. It is a process that applies both a formula and an assessment of reasonableness both in relation to the time spent and the work done.

Law: law is created in two ways - by *legislation* or by the *courts*. Arguably, there is a third way - custom - but for all practical purposes, this is obsolete, requiring, in England and Wales, the party alleging custom to prove that the supposed practice has been in use for "time immemorial" which originally means going back to 1189 - the coronation of Richard II. Under The Prescription Act, 1832, it was refined to mean "since time whereof the Memory of Man runneth not to the contrary" i.e. not a fixed date. That was held to be uncertain and so it was later fixed as being not less than 20 years (unless the other party was the Crown in which case it was not less than 30 years).

Legislation: the making of law by Parliament. "Acts" are "passed" and are the superior form of law. "Regulations" are "made, " under authority delegated to part of Government e.g.

a Department. Regulations are termed "secondary legislation." In some countries, they are called "statutory instruments." It is important to differentiate between Regulations that are Statutory Instruments and regulation in the sense of industry regulation as imposed by "regulators."

Settlement: an agreement between the parties to dispose of the litigation upon terms that both accept. It may be subject to court order but (unlike criminal proceedings where an agreement is reached) it is generally not subject to court scrutiny and approval unless the Judge considers it to be so outrageously one-sided that he suspects undue pressure has been brought to bear.

Instructions: a client "instructs" his lawyer. This reflects the relationship in which the client specifies the objective and his lawyer defines the way in which that objective is achieved. The instructions will depend upon the client's own requirements and the *advice* he receives from his lawyer.

Advice: a lawyer gives advice to ("advises") his client as to what is achievable, what means are available to reach those achievements and the risks, including risks as to costs, of each of those means.

Litigator: a *lawyer* who conducts litigation

Lawyer: a generic term for a legal practitioner.

Litigant: a party to litigation

Litigant in person: a party who represents himself in litigation

Litigation: proceedings undertaken in a Court.

Advocate: a person who presents a case in Court. He may or may not be the litigator who has had conduct of the case.

Judgment: the Order made by a Court when determining a case, usually including the reasons for the decision. Note the spelling compared with the non-legal "judgement."

Pleadings: the formal documents that state the case, for example the writ, the defence, the counterclaim, defence to counterclaim and replies to defences.

Striking out: A pleading may be struck out if it fails to disclose e.g. a *cause of action* or a *defence*. If the *statement of claim* is struck out, then the action is struck out. But it is not dismissed. Therefore it may be recommenced.

Real Evidence: physical, tangible evidence. Compare with "demonstrative evidence."

Demonstrative evidence: this American term encompasses both oral (witness) and documentary evidence.

I love it when a plan comes together

Hannibal Hayes,
The A Team.

1. Laying Plans

Chapter I. Laying plans

1.1. Sun Tzu said: the art of war is of vital importance to the State.

In litigation, the client is king. He issues instructions to his lawyers. It is the function of the lawyer, if he accepts instructions, to develop and implement strategies to give effect to those instructions. Most clients do not enter into litigation lightly, either as plaintiff (claimant) or defendant. Litigation is costly in terms of money and, often more importantly, time and emotional involvement. By definition, therefore, the case and the strategies adopted, are vitally important.

It is therefore essential that lawyers recognise that, while the case they are handling may be one of dozens of actions in the lawyer's hands, it is very personal to the client.

Managing client's expectations and attitudes becomes a core part of the relationship where there is a disparity of involvement.

1.2. It is a matter of life and death, a road either to safety or to ruin. Hence it is a subject of inquiry which can on no account be neglected.

Litigation is (at least on the face of it) a zero-sum game. There is a winner and a loser in what is often seen as a "winner-take-all" battle. Therefore, to be successful, there must be a thorough examination of the facts and law before engaging the enemy.

One of the most common reasons for failure, or for making life much more difficult than it need be, is to take preliminary steps without adequate preparation.

All too often a client will say "I just want a lawyer's letter." And all too often poor litigators will fire off a threatening letter based upon scant facts presented by the client at a short, in effect a preliminary, meeting or, even, a short letter of instruction from the client.

This leads to several potentially adverse consequences.

First is that the facts, as the client sees them, are often incomplete. That means that the Letter Before Action does not take full account of the possible responses.

Secondly, a properly constructed Letter Before Action inevitably includes a demand failing which consequences will follow according to a timetable set out in the letter.

For example: "unless you pay the sum x within seven days, we will issue proceedings on our clients' behalf."

If full instructions were not taken before issuing the Letter Before Action, then the lawyer is unlikely to be in a position to give effect to his threat.

The phrase is defective in other ways, too, which will be examined later.

Third and worse, if the litigator does not fully consider the case, he will have no indication of what his client's opponent may claim and that will prejudice his ability to properly phrase his Letter Before Action and the claim which will be filed in Court.

1.3. The art of war, then, is governed by five constant factors, to be taken into account in one's deliberations, when seeking to determine the conditions obtaining in the field.

1.4. These are:

> *(1) The Moral Law;*
>
> *(2) Heaven;*
>
> *(3) Earth;*
>
> *(4) The Commander;*
>
> *(5) Method and discipline.*

1.5, 1.6. The moral law causes the people to be in complete accord with their ruler, so that they will follow him regardless of their lives, undismayed by any danger.

The lawyer must carry out his client's instructions without question. This is, of course, tempered with the over-riding obligation to act in accordance with the Law and professional etiquette as well as the Rules of Court.

It is, therefore, incumbent on the lawyer to challenge the client when the client's demands fall outside those boundaries.

Sun Tzu himself, reportedly, was not above challenging the Rulers. When preparing citizens for civil protection, the concubines of the Royal Household were ordered to prepare, forming their own units each under the command of a senior concubine. Given orders to "turn right," they did not. Nor did they when ordered to "turn left." Sun Tzu said that if orders were not clear that was the fault of the commanders but if they orders were clear and the troops did not comply, that was a failure of discipline. A failure of discipline is a serious failure in the command structure. Therefore he ordered the senior concubines to be beheaded. The King said that to behead the senior concubines would cause disruption in the Household. But Sun Tzu said that a failure to control subordinates would mean that discipline would fail. The senior concubines were beheaded and the next most senior installed in their place. There were no further incidents of disobedience.

The phrase "undismayed by any danger" can be seen in the light of the expectation that a lawyer will prosecute his client's case "without fear or favour before the proper tribunals," an expression to be found in the professional ethics statements of lawyers all over the world.

The concept is expanded by the phrase "they will follow him regardless of their lives" - which is allied to the professional conduct requirement that the client's interests are always to be paramount, even at the expense of those of the lawyer.

Claud Adrien Helvétius (1715 - 1771) was a French philosopher - a polite word for someone who jotted down his thoughts and got them published. He was actually a well-to-do Parisian who first went into what has been termed "finance" but he was really a tax collector, then decided to write poetry, had a life at court, got bored with that in 1751 and declared himself a patron of the French group of "thinkers" known as "les Philosophes." part of The Enlightenment. The group included John-Jacques Rousseau and Voltaire. Helvétius' main claim to fame, aside from his patronage, appears to be the ability to turn a pithy phrase. He said "discipline is simply the art of making the soldiers fear their officers more than they fear the enemy. "

1.7. Heaven signifies night and day, cold and heat, times and seasons.

Law, especially case law, is never finally fixed. Courts interpret laws according to the moral stance of the judge (or jury) and the prevailing general morality.

It seems melodramatic to say it, but the decisions of courts are often political (small "p"), almost a matter of fashion. In the depths of the global financial crisis of the late 2006 to ? (it's not finished yet), courts began to find ways to avoid giving effect to clear contract terms - and even express provisions in laws and the Rules of Court - to prevent banks repossessing properties of those who had been caught in the cross-fire of a financial meltdown which was not of their making.

Litigators, therefore, needed to think carefully whether they would be able to secure a repossession and, if not, what the fall-back position might be.

Therefore, policies were developed to negotiate payments holidays, reductions of repayments and a range of other measures designed to avoid throwing people out of their homes and leaving the bank with a property that it could not sell or, if it could, would be likely to sell for less than the amount of the outstanding mortgage.

But they would seek to tie those revised arrangements to an order for repossession - that is the property was ordered to be repossessed but the taking of possession would be suspended provided the revised arrangements were adhered to.

In some countries, governments intervened to prevent such action, requiring the Court to order a revised plan but with an order that the matter be brought back before them in the event of failure, with no repossession order being made when the revised plan was ordered.

Thus litigators lost all the pressure points that they were able to apply under the previous concept.

This then threw the questions of planning for failure back onto those who draft mortgage documentation. And the repossession provisions in all existing mortgages were, in effect, frustrated.

In this way, the question of preparation for all eventualities can be seen as applicable to the original agreement just as much as to the enforcement of it.

In contract disputes, it is the litigator's job to unravel the client's bad decisions without making the client look or feel bad. Indeed, the litigator can boost his own standing in his client's eyes if he can find a way to make his client look and feel good.

That means making his opponent or his opponent's client look bad or, at the very least, worse than his own client.

1.8. Earth comprises distances, great and small; danger and security; open ground and narrow passes; the chances of life and death.

This principle might be read as referring to "forum shop-ping:" the choosing of the correct venue for litigation.

There are often choices of venue. For simple small claims this is less so but for larger claims, there are potentially several different fora. For example, in England and Wales, cases might be found in the County Court (which has a geographical juris-diction), in the High Court (where the case can be brought in a District Registry where there is a geographical aspect or in London where there is no geographical restriction). But within the High Court, depending on the facts and the remedy sought, it can be brought in any one of several "Divisions" or discrete courts for specific types of case e.g. the Commercial Court

The decision as to which Division might also be influenced by the known attitude of "Masters" - a grade of Judge. Masters in London are well known for being cantankerous and opinion-ated and for making rapid-fire decisions, often without allow-ing an advocate to make all the points he wishes to make.

There are other possibilities, too. In international cases, there is the question of which country to bring an action in. Although many contracts include a "choice of law" clause, some countries say that, if they can find that the facts would give them jurisdiction, they will over-ride a choice of law clause. This is often the case where a national of their own country wishes to commence action against a foreign national, in order to save their own national the costs and risks of fight-ing an action overseas.

In addition, there is also the possibility of taking a case to arbitration or mediation rather than to a formal court. There are advantages and disadvantages and, again, a formal court may over-ride a clause in a contract that specifies arbitration or mediation. Often, for example, the Court will accept jurisdiction despite an agreement to the contrary if one party alleges fraud.

In countries where civil actions are tried by jury, the venue can be extremely important: for example, a jury in a city dependent on the automotive industry is likely to be more sympathetic to the car company than a jury in a city where the livelihoods of families (even if only a matter of perception not reality) will not be put at risk.

Earth also means being aware of all the circumstances, being prepared for the unexpected and being aware of the traps that are always present in litigation.

1.9. The commander stands for the virtues of wisdom, sincerity, benevolence, courage and strictness.

In a law firm, it is the partners who set the ethos and ethics of the practice. Those firms that are unethical are well known within the profession. Often those firms are the same firms that do as their clients tell them without question.

A lawyer is dependent on his professional reputation. Those with a reputation for winning at all costs, even dishonourably, tend to attract dishonourable clients.

In litigation, there should be no room for trickery. The Rules of Court are designed to limit the opportunity but some litigators still try to evade the spirit of the Rules while still remaining within the word of them.

It follows that the partners define how a case will be conducted. It is for them to ensure that cases are properly researched, that the Letter Before Action and the writ (or other claim document) contains only provable facts. The partners have to control their associates and employees, making sure that litigation is conducted in accordance with the firm's ethical principles but also "without fear or favour."

1.10. By method and discipline are to be understood the marshalling of the army in its proper subdivisions, the graduations of rank among the officers, the maintenance of roads by which supplies may reach the army and the control of military expenditure.

Complex or large litigation is the work of a team. This principle says, simply, that any team must have clearly defined roles (the proper subdivisions), a hierarchy, internal systems including lines of communication and controls.

Today, we would put these under the headings of human resources management and compliance.

It is surprising how smaller firms, perhaps swayed by the notion of a "flat structure," fail to realise that a flat structure only works if everyone knows their place and their function.

While computerised case management systems have removed some of the risks of timetables and even relevant information falling between the cracks, information flows are essential.

Many people laugh at the concept of "morning prayers." But team or departmental meetings are an important fail-safe under which supervisors can be assured that priority is given to activities even within that day. For example, if a deadline will be reached at 3pm that afternoon, then the relevant team members should be prepared to impose the consequences at 3pm, not to begin to prepare the required action at 3pm.

Diaries should show the start time for that preparation in addition to the time the deadline expires.

1.11. These five heads should be familiar to every general: he who knows them will be victorious; he who knows them not will fail.

Sun Tzu is blunt: if any lawyer fails to prepare properly, he will fail. Of course, that does not mean that, at each and every step, he will lose the case (although there are always some stages at which a claim or a defence may be knocked out on technical grounds). It does mean that, at any given stage, a complexity may arise as the result of an error or omission. Therefore there must be constant attention to all these factors not just at the commencement of a case but at all times until its end.

In short, in litigation, there is no room for complacency or laziness.

1.12. Therefore, in your deliberations, when seeking to de-termine the military conditions, let them be made the basis of a comparison, in this wise: —

1.13. (1) Which of the two sovereigns is imbued with the Moral law?

Litigation is a battle of champions, each representing their clients.

If your client is your king, then your opponent's client is king to him. Right at the outset, even before the Letter Before Action, the merits of the case must be fully considered. The merits of the case are not the same as the facts.

Considering the merits of the case means looking at the facts and law and all other relevant factors. It's called "litiga-tion risk" and, translated into simple terms, it means that even a cast-iron case can rust away.

(2) Which of the two generals has most ability?

Everyone comes up against someone that they think is a better litigator than they are. But simply because one's oppon-ent is from a large firm or attended a particular university or law school does not mean he has more ability. However, some judges - even though to do so is fundamentally wrong and arguably corrupt - will place more weight on a case presented by a large firm, or a senior lawyer (in some countries, a QC, for example) than by a small firm or a junior lawyer.

This is something over which a litigator has no control.

There is one simple tactic for dealing with this situation: be as well prepared as possible and advise the client that the case may have to be appealed if the Judge proves to be partisan.

Taking that variable out of the equation, the Rules of Court are, generally, designed to ensure that lawyers of disparate ability have an equal chance of presenting their case.

What the Rules do not do is protect a client against an inadequate lawyer who fails to properly build or prepare his case or one operating outside his sphere of competence.

Of course, there are some lawyers that are significantly more successful litigators than others.

This principle says to be aware of that risk and to assess it as part of the overall strategy.

For example, it may be that a particular lawyer has a fearsome reputation in court. Therefore the strategy would be to find a way to bring the case to a satisfactory conclusion without proceeding to a final hearing.

Some very successful litigators consider that ending up in a final hearing is, in itself, a form of loss because of the costs of preparation for trial and the costs of the trial itself.

(3) With whom lie the advantages derived from Heaven and Earth?

Litigators like what is, literally, home Court advantage. It is easy to underestimate the value of being familiar with the building, local customs, the court staff and, even, the Judge.

For example, a Judge may have a particular dislike of mobile phones (one, when hand-held mobiles were new, threatened to drop my phone into the water jug on his desk). Home court advantage can be gained by something as simple as taking the phone out and pointedly turning it off or to silent.

Others become very agitated if the parties for the next case go into their court while a case is in progress. In other courts, even in the same building, a Judge may have a different preference and like the parties for the next case already "teed up" to be called forward as soon as possible.

In some courts in England, "local" solicitors are permitted to use the barristers' robing rooms, while non-local solicitors are not without invitation from Counsel (i.e. a barrister).

Many judges have a great sense of humour - but are, of course, required to suppress it, at least publicly. Local knowledge allows the advocate to know what he can do to brighten the Judge's day without causing him to lose his dignity. And brightening a Judge's day is often a way of building a rapport which translates, sometimes, into a little more leeway than would otherwise be given. An out of town lawyer, trying to achieve the same, may be viewed as trying to be just a little too cocky and so alienate the Judge. Fair? Of course not. That's why it's a home court advantage.

Home court advantages also include the convenience of issuing proceedings and applications. Out of town litigators have to travel or appoint a local agent - both of which involve cost and time. Or to issue by post which causes delay. In the case of agents, it also involves a risk that the agent will not issue at the expected time.

Home court advantages also include where there are "local directions" by which a court varies or supplements the Rules of Court as they are applied as a standard. Often, local directions are unknown to out-of-town lawyers until they fall foul of them.

Apart from home court advantages, there are other factors that need to be considered: does the court of choice have a cut-off time for the filing of applications? Does it have a long queue on Friday because a particular firm handles debt collection for a large company and chooses to issue proceedings in batches (less of a problem where electronic filing is possible).

Does a particular court have a long waiting time for the hearing of applications? As a plaintiff, this is something you do not want, especially if your opponent adopts the tactic of finding excuses for adjournments.

What are the profiles of different courts when they assess costs payable to one party to the other i.e. is one stingy and another generous?

Does a particular court dislike making interim costs orders i.e. for the payment of costs orders made in interlocutory applications to be paid within a very short time of the conclusion of the hearing?

(4) On which side is discipline most rigorously enforced?

Unless there has been prior legal conflict between your client and his opponent, a litigator may have no idea who his opponent will be. Therefore he cannot assess this.

But if the litigator does know, is he aware of the ethics, ethos and tactics of the opposing firm? Can he find out by asking colleagues?

Can that information be used to aid in assessing litigation risk?

(5) Which army is stronger?

This is not just a question of numbers. It's a question of capability.

Many solicitors (who are often general practitioners) take on work that is outside their area of expertise, relying on the abilities of a barrister (who declares a specialism).

The basic rule should be "If you don't understand the business, don't do the business," but there are often commercial pressures and firms, especially small firms, can rarely afford to turn work away.

Also long-standing clients who have an isolated piece of litigation may not want to instruct other lawyers. And, of course, no firm wants to have to send their clients to another firm where there is a risk of the client being encouraged to take some or all of their other work there.

But there are inherent risks in trying to have day to day conduct of work that is outside that with which a practitioner is familiar.

A solicitor who specialised in small business matters and conveyancing took on a criminal case because a long-standing client asked him to. The case related to drug smuggling. The solicitor believed his client innocent. The solicitor was jailed for failing to report, under laws designed to combat money laundering, a suspicious transaction i.e. the payment of legal fees in cash. He had no experience in criminal matters and had, in effect, handed over the conduct of the case to a barrister who did know know that the fees had been paid in cash. This disconnect was the root cause of the solicitor losing his free-dom and his practice.

All litigators should consider if they have the expertise in that particular type of litigation e.g. a specialist subject such as medical negligence, intellectual property before accepting instructions and not to rely on "bought in" expertise, especially if there is a hint that one's opponent may be a specialist. E.g. in a libel case, an individual may consult a general practitioner but the publisher will almost certainly have specialist libel law-yers available.

(6) On which side are officers and men more highly trained?

Just because a lawyer went to a well-known university or particular law school does not automatically guarantee that he is properly trained. They provide a very general background. The real training comes in the form of specialised courses in house or on the job training as well as external courses. And most importantly, real experience.

Hint: even though most professional bodies require lawyers to maintain a certain number of hours of continuous professional development, most take the minimum number and then often at the lowest cost. They are looking to tick boxes.

It is in this area that most large firms do have an advantage: their in house training does instil knowledge, systems and discipline.

They also provide a wider range of training than most small firms either provide or send lawyers to so that their litigators are always up to date on the changes in Rules and relevant laws.

They also conduct mock-litigation exercises and mock trials.

Only each individual litigator can tell whether he is properly trained and fully up to date. It is almost certain that those in small firms do not take part in mock litigation and mock trials.

There is, therefore, a significant mismatch between large and small, general practice, firms in this area.

But specialists in small firms are often at least as well trained as those in large firms and often more experienced, hence the growth of "boutique practices."

So the assessment in relation to the litigator's own capability will relate to the person having conduct of the litigation not the firm as a whole.

While law and even technique can be learned from a course or a book, only experience creates true skill. True, some have natural talent but even then it must be honed by practice (with a "c" as distinct from "practise"). Young bloods may be enthusiastic and thrusting but it is the wisdom of experience that allows the commander to best deploy his resources to secure an economical and swift victory.

(7) In which army is there the greater constancy both in reward and punishment?

Litigation is a combination of three things: superior fire power (in the form of a better presented case), superior tactics (which arise from a better grasp of what can be achieved and when and how best to make and defend attacks) and better preparation (which results, in part, from better systems and controls within the litigation firm).

This principle refers to the question of systems and controls.

A litigator needs to make sure that all opportunities for advantage are taken and to be sure of that, there has to be a plan for the conduct of the case.

This principle says that there has to be a strict adherence to those systems and controls to make certain that the plan for the conduct of the case is followed and that, where the plan needs to be modified, those changes are documented and the new plan followed.

If it is not, then there must be punishment.

If it is and if success is achieved, then there must be rewards.

The principle says that consistency must be applied if those working on a case are to be loyal.

It is a well established fact of management that nothing creates disunity within a workforce more than some receiving treatment which is more or less favourable than that afforded to others.

It is therefore useful to know if an opposing team are united (in which case they work as a single, effective unit) or disunited (in which case, intra-team rivalries or tensions will create the risk that the systems and controls will fail.

That often results in missed deadlines or failures to comply with e.g. orders to serve specific documents, with one person saying that responsibility for a specific task lies with another.

1.14. By means of these seven considerations I can forecast victory or defeat.

This principle is, perhaps, a little simplistic. But the principles do provide a good idea as to how litigation will be conducted. A poorly managed firm will make mistakes which they will need to rectify. That costs time and it costs money. It provides an opportunity to divide one's opponent from his client by means of e.g. costs orders.

1.15. The general that hearkens to my counsel and acts upon it, will conquer: —let such a one be retained in command! The general that hearkens not to my counsel nor acts upon it, will suffer defeat: —let such a one be dismissed!

This principle is addressed to the king i.e. the client. In summary, it says, "if a lawyer fails to properly prepare, to devise and implement a plan and to follow it and to ensure that the team is properly managed, then clients should find another lawyer who will do these things".

So it's a warning to lawyers to make sure that they know what they are doing, know how and when to do it and to make sure they do what they say and, perhaps equally importantly, to demonstrate it to the client.

This is a function of the client engagement letter but also of correspondence in the course of the litigation.

Clients need to know what is expected to happen and what the possible pitfalls are so that they understand the assessment of success or failure.

By keeping the client fully informed, of the bad as well as the good, litigators demonstrate to the client that they are on top of the situation, even if it's going badly.

And if they cannot be assured of that, then clients are not only entitled to change representation but should do so.

1.16. While heeding the profit of my counsel, avail yourself also of any helpful circumstances over and beyond the ordinary rules.

1.17. According as circumstances are favourable, one should modify one's plans.

These two principles can be regarded as part one and part two of the same idea. 16 says not to be too rigid in the application of Sun Tzu's stated ideas. 17 says not to be blinded to opportunity by slavishly following a plan.

The 16th principle is rather garbled.

However, its core concept is simple: no General can think of everything.

Remember this from Donald Rumsfeld?

> "As we know, there are known knowns; these are things we know we know.
> We also know there are known unknowns; that is to say we know there are some things we do not know.
> But there are also unknown unknowns - the ones we don't know we don't know."

Many people who were either too arrogant to read it properly or to stupid to understand it laughed at it.

But then many of those same people went on to buy and applaud "The Black Swan" by an academic, Nassim Taleb, that said the same thing in a hundred thousand words or so and cost them several dollars and lots of hours to reach the same point.

Was this little more than herd instinct? Herd instinct is important for litigators and we will return to it in due course.

The principle says that even a well prepared General can be taken by surprise and that when he is and an opportunity for an advantage presents itself, it should be taken.

For example, a sole practitioner may be taken ill and miss a deadline. It's harsh to say so but the effective litigator will take that chance to press for an early application, perhaps even to strike out the claim or defence or enter judgment.

Is it ungentlemanly to do so? No, it is not. Every litigator, no matter what the size of his firm, must have a Plan B in case he is unable to act for reasons of unforeseen circumstances. Indeed, many professional bodies expect such a plan to be in place.

If the case is lost by reason of the inability of the litigator to properly conduct the case and a failure to have an alternate able to step in (even if it is nothing more than an associate who is able to make an application for an extension of time), that is seen as professional misconduct.

Is it ruthless? Yes, it is.

Is it "playing the man not the ball?" Yes. But think of litigation as rugby (or one of its variants) instead of soccer and it makes sense.

The simple reality is this: unless a specific court will penalise the litigator for such harsh tactics, he has a duty to his client to take the advantage when it is presented. If he fails to do so and misses an opportunity for a "quick kill," then he does his client a disservice and the client - and the litigator's regulator - would be fully justified in criticising the litigator for failing to bring the case to a quick and cost effective end.

To return to the gladiatorial analogy: no points are gained for allowing one's opponent to get to his feet when he slips. The advantage must be pressed home. And while the crowd might respect the sportsmanship that comes from allowing him to recover and fight on, the only person that actually matters is the person whose champion the gladiator is.

Therefore, if the litigator feels that to press home such an advantage is too harsh, then he must ask his client if he may afford his opponent time to recover (or to find an alternate).

But if he does not ask for and receive those instructions, he has no alternative but to press home the advantage.

1.18. All warfare is based on deception.

It is important to remember that the conduct of litigation is or at least should be, perhaps above all else, a matter of honour.

It is unprofessional to lie to your opponent or to the court.

Therefore do not imagine that this principle permits or encourages dishonesty or untruths.

But, all good litigators aim to gain the advantage of surprise.

There is a saying that "everything before a *but* is a lie." Not in this case.

There is absolutely no duty upon any litigator to reveal to his opponents what his tactics are. He is perfectly entitled, in military terms, to "keep his powder dry."

A good litigator may issue an application and during the hearing of that application, modify or add to it.

It is a brutal and unusual technique but it is one that a Court will rarely criticise provided it is done with subtlety and finesse. And due (if slightly disingenuous) humility.

Every criminal defence advocate learns very early in his career that he does not have to tell the truth, the whole truth and nothing but the truth, even when his client has been cautioned that he must tell investigators everything and that a court may be invited to draw adverse inferences from his late disclosure of facts, particularly, for example, alibi.

The advocate exercises his skill to invite the Court (which may be a jury or a Judge alone) to consider alternative explanations, even if there is little or no basis for them. He says "is it possible that....." so sowing the seed of doubt. So long as he does not represent a fictional example as fact, he does nothing wrong.

In civil litigation, that is more difficult because the burden of proof is very different.

In a dispute over the interpretation of a document, every word, every phrase is either an opportunity or a threat. A preamble sets out the intentions of the parties at the time the agreement is made and, even though often regarded as not forming a part of the agreement proper, it is nevertheless an aid to interpretation - and to fix what the parties thought so as to undermine claims of a different interpretation found later; words such as "may," "should" or "will," are indicative of the level of discretion allowed (with decreasing discretion as one moves up the scale), amounts of money and other quantities should be carefully defined: whose dollars are referred to? What is "a billion?"

An opportunity is only an opportunity if it is identified and acted upon. A threat is always a threat. And a missed opportunity can be turned into a threat.

This is not a matter of evidence but rather of rhetoric, editorialising and advocacy.

Therefore, it is always possible to posit alternatives to the interpretation of facts put up by the other side. Civil litigation is all about interpretation of facts and who has the most convincing explanation.

While facts must, in most courts, be declared in advance, explanations are not subject to the same requirement. Although the pleadings must make the case, there is still room for the introduction of new interpretations at trial.

It is these that the litigator - within the bounds of the Rules of Court - keeps secret until he needs to use them.

How far can the litigator go with this tactic? There is no clear answer. It is a matter of skill, judgement and knowledge of the Judge and of his opponent. A weak opponent may be blind-sided and have no answer to the introduction of an alternative interpretation.

However, such tactics are dangerous: an advocate cannot lead his witness nor can he lead evidence. Therefore, usually, the new interpretation must be introduced during cross-examination of his opponent's witnesses.

The advocate must be alert to the oft-quoted phrase "never ask a question unless you know the answer."

Therefore to ask a witness of whom the advocate has little knowledge a question to which the answer may be a bald "no" can cause serious damage to the presentation of a case.

It follows that the question must be asked very carefully, often having led up to it so as to gauge the likely response.

And if the probable response would be against the advocate's interests, he should abandon the line of questioning.

If, however, he is confident of getting the answer he wants, then he puts his opponent on the back foot and in the position of having to redress the position in re-examination.

However, often, the damage is done by the first answer and an attempt to apply a sticking plaster to a hole in a case is often seen as a desperate move and can have the effect of increasing the effect of the original answer.

The potential benefits, therefore, are considerable so long as the risks are managed before the question is asked.

And, in doing so, the litigator has not misled the Court nor told an untruth, he has merely posited a potential explanation to a witness who had no notice of the question.

1.19. Hence, when able to attack, we must seem unable; when using our forces, we must seem inactive; when we are near, we must make the enemy believe we are far away; when far away, we must make him believe we are near.

It is a well established tactic to delay litigation, often buying time to prepare. But the well prepared litigator may want to lull his opponent into a sense of false security. Therefore, if he knows his opponent does not pounce on delay, the litigator may choose to allow that delay to arise. Depending upon which side he is on, he is using the maxim "justice delayed is justice denied."

A litigator may allow his opponent to issue an application and to obtain a date then, as the date approaches, issue at the last moment allowed by rules as to good service a cross-application, so gatecrashing the date already fixed.

Once his own application is listed, he may then comply with whatever it was that he had defaulted on in order to sidestep the original application, leaving only the matter of costs to be dealt with but then, having taken his opponent by surprise with what may be a very substantive application, he puts his opponent under pressure.

The opposite side of the coin, as the principle says, is to make one's opponent feel that one is more ready than is actually the case. Therefore applications may be issued for little more purpose than to harry and hassle one's opponent. Of course, the applications must have purpose and substance. Applications can be withdrawn leaving the question of costs to be dealt with at a later date. An offer to withdraw an application with that proviso as to costs may be rejected but if such a rejection is made and the date is not vacated the Court is likely to take a very dim view of the party that rejected it.

Litigation involves harrying one's opponent, within the bounds of the Rules of Court and unsettling his preparation - and unnerving his client who must, at least initially, bear his own costs even if, at the end of the day, he obtains an order for costs.

1.20. Hold out baits to entice the enemy. Feign disorder and crush him.

Staying with the theme of deception, the making and withdrawing of an offer is a tactic that harries one's opponent and causes him to risk potential conflict with his client.

Offers may be made with an unrealistic time-scale for acceptance or be so far away from the likely award that it will not be accepted. However, the offer should look sufficiently substantial to suggest that you recognise that your client has a weak case and therefore wishes to settle.

Then, once your opponent is destabilised, a second offer, this time more attractive but still within your own client's comfort zone, can be made, perhaps backed by a payment into court or other means by which your opponent's client is put at risk as to costs if the offer is not accepted.

This focusses the mind of the opposing client: once he realises that he can walk away - if he acts quickly - with x or risk getting less and having to bear both parties' costs from that point on, he is likely to want a very convincing explanation from his lawyers to continue.

In cases where there is a "no win, no fee" arrangement, the lawyer is, by definition, in a position of conflict with his own client. He may wish to risk going for a higher settlement because his own percentage will result in a higher fee. Everyone is aware of cases where the lawyer has said to his client little more than "I think we can get more."

Clients are either scared or ignorant at this point. The scared will want a full explanation of the prospects and risks, the prognosis if you will. The ignorant do not think to question their lawyer and have blind faith in his representations.

It's time to play the man instead of the ball, again.

Lawyers are not permitted to make direct contact with their opponent's client. But, in most jurisdictions, there is nothing to prevent them making contact with witnesses. The basic principle is that "there is no property in a witness."

Very shortly after the offer is made, an approach can be made to the witnesses in the opposing case, setting an appointment for a meeting. It may not matter whether the witnesses - or even potential witnesses attend the meeting. That is not, at least initially, the point of the exercise. The point is that the witnesses and potential witnesses contact the opposing litigator or, better still his client and - to use a term from the intelligence sector - run interference. Half a dozen people phoning the lawyer or his client demanding to know why they have been told to attend a meeting at another lawyer's offices is a very effective form of pressure.

And pressure creates uncertainty and unsettles both the opposing litigator and his client.

Unsettled people lose confidence in their own judgement and in this way the opposing client may instruct his litigator to compromise the action rather than suffer additional disruption.

1.21. If he is secure at all points, be prepared for him. If he is in superior strength, evade him.

Where an opponent is fully prepared (or, rather appears to be), then any litigator must be ready for a full frontal assault. However, if there is a way to avoid the confrontation, so as to be more ready next time or to choose a more favourable battle-ground, then it is a good idea to take it.

There is no point in being beaten up if you could have run away.

1.22. If your opponent is of choleric temper, seek to irritate him. Pretend to be weak, that he may grow arrogant.

I wonder if I if he should tell this story. But as all those (except me) who were party to it are either dead or in their dotage, it's probably safe.

A lawyer was famous for berating his opponents, often reducing both men and women to tears of frustration (when they got back to the office). It reached the point where the advocates in the firm I was working with would go so far as to take a day off "sick" if they had to face this bully. He won almost all his applications by preventing his opponents from presenting their case and the particular District Judge was not sufficiently strong to control him.

I, just 17 years old but a veteran of many applications in chambers, was given a case where the bully would be the advocate.

Without reading the papers, the first questions I asked of those who had come up against the bully before were about the him and his conduct. It appeared that the merits were irrelevant if it was impossible to present the case.

It turned out that the advocate had just returned to work after a period of sickness for which he was on medication. It was supposed to calm him but it appeared that he was just as irascible as before.

Before the District Judge (in those days called a "Registrar"), I began to reply to his application only to be interrupted over and over again. I opened my file and handed a piece of paper to the District Judge who read it but clearly did not understand its relevance.

The bully demanded to see it.

"No, you can't. It's privileged," I responded, directly to him, in a clear and deliberate breach of etiquette. Then to the District Judge "he can't see it."

The bully became increasingly agitated and he and I argued with us both becoming more and more heated (although on my part, it was all acting) leaving the DJ looking entirely at sea, still completely unaware of the relevance of the paper. I reached across the table, snatched the paper out of the DJ's hand and threw it along the table to the bully who read it and spluttered.

"It's got nothing to do with this case," he yelled.

"I didn't say it had."

He literally sat and spluttered, unable to form words.

He could not argue, could not present his argument and I calmly and quietly defeated his application.

I was later told that he never again appeared in any application against the firm I worked for, saying that he did not wish to ever find himself opposing me.

I don't think the DJ ever worked out what happened.

I didn't hear about Sun Tzu until perhaps 15 years later but I think he would have approved. After all, elsewhere in his principles, he labours the point that one should know one's enemy.

I'm not sure that too many other people would have approved.

The point is simple: there are many weaknesses that one can exploit and not all of them are to be found in the case papers.

It is also true that one can create a sense of complacency in one's opponent by appearing to blunder about. Imagine US TV detective Colombo.

There have, over the years, been many advocates who have pretended to be confused by their papers, particularly during cross-examination. And many more who, with a weak case before a jury, have elicited sympathy for themselves (and by association, their client) but appearing to be, not to put too fine a point on it, a bit thick.

One advocate of this author's acquaintance used this tactic so often that other advocates joked about his catchphrase "I'm sorry, I don't understand. I'm not that clever. Can you explain it more simply."

Of course, he was actually very clever and what he was actually saying, in code, was "the Judge hasn't got that point."

Here is not the place to theorise as to why the Judge had not understood.

1.23. *If he is taking his ease, give him no rest. If his forces are united, separate them.*

The first part of this principle has been discussed above: harry one's opponent non-stop so as to keep him under pressure.

I do not advocate the use of "death by paper." This is the production of massive amounts of documentation to soak up an opponents' resources. In many cases, it creates an unnecessary risk as to costs for one's own client as well as a great deal of pointless work within one's own office which, at least initially, one's own client has to pay for, except in a no-win, no fee arrangement in which case the additional work has to be paid for out of the fee, so reducing profit. Yet I do support the use of "interrogatories."

Interrogatories are, in layman's terms, questions posed to the other side in litigation. They are served, with a realistic time-scale for answers to be given and, if answers are not given in time, then an application can be made.

Playing right to the edge of the Rules and depending on whether a notice of hearing is served by the Court or by the litigator, a forceful tactic is to issue the application as soon as the interrogatories are served.

Usually, such a hearing will require only a short period of notice - but the court lists may be so long that a hearing date may be several weeks away.

If the required period of notice for the hearing is three working days, then an application can be made even before the interrogatories are served and the application can be held in reserve. Now the litigator works backwards from the date when the application is due to be heard.

The litigator counts back three working days (usually said to be "clear days" which means three days not including the day of service or the day of the hearing) and then counts back the number of days that will be allowed for reply, for example seven days.

The interrogatories would therefore be served ten clear days before the hearing date which the litigator knows but his opponent does not.

If no answer is received on or before three days before the hearing date, then the application is served at the last minute. Many Rules of Court specify that applications must be served before a certain time, often 4pm, in order to qualify for service that day, otherwise they are deemed served the following day. It is therefore imperative that the application is served before the cut-off time using whatever method of service is considered appropriate. There is more on this in the penultimate chapter, *The Attack by Fire.*

A vicious tactic is to serve by fax, to a general fax machine in a large firm not to the fax machine dedicated to the department dealing with the case. Provided that the Notice of Acting filed and served by the other side has not specified a particular fax number, then service is good. By the time it reaches the department concerned, significant time may be lost, especially if a file reference is omitted from the covering letter. Indeed, it might not make it to the litigator concerned until the following morning.

The pressure is now on on the firm that thought it had, say, the seven days in the notice containing the interrogatories, plus however long it took to issue the application and then however many days or even weeks it would be before the application date came around. Now it finds that it has only some three days to reply failing which it has to explain its dilatory behaviour to the Court.

Where the Court serves the notice, this is not possible, but some courts do permit the parties to serve their own notices of hearing, even when the normal practice is for the Court to serve. In such circumstances, such an option should be taken.

I, incidentally, used to specify in the notice of acting that service by fax was not accepted and refuse to specify any fax number for service. This made it difficult for this tactic to be used against me, even though my opponents might allow service on them by fax. Service which is not in accordance with the notice of acting is not good service: very few firms, especially large firms, ever bothered to read the notice properly with the result that their efforts at last minute service were generally frustrated. That left it open to me to arrive at Court and have the hearing adjourned for short notice and to secure a costs order causing them both cost, delay and embarrassment with their client.

There are two interpretations of the second part of this principle.

Some say that Sun Tzu says to divide the members of the opposing force. Others say that he means to divide the sovereign from his generals, in our terms the client from the litigator.

It is here argued that the latter interpretation has more relevance to litigation but there are possibilities for both.

If a member of the opposing litigation team has a specific weakness, then it might be possible to play on it. However, one has to be careful not to be gratuitously cruel. I do not suggest that one should go so far as to actively target the life of one of the team to cause him upset: this is not Hollywood and its famous crazy silver-screen gun-slinger lawyers who have somehow managed to find a dictionary with the word "ethics" missing.

But there are fair and legitimate ways to target an individual in the opposing team. For example, if one member of the team always takes the role of advocate for applications, he is isolated from the herd by the simple act of being sent to Court. It is possible to engage him in conversation while waiting to go in and to discuss some peripheral aspect of the case where you think his case is especially strong. But by presenting to him the suggestion that it is the weakest part of the case, you can begin to undermine him and his team.

Questions such as "I see you plan to .... We can't see that. How do you think you can prove it?" may not elicit any response. But, one of three things will happen. First, he will forget all about it and the tactic has been unsuccessful. Or he will go back to the office and discuss it. The third option - and the one that is the aim of the plan - is that he will go back to the office, say nothing and investigate the supposed weakness himself, looking for the problem (which so far as you know does not exist) and therefore focussing on that instead of the areas of the case that you know are weak and where you believe you will be able to attack later.

Eventually, out of frustration or worry that he has missed something he will begin to discuss it with the rest of the team. But by then, he already feels that he is not doing his job properly and that leads, ultimately and perhaps only in a tiny way, to him losing confidence. Because confidence is of core importance to a litigator, he will begin to under-perform.

If he refers it to others, lawyers being a highly competitive bunch, the likely response is that those who know there is nothing wrong will ridicule him and the team leaders will be angry at the wasted time - all the while wondering how to justify billing it.

In this way, it is possible to begin to undermine the unity in the team.

The second interpretation is that Sun Tzu means to try to drive a wedge between the client and the litigator.

This is much harder than it seems. Clients appoint lawyers because they trust them to do the best possible job. If they do not trust the lawyer, the relationship is fractious and, often, fractures. But, in general, the relationship is pretty solid.

Given that it is unprofessional to approach another lawyer's client (especially in the course of litigation) how can one litigator begin to undermine that relationship?

Again, let's stay away from the goggle-box view of lawyers and the dramatic stunts as seen on TV. The reality is much more prosaic.

Clients sue for money or for "principle." Clients who sue for money are business-like. They make a cost-benefit analysis and decide what the financial and opportunity costs of litigation are likely to be and balance that against the expected (perhaps it is better to call it hoped-for) gains. Provided there is sufficient margin to take account of litigation risk, then clients go ahead.

If during the litigation the balance is disturbed, especially where there has been some change to the costs that have to be provided, by the client, for periodic billing and to keep topping up the balance the litigator keeps "on account," then the client will think - each time he writes a cheque - "how much more money do I want to put into this? "

Therefore any strategy that causes one's opponent to keep having to go back to his client for money will cause friction.

If one's opponent has (inexplicably but some do) agreed to charge a flat rate for the whole case or even for specific stages, then to compel him to erode his profit margin will, in many cases, cause one's opponent to cut corners, to de-prioritise the case or, simply, to lose interest in it unless something dramatic happens - he will become reactive not pre-active because being pre-active means spending time that he does not have the budget to cover.

If the case is being funded by the lawyers themselves on a "no win, no fee" basis, then they are inevitably in conflict with their client's interests if the case becomes large and complex but the likely benefits are not substantial.

Finally, if one's opponent is funded by a third party e.g. the state or an insurance company, they will have some say in what one's opponent is allowed to do. This conflict puts the litigator in a very difficult position: he is professionally bound to give all clients the best - and highest he can manage - standard of service. This is a duty that is honoured more in the breach than in reality, at least in relation to state funded work where the pay rates are low and the allowable work is often second guessed and work done disallowed for payment. But although the duty as to careful husbanding of costs and fees is owed to the indemnifying party, the duty as to performance is owed to the client and the client wants to see results.

This is a golden opportunity to create a three-way conflict.

Earlier, I said that I do not approve of "death by paper," and I don't. However, sometimes, there can be a benefit.

One has to be careful not to behave in a way that the Court will criticise. So the idea of sending a container lorry up to the door of a law firm and using a fork-lift truck to unload pallet after pallet of boxes of documents will never be acceptable in most courts.

Also, one has to remember who is liable for the initial cost of production of those documents.

If there is a system in place under which each party pays for the copies of the documents he wishes to have made, then self-interest tempers the demand. However, where the system of "inspection" is adopted, a litigator visits the offices of his opponent and examines the documents that have been listed in order to decide what to take copies of.

So, death by paper can be a weapon that can bite back.

But a smaller version can be useful. If one's opponent serves interrogatories, then - depending on the opponent's resources - replies can be submitted accompanied by documents with the reply being to refer to a bundle, not necessarily to a particular page. Depending upon one's opponent's resources just two or three thousand pages can cause considerable disruption. If that is followed up with a series of applications and, perhaps, one's own set of interrogatories, then considerable pressure can be put on resources and the budget in one's opponent's office.

1.24. Attack him where he is unprepared, appear where you are not expected.

All litigation proceeds in fits and starts. But of more interest for this principle is that a case is made up of a number of streams. Those streams do not, always, move at the same speed.

Often, the interviewing of witnesses takes place after a claim has been issued, despite the general rule of being fully prepared before issuing proceedings and, ideally, before the Letter Before Action is despatched.

All too frequently, litigators do not test the evidence before issuing proceedings.

Where the client is funding the action, bills are often delivered at the end of the month and charged against a sum held on account. However, many firms do not like to ask established clients for moneys on account, trusting instead that the client will pay promptly usually within 14 to 28 days.

All of these provide an opportunity to attack.

Earlier reference was made to contacting the witnesses for the other side. Considerable disruption can be caused by getting to the other side's witnesses first. Therefore as soon as a claim is served, a litigator should discuss with his client who might be able to support the statement of claim. The litigator should not delay - he should immediately contact those persons and ask them to attend a meeting. This is a different approach to that described earlier - there the plan was to destabilise relationships; here the plan is to discover if a relationship can be built between the litigator and the person who - at this stage - is only a potential witness for the other side. Therefore, instead of writing demanding attendance at a fixed appointment, one would write asking the potential witness to call to make an appointment.

While a statement of claim does not include a statement of evidence, it must give sufficient information to allow the claim to be answered. As a result, there will be clues as to the evidence that will be presented later. These clues must be carefully examined and where possible the actual evidence determined.

If the evidence is available for inspection without the consent of one's opponent (e.g. in a public car park rather than in a gated factory) then it must be inspected and comprehensive details taken. This prepares the litigator in readiness for the evidence - and provides an opportunity to make an application for its preservation. Often, where property is damaged, it will be repaired before trial. But if a case can be made for its preservation in order that it can be examined at trial, considerable inconvenience can be caused to the opposing client. At its simplest, he may be without his car, or have a wall knocked down or, in more complicated cases, find a factory at a standstill while machinery is ordered to be preserved. He may well be forced to make an admission, express or implied, of fault. For example, he may put up safety signs, new guards or issue new training or other manuals in order to get the machine back into service.

There is always a valid argument for preserving real evidence rather than relying on reports and photographs. However, there has to be a good reason for doing so where there is a risk of loss arising from the preservation.

The third point was to do with billing and payment schedules. Again returning to the question of applications and the time for service, it is useful to consider holding back service until after the expected billing period, then to serve the notice with the minimum period before the hearing, ideally with the hearing set approximately in the second or third week of the month. This will cause an immediate question as to whether the funds in hand (where there is a payment on account) are sufficient to cover the outstanding bill plus the additional, surprise and urgent work. If one's opponent can be compelled to go back to the client and ask for additional sums on account in addition to the prompt settlement of an outstanding periodic bill, then the litigator looks bad in his client's eyes.

It looks as if the litigator did not plan properly (even though on the facts available to him, he did) or that his management of the finances is not as good as it might be. Neither of course is true but clients, when confronted with an urgent demand for money, will often feel the need to blame someone and the nearest someone is their own lawyer. The client is often prone to being suspicious of the explanation provided by their lawyer even though it is demonstrably true.

The fact is that most lawyers are really bad at asking clients for money; we find it embarrassing. It's akin to being in trade when being in law is a profession. It is, of course, a business and has to be run like one. No one expects to leave a shop without paying, nor even a dentist's surgery. But clients often expect lawyers to give them credit.

It is therefore always a valuable tactic to disrupt the financial planning of one's opponent because the effects are complex and go the heart of the lawyer-client relationship.

1.25. These military devices, leading to victory, must not be divulged beforehand.

Just as any field commander (at least in war as Sun Tzu knew it) can assess the fire-power and manpower of the opposing army. He also knows the available strategies. But he cannot know what his opponent will do and when (except in the rather dance-like set-piece battles that dominated in Europe and the England for several hundred years), a litigator knows, in broad terms, what his opponent can bring to bear - the exchange of evidence is akin to making visible the available resources. But he does not know and cannot compel his opponent to reveal, his strategies. And each litigator should keep those strategies secret until they are deployed.

1.26. Now the general who wins a battle makes many calculations in his temple ere the battle is fought. The general who loses a battle makes but few calculations beforehand. Thus do many calculations lead to victory and few calculations to defeat: how much more no calculation at all! It is by attention to this point that I can foresee who is likely to win or lose.

The "temple" referred to was a portable temple that was set up away from the battlefield for Generals to pray and formulate their strategies in peace and quiet. It is, to all intents and purposes, the same as the litigator's office. Sun Tzu says that the general who wins is the general who develops multiple scenarii, who has alternatives for when things go according to plan and when they don't. And it cautions against trying to do battle without a plan.

It is surprising that, today, we still use this same maxim, albeit simplified: "He who fails to plan, plans to fail."

In short, your chances of success are slim indeed if you choose to just "wing it."

A badly formed battle plan is almost impossible to turn around and if it can be turned around it will be at huge cost. Sometimes, the cost of trying to turn around a bad plan and failing can be catastrophic.

At the Battle of Waterloo, Napoleon, France's greatest leader and self-proclaimed Emperor, turned up with an army already weary from a succession of battles. Aware that the English, under Wellington, had set up camp on - and beyond - a ridge, he marshalled his forces in readiness. Over a period of about eight hours, his army, which had a history of spectacular successes and a small number of failures, had been routed. The total number of dead on all three sides (the Prussian Army had arrived half-way through the battle after a rapid march to re-engage Napoleon after, he wrongly thought, he had defeated them) is estimated at some 50,000.

A simplified history of the Battle is instructive, demonstrating as it does many of the principles set out by Sun Tzu and clearly applicable in the art of litigation.

Wellington won not by superior fire power nor by weight of numbers but by clever use of terrain and effective use of simpler technology.

Napoleon first lined up his heavy artillery, known as the "Grand Barrage" or Grand Battery. His first problem was to manœuvre the guns into position: they were in a muddy meadow and they bogged down.

The Grand Barrage was a tactic of shock and awe. The thundering guns shaking the ground and making a huge noise and a lot of smoke. And their use was intended to maximise the effect by co-ordinated firing, all at once.

It fired heavy, slow moving cannonballs and exploding ball-like shells. The shells were, in effect, grenades, intended to kill, injure and maim by shrapnel. If a gun was pointing in the wrong direction it was incredibly difficult to move in normal times and, in mud, exponentially worse.

But the muddy ground was on both sides of the hill and the exploding balls sank into the mud. Not deep, but deep enough to contain the shrapnel effect.

Worse, the guns took a long time to re-load. And so there was a barrage, then nothing, then a barrage, then nothing. Shock and awe doesn't work with periods of respite.

Far from creating fear in the British ranks, the failure of the tactic heartened the British.

The French did not know that when their cavalry raced up the hill only to find, on the other side, the massed British forces, far from cowering, formed into the standard four-square formation which is all-but impregnable to cavalry and can cause considerable harm in response to any attack.

And, as the horses got too close to turn around, the British blocks moved into defensive position: one row dropping to their knees, muskets loaded, bayonets fixed, ready to attack upwards, under the necks and bodies of the horses; a second row, similarly armed, aimed higher, at the riders.

Several attacks were mounted on the squares, but each was repelled in short order. The British, aware of Napoleon's habitual strategies, expected the next move from the French, watched the horses withdraw and rolled their lightweight artillery to the top of the ridge but just out of sight. As Napoleon's foot soldiers, his infantry, under the command of General Ney walked forward, the light cannon were brought into effect. They shot a six pound (2.75kg) ball which relied on velocity rather than mass. Just to prove that all your struggling in physics class at school was not entirely wasted on those planning a non-scientific career, we can get some useful information here.

At *velocity* approaching 320kph - the speed of a Formula One car - a ball with a 2.75kg *mass* hits with a *force* (or "momentum") of 2.75 x 320 = 8800 *kg•km/h* (a very unwieldy term).

So what does that tell us?

Because of the high speed and the small profile of the ball, it punches holes in things and the things it punches holes in are people. On some estimates, the smaller British ball travelling at a much greater velocity could put a hole in somewhere between ten and fifteen soldiers marching in close-packed formation.

As they approached the hill, the French were in close packed formation.

The British also engaged a much less sophisticated shrapnel device than that of the big barrage: called "container shot" a container that looked like a second hand baked bean tin (of course, it wasn't) was filled, on a good day, with dozens of small balls, turning the cannon into, in effect, a large scale shotgun. As the container flew out, the balls spread, dissipating some of their energy but they were smaller and so needed less energy to penetrate. On a bad day, if the artillery had run out of shot, the containers would be filled with anything they could find: pebbles, sharp stones, pieces of metal, nails.... In short, it was an early version of today's "nail bomb" that so strikes fear into civil security forces everywhere. A single container could kill or seriously maim as many as 20 soldiers, on some estimates. Unlike the single-shot which penetrated deep into the lines, the container shot brought them down in a horizontal line, so that those behind had to step on or over fallen colleagues. The much smaller guns were faster to reload than those of the French and they were more easily moved in the mud, so allowing re-aiming. Finally, they were fired in volleys, not all at once, keeping up a constant pressure on the French until they recognised the futility of that form of attack and pulled back.

Napoleon, before the infantry march, had left the field of battle and headed home due to a stomach upset, a condition which - with others - had been a problem for several months. But even so, to go away for a couple of hours in what was shaping up to be the most decisive battle of his career was strange. Some commentators argue that he knew a loss was inevitable and so, by leaving General Ney, a veteran of the Prussian front and, according to many historians, suffering from battle fatigue, Napoleon would have someone to blame when it all went horribly wrong.

As it did: the Prussians attacked from the flank, taking territory almost at will. Against that attack, the French deployed The Old Guard depleting their forces for the assault on Wellington. But it was too late: the defence was reactive and ill-considered.

The final assault was by the Imperial Guard, Napoleon's elite troops. Basically, they were the final attempt to overcome the British. If they were lost, the war was lost.

It was not as if Napoleon did not plan: he was, after all, a master strategist. He waited three days before engaging Wellington, worried that the ground was too muddy. But his hand was forced by intelligence that said that the Prussian Army was getting closer. And he appears to have entirely underestimated the speed and even the strength of the Prussians, as well as their preparedness for battle and their willingness to fight.

Also, Napoleon over-estimated the effect of his Grand Barrage.

There was another factor at play: the British operated on a system of delegated authority. Once Napoleon's plans were known, Wellington (who had previously famously said that he could not form a plan until he knew what Napoleon's plans were) gave his commanders (various ranks for various units) orders and authority to act independently when circumstances demanded it.

The benefit to the British was that, within Wellington's broader parameters and the training that the men had, were not entirely predictable. But there was close communication between the commanders, ensuring that they were available both to assist each other when required and to make co-ordinated attacks.

Napoleon was a micro-manager.

So while Napoleon wanted to know exactly what was happening and to direct individual units in real time (at least until he went away for a few hours' potty break), Wellington wanted to know what was happening but not to interfere unless his bird's eye view had identified something his commanders, closer to the action, could not see.

Ney, increasingly battle weary, was even worse, storming around the lines, berating individual soldiers, smacking his sword on cannon in frustration at the reloading time, racing his horse up and down the lines yelling at the men who were trying to steel themselves for the walk into gunfire and, for the front row at least, a very high probability of death or serious injury.

Napoleon failed to assess the mental state of Ney (or did so and, as noted above, set him up for failure) and his ability to lead. There is little doubt that Ney was not fit to lead the French that day despite his previously excellent record.

The lessons for litigation are clear: if you make an attack, lots of smoke and noise might provide a short term distraction but when those clear and your opponent can assess the damage, it is he who will know how much harm has been caused not you. And while the battlefield may look a mess, even your heavy guns, if not used properly might cause only superficial damage.

The failure to properly assess the risks posed by the Prussian army was a major error: Wellington knew where they were, how they were armed, what their capacity was, where they were going and when they would get there. He knew because, despite the numbers of French in the vicinity, he and the Prussian generals were in correspondence several times during the days leading up to the battle and, even, during the battle itself.

Napoleon failed to secure a perimeter around the British : he had enough men to provide skirmish groups who could police an area around the British who were on foreign soil. But he did not have sufficient to encircle the British. Couriers were able to carry letters back and forth with impunity. Supply lines were not subject to any significant interference. Instead, Napoleon preferred to focus on what amounted to an invitation to take part in a set-piece battle.

There are few explanations for why he chose to engage in such an unfavourable place and in such unfavourable conditions. One is that he considered himself infallible, that he was too arrogant to think he could lose.

The next day, he surrendered to the British and was exiled to St Helena, a fallen Emperor who had lost his life's achievements in somewhere between eight and twelve hours due to uncharacteristically poor planning, poor execution and failure to properly assess the threats he faced.

Use one's commanders wisely: if they are hand picked and able, then once they have been given direction, leave them to do their job, overseeing and guiding from a strategic point of view but not trying to be involved in every single decision. A good General places his trust in his commanders.

But he also reviews that trust because, especially in long litigation, everyone has an off day. And like in war, in litigation there is rarely a chance to recover. Better to remove a badly performing commander from the field and bring him back rested than to let him run the risk of losing the battle.

But most of all, Napoleon might have won if he had decided not to fight on the terrain and in the conditions chosen by Wellington.

Wellington's men simply waited for Napoleon's men to tramp or ride through the mud and up a hill, either to be met with a hail of gunfire or, if they charged over the crest of the hill,, a mass of muskets and bayonets.

Napoleon, the great strategist, initially probably thinking he could not lose, rushed in, lost his head and lost the battle and, as a result, lost the war.

There, in the abbreviated story of just one battle, is the encapsulation of many of Sun Tzu's principles and an object lesson for litigators.

Slightly missing the point that his countryman had trounced Napoleon in the final battle, Col. George Francis Robert Henderson (1854–1903 and therefore a contemporary of Giles) is quoted by Giles in the notes to the original translation. "The rules of strategy are few and simple. They may be learned in a week. They may be taught by familiar illustrations or a dozen diagrams. But such knowledge will no more teach a man to lead an army like Napoleon than a knowledge of grammar will teach him to write like Gibbon. "

Well, Napoleon had had a tremendous run of success until the British turned up in a muddy field wearing their wellies.

"Nobody remembers who came in second."

Charles Schulz,
creator of cartoon strip Peanuts

(But it's not true in litigation
where the loser often attracts
more attention than the winner.)

2. Waging War

2. Waging War

2.1. Sun Tzu said: in the operations of war, where there are in the field a thousand swift chariots, as many heavy chariots and a hundred thousand mail-clad soldiers, with provisions enough to carry them a thousand LI, the expenditure at home and at the front, including entertainment of guests, small items such as glue and paint and sums spent on chariots and armour, will reach the total of a thousand ounces of silver per day. Such is the cost of raising an army of 100,000 men.

The title of this Chapter is almost a pun. The chapter is about the securing, managing and use of resources. And so, when Sun Tzu says about chariots, mail-clad soldiers and the cost of the minutiae of life, even before reaching battle, he is planning for the most important aspect of battle: to make sure that his men are properly provisioned, properly equipped and that they have been paid and are not concerned that they (or their families) will not be paid after the battle - assuming, of course, that they win.

In Sun Tzu's time, if they lost, the chances were they would be killed along with all the officers and anyone else the victors could find.

Litigation is often like that: to the victor the spoils. The winner not only gains his prize but also a significant proportion of the costs of battle. The loser, well, loses.

Note, too, that Sun Tzu recognises that there is expenditure at the front - i.e. where the war is fought - and back at home.

Sun Tzu says to prepare provisions, or at least the means to pay for provisions, for a long way and a long time to come. Of course, there is a degree of rhetoric in what he says when he refers to "1,000 li" - that's about 2,750 miles or 4,400 kilometres. The amounts he talks about seem out of kilter with the numbers: to march 100,000 men, with their equipment and horses and their provisions for 1,000 li at a cost of only one ounce of silver for every 100 men seems very optimistic, again suggesting that there is rhetoric.

But whether his calculations stack up is not the point. The point is whether, in a case which a litigator is conducting, he is able to produce a budget at the outset and ensure that the funding is available.

Of course, some funding may come from the state or from insurance but in the majority of cases, funding comes from one's own client either in the form of a no-win, no-fee agreement or in the form of stage payments paid by the client as the litigation progresses.

The single most difficult area to manage of the client-lawyer relationship is that of costs. The client will, in many cases, simply not see where the time has gone (and here, no account is made of "creative" activity on the time-sheets). Clients do not, in general, understand that, in order to strategise, lawyers need peace and quiet and that, clichéd as it is, an afternoon fishing or weeding the garden is, genuinely, valid thinking time.

People think in different ways. Some like to make lists, some like to talk in groups, some like to put some seriously loud rock music on big speakers and shake the walls, some like to play golf, some like to do dangerous sports (or at least a bit risky - no point in being so injured you can't work!)

Others like to lie in a hot bath or to sit at home on the sofa with their arms around a loved one who is reading a book while they stare out of the window, letting complexity sort itself out, piece by piece and forming a logical pattern.

The fact is that there will, always, be time spent on a case that a client will question. Rarely will the client see the irony that the litigation is often due to the fact that, at an earlier date, the client did not allow sufficient time for contemplation before following a particular course of action or entering into a particular contract.

Time like this is notoriously difficult to budget for.

It is difficult to budget for how long it will take to draft a pleading or an affidavit.

All litigators come up against a client or witness who is, without meaning to be, almost impossible to interview. And when that happens, time disappears with very little to show for it.

I had this problem: a client in a small matter was incredibly difficult to secure instructions from. Although the issues were simple and the amounts of money small, she was beside herself with worry. There were many telephone calls, sometimes only minutes apart, asking questions or asking as to progress. She paid no heed to written advice, demanding to be seen even though in the meeting even less was said than in detailed written advice. In short, she needed her hand holding constantly, even though she was repeatedly advised that, at the end of the case, all the wasted time would be paid for out of her damages because the other side could not be expected to pay for her excessive demands.

At the conclusion of the matter, when it came to having our bill "taxed," i.e. assessed by the Court for reasonableness, the District Judge who examined the bill could not understand where the time had gone.

Historically (and as a party trick) old litigators used to weigh a file in their hand and estimate the likely fee. Some of us were very good at it. In this case, however, the fee far outweighed the expected amount.

It was only by detailed examination of the attendance notes which detailed frequent and long meetings at which very little actually happened, that it was clear where the time had gone.

Rightly, the District Judge moved huge chunks of time from "party and party" costs to "common fund" - a term used under the UK's legal aid provisions which means that she bore the costs out of her winnings.

The District Judge asked me why she had been able to run up such a large amount of time. I explained that trying to interview her was "like swimming through treacle" and that everything had to be explained over and over again.

Ultimately, she paid the price for her excessive demands.

Sun Tzu reminds us that there are all manner of expenses that arise during war and it is the same in litigation. Everything from courier's fees through copying charges to the cost of transport has to come from somewhere. And that somewhere is the client or third party payer.

In some cases, passing on those charges to the client is not acceptable: they are part of overhead. The stories of firms charging for new shirts for staff after an all-night session and, in one particularly widespread anecdote, for a pop-up toaster and some bread are legion. Clients have become fed up with such antics and are now much more alert to what is included in "disbursement" items and, as a result, things that in simpler (and more dishonest or at least opportunistic) times would have been added to the bill are routinely and rightly tossed out by clients.

2.2. When you engage in actual fighting, if victory is long in coming, then men's weapons will grow dull and their ardour will be damped. If you lay siege to a town, you will exhaust your strength.

2.3. Again, if the campaign is protracted, the resources of the State will not be equal to the strain.

2.4. Now, when your weapons are dulled, your ardour damped, your strength exhausted and your treasure spent, other chieftains will spring up to take advantage of your extremity. Then no man, however wise, will be able to avert the consequences that must ensue.

Principles 2, 3 and 4 sit together, as one.

Sun Tzu is a believer in a quick kill. He's right. A good litigator does not view the Letter Before Action as a preliminary step leading to a possible negotiation or litigation if negotiation fails. The Letter Before Action is the first step in litigation. And, if it is done right, in many cases it will be the last.

It must be clear, precise and demand exactly what the litigator's client wants (or at least what he wants and is, so far as the litigator can tell, entitled to), a clear deadline and a clear note of the consequences.

And if the "what" is not done by the "when," the "then" must follow without hesitation and without mercy.

A good litigator knows that the first strike is one of the most important steps in litigation. That is why he must prepare thoroughly before taking that step. It is like the gladiator who has to lift his sword and make sure it is in the strike position before making the strike.

A Letter Before Action is a statement of intent. If weakness is shown by the writer of the letter, then his opponent knows that he can be weakened elsewhere, perhaps even by the simple tactic of not replying.

I have seen examples of litigators who write a Letter Before Action and, getting no reply, wait a few days then write a second letter, this time by recorded delivery or some other form of provable delivery system. The element of surprise is lost, the ability for a quick strike is lost and the ability to demonstrate a strong will is lost. This is not the way to conduct litigation.

Later in the litigation, whenever there is a chance for a "technical knock-out" it must be taken.

A long siege is both exhausting and generally debilitating for the army outside the walls which, not to put too fine a point on it, get bored, especially after they have plundered all the surrounding villages and eaten all the livestock they found.

It's exactly the same in litigation: if you have a large case, it takes up a lot of your time, even if you are not doing very much or making much progress. And soon all you are able to handle is a succession of little things on the side which are more interesting but not very profitable or career enhancing.

And, to return to the question of costs, principle 3 is wonderfully clear: long litigation costs a lot and eventually the client is likely to run out of money. Or the will to keep paying. Or in the case of corporate litigation, new management may decide that to continue is not in their plan.

The consequences of running out of money are severe. His lawyers withdraw because they are not being paid. His action is likely to be struck out and he is likely to be left with a massive bill for his opponent's costs. Bearing in mind that the reason he did not continue with the litigation is because he has no money, a substantial costs order could drive him into penury.

This is exactly what some litigators - and some clients - try to do. To simply make a client who has a good claim run out of money and then to grind him into the ground.

That is why it is the duty of a litigator to win quickly and cheaply whenever possible.

Incidentally, while much is made in this work of the use of the Letter Before Action, there are circumstances, discussed later, where a Letter Before Action may actually be counter-productive.

Principle 4 is a beautifully phrased analysis of the consequences of long, draw-out litigation. As litigation fatigue sets in, as the money runs out, one's opponents are able to take advantage of the weaknesses that are created.

How much better, then, to avoid getting into that state in the first place by being a forceful and effective attacker right from the outset and at every point where your opponent can be weakened.

2.5. Thus, though we have heard of stupid haste in war, cleverness has never been seen associated with long delays.

There is a theory that litigation can be won by wearing down your opponent.

Some have tried to apply the same idea in boxing: allowing oneself to he repeatedly punched in the hope that one's opponent will eventually tire. Usually, the one taking the punches is the one who gets worn out - or beaten up - first.

Of course, some boxers recognise that they can tire their opponent by dancing around the ring, making their opponent take wild swings that miss. It's true: getting out of the way takes less energy than winding up and throwing a punch. But the risk is that the dancer doesn't see one of the punches coming, that the puncher is applying the principle discussed earlier, of applying a subterfuge. In sports, including boxing, it is known as a "feint," to make one's opponent think one is going to do one thing, then doing another.

It can be seen, then, that the idea of allowing the other side to have control of the pace of the action while you are in fact slowing it down has a substantial potential downside.

That downside can be to be taken by surprise and to be knocked out.

Clients do not like that.

Sun Tzu also talks of "stupid haste." A more modern phrase is "fools rush in where angels fear to tread."

It reinforces the concept that no action should be taken without full preparation and consideration.

2.6. There is no instance of a country having benefited from prolonged warfare.

Principle 6 does go a little further than 2, 3 and 4 in that it says that, even if the war is not lost, the cost of winning may be so great as to make the victory hollow.

Costs that are not recoverable from the other side at the conclusion of a long action are one aspect of this but, often, even more important are the indirect consequences.

Litigation is mentally stressful for clients. It causes them problems at work and at home, particularly during the preparation and pre-trial phases. The actual trial (and any appeals) create stress levels that most people do not expect to meet in their working lives.

For the lawyers, it's a serious business but it's also a game. There is little more stimulating that a good case.

And it is a game that the lawyer rarely loses in that, even if he loses the case, he will - mostly - get paid.

Clients have to put the management of their businesses on hold, or engage additional managers to do work they would ordinarily do themselves. These costs are not recoverable.

At home, clients find themselves thinking about the litigation when they should be playing with their children or taking their wife out for dinner. Instead of going out to weed the garden, they sit making lists, thinking of questions to ask, of ideas to present, even blaming themselves for having got into the situation where the litigation arose.

The risks can be extreme: so extreme that the Canadian Bar Association published an article called "Lawyers: Gate-keepers For Psychological Issues " regarding the stress of litigation and the risk that, in some cases, the client may consider or even commit suicide.

The longer litigation continues, the more serious the stress on clients becomes.

It is all too easy to think that litigation is all about huge cases involving major corporations. It is not. Looking the cause list in almost any court - and every criminal court - shows that the vast majority of cases involve individuals and small business owners.

Small business owners are a special case: if they lose, they risk their family's livelihood and the livelihoods of all those they employ and, in a small business, the staff are generally quite close knit, almost a secondary family.

Lawyers rarely see that. Lawyers see the client as a means to an end - to have a bit of fun and get to get paid for it.

And, to a degree, it's right that they should. Although it is right that lawyers advise clients of the consequences of a win or a loss, they should not become in the client's domestic affairs, in the client's emotional state.

The effective litigator is driven by the desire to excel and to achieve the best possible result for his client. He must remain objective.

But even if he closes his eyes to it, to practice his art without dilution by other factors, the big picture is still there.

The stress suffered by the client can be aggravated by other factors - for example, a client in a personal injury case may be unable to earn his full, or any, income and the financial pressures may be building up.

Or a business may find that an injunction has frozen important assets (perhaps even the means of production) or blocked the sale of product due to e.g. a patent claim. As a result, cashflow might be reduced or entirely stalled.

Litigation is not fun for clients. It's horrible.

Their integrity is under attack, their way of life is under threat, their time and mental energies are diverted to things they don't want to do, preventing them enjoying their work and life.

For direct and indirect financial reasons and for the social and mental health reasons outlined, litigation should be conducted with proper (not undue) haste, even if it's not as much fun for the lawyer or if it means that the case will not generate as much in fees as it might in other circumstances.

A bankrupt or dead client is not, as Sun Tzu implies, an ideal outcome.

The Canada Bar Association article referred to is at http://www.cba.org/cba/practicelink/careerbuilders_clients/psy ch.aspx

2.7. It is only one who is thoroughly acquainted with the evils of war that can thoroughly understand the profitable way of carrying it on.

It is logical to assume that a seasoned litigator will have more experience in the economical exercise of his art.

The purpose of litigation is either to produce some benefit for one's client or to defend against a party who is trying to make a benefit at one's client's expense.

It follows that, either as a gain or as limiting or preventing a loss, litigation is conducted with a view to, in broad terms, profit.

The profit may not be financial: it may be to enforce a right e.g. over a boundary dispute where there is no obvious fiscal gain to be had.

Drawn out litigation in such circumstances is doubly costly because there is no back-stop in the form of damages (or, at least, sufficient damages) to cover any shortfall in costs between the full bill charged by the litigator and the costs recovered from the other side.

An experienced litigator will understand this and, depending on which side he is on, do everything in his power to bring the case to an early and cost-effective conclusion or do everything in his power to put financial pressure on his opponent including dragging it out unecessarily.

2.8. The skilful soldier does not raise a second levy, neither are his supply-wagons loaded more than twice.

Wars are financed by a levy: today, it is a general levy charged to the population through the taxation system but in times past it was by a specific "war chest" that, usually, Nobles were required to fund by a mix of money and in kind - usually soldiers and their provisions.

Principle 10 speaks to this:

2.10. Poverty of the State exchequer causes an army to be maintained by contributions from a distance. Contributing to maintain an army at a distance causes the people to be impoverished.

Returning to principle 8, Sun Tzu says that a properly prepared battle plan must include a budget and that if the plan is properly prepared and executed, there should be no need to go back to raise further funds or additional resources.

And so it is with litigation. Any good plan will include sufficient funding to cover contingencies.

The estimated total cost of litigation should be presented to the client. He should not be taken by surprise. Clients are naturally suspicious that they may be taken advantage of in a situation where they have no second opinion nor any realistic alternative but to carry on with the course of action that they have embarked upon. Where they are told that the initial funding requirement was inadequate and more money is needed, they often feel - even if they do not express it - that there is "charging by ambush."

It is therefore important that a budget is set and adhered to.

There is a method of supporting litigation without recourse to the client - that of demanding and obtaining costs orders during the conduct of litigation.

This is outlined in principle 9:

2.9. Bring war material with you from home but forage on the enemy. Thus the army will have food enough for its needs.

It is therefore essential that, wherever possible, costs on every application are secured and that every opportunity is taken to avoid orders of "costs reserved" or "costs to follow the event."

"Costs reserved" means that the costs of the application are to be argued at trial. This is unsatisfactory in part because payment will be delayed but also because the Judge at the final hearing will have regard to the eventual decision and, human nature being what it is, that will have some impact on how he considers the question of costs in earlier applications, regardless of who was successful in them. But even more important is that the Judge will not have the benefit of context - and a sense of the conduct of the parties and their lawyers at the time the application was made.

To aid the Court in making a decision when the application is heard, a litigator should have a costs statement ready prepared and served on the other side in support of his application for costs. In fact, in recent years, this has become required practice in some English courts. Aside from the psychological benefit of being well prepared, the Judge hearing the application will not, then, be in the dark over what he may be ordering. Furthermore, the costs statement will demonstrate that the litigator has acted properly, that he has been fair but firm and that his opponent has been, for example, dilatory which is why the application was necessary.

"Costs to follow the event" is desirable where a party has lost an application but undesirable for a party which has been successful. Often, this Order is a form of mild rebuke because the Court feels that the party making the application had adopted strong tactics. It says "you will get the costs of this application if you win at trial; if you lose at trial, you will pay both sides' costs of this application."

It is therefore essential that a litigator is prepared to argue why strong tactics were essential, why what is euphemistically called "professional courtesy" was not extended.

"Professional courtesy" means allowing one's opponent leeway that the Rules do not provide for.

It is here argued that, in litigation, there is no room for such leeway unless it is specifically requested and there is good reason for it. A request that amounts to "I'm too busy to deal with this for a few days, can I have an extra week?" is not, in this author's view, a good reason.

But there are two other dimensions to Sun Tzu's principle.

First, we can view the question of provisions as relating to instructions or to information that can be turned into evidence. Going back to the beginning: it is incumbent on the litigator to make certain that he has the full story before embarking on a campaign, even before writing the Letter Before Action.

It is, by definition, a failure of that policy if it becomes necessary to go back to the client for further instructions. Of course, there are times when it is necessary to clarify information that the litigator has received but that is not the same as being taken by surprise and having to address an entirely new area.

Secondly, if there is a call for funds (or, for that matter, information) and one's own client does not provide it, then that causes delay. That undermines the principle that one should act quickly and decisively at all times.

2.11. On the other hand, the proximity of an army causes prices to go up; and high prices cause the people's substance to be drained away.

This principle has little application in relation to litigation save to say that, as pressure mounts and time becomes an increasingly precious resource, less care is taken to minimise expenses. Instead of searching the internet for an inexpensive flight or hotel, it's faster to phone a travel agent, book whatever flight and hotel they recommend and to get on the move even if the costs are significantly higher than they otherwise would be.

What Sun Tzu was warning against is that when an army is preparing for battle, there is always profiteering. That much is undoubtedly true: copy-shops next to a court house almost routinely have a higher per-copy and binding charge than one a few hundred metres away.

He then warns that this dissipates the war chest and may require additional funding.

In long trials away from home, we would take a clerk and a photocopying machine and set them up in a hotel room or, if the expectation was for very substantial copying, rent a copier. The usual plan was to rent normal hotel rooms for everyone except that clerk who got one suite, the latter providing a "sitting room" that was turned into what amounted to a war room for meetings, document preparation and such other work as may be necessary including tracking down last minute witnesses. The clerk or assistant who was allocated the suite soon found it to be a double edged benefit as half of the suite would be in near constant use by other members of the team.

2.12. When their substance is drained away, the peasantry will be afflicted by heavy exactions.

It's not nice to think of one's clients as "the peasantry" but in the context of Sun Tzu's writing it makes sense. And it supports what was said earlier: clients can be driven to penury by long litigation and it should be avoided wherever possible.

Principles 13 and 14 support this point in a graphic manner.

2.13, 2.14. With this loss of substance and exhaustion of strength, the homes of the people will be stripped bare and three-tenths of their income will be dissipated; while government expenses for broken chariots, worn-out horses, breast-plates and helmets, bows and arrows, spears and shields, protective mantles, draught-oxen and heavy wagons, will amount to four-tenths of its total revenue.

2.15. Hence a wise general makes a point of foraging on the enemy. One cartload of the enemy's provisions is equivalent to twenty of one's own and likewise a single PICUL of his provender is equivalent to twenty from one's own store.

Here, Sun Tzu is alluding to the fact that there are costs associated with re-provisioning at a distance. A locally sourced product is already there, one that has to be shipped in takes both time and money (and the risk of loss) to get it to where the army needs it.

Thus, producing a thousand pages of documentation on one's own office, then producing sufficient copies for witnesses, the parties and the Court, might cost roughly the same as producing them near the Court. However, the cost of shipping, especially if it is necessary to ship by courier, will result in a cost that is - in total - much higher than the cost of production near the Court even at the inflated prices that are charged there.

2.16. Now in order to kill the enemy, our men must be roused to anger; that there may be advantage from defeating the enemy, they must have their rewards.

Sun Tzu does not mean that crazed fighters win wars. In fact, the opposite is true. But he does mean that they must be prepared for battle and that a soldier "with his dander up" will be more aggressive and that, in war, aggression is an advantage where being passive is not.

And so it is in litigation. A good litigator thrives on the thrill of battle, he performs better when the adrenaline is flowing.

This is not to suggest that a team of lawyers should engage in pre-match locker room aggression building but rather that they should be ready for anything that their opponents may throw at them and also to act, without delay or fear, on the orders of the General.

But Sun Tzu recognises that there is a mix of carrot and stick and that the carrot is that there are bonuses to be had for good performance.

He therefore suggests that, where there are victories those who have provided outstanding service should be rewarded, so as to encourage continued excellence. He makes a very precise suggestion in principle 17.

2.17. Therefore in chariot fighting, when ten or more chariots have been taken, those should be rewarded who took the first. Our own flags should be substituted for those of the enemy and the chariots mingled and used in conjunction with ours. The captured soldiers should be kindly treated and kept.

In addition to sharing the benefits of the win, things which are won should be added to the victor's resources, to his war chest.

He also says that one should be magnanimous in victory, particularly to junior soldiers. They are, after all, following orders and are not the instigators of the battle.

For this reason, one should be courteous to one's opponents after a win, even a win in an interlocutory application.

This is not only a question of good PR. It destabilises the other side to know that they are dealing with a hard but fair opponent.

The other side wants to be angry: by treating them well after a win, it takes away much of the motivation to be angry.

And that refers back to principle 16: if a litigator can behave in such a way that his opponent behaves passively, then the next win will be easier. Sun Tzu expresses this in principle 18

2.18. This is called, using the conquered foe to augment one's own strength.

In short, a litigator can use his own generosity to build up his own case and, given that litigation is as much a mind-game as it is a battle of facts, this equates to tipping the balance in his own client's favour.

2.19. In war, then, let your great object be victory, not lengthy campaigns.

Sun Tzu says, in effect, hit hard, hit fast, show no mercy on the battlefield but be merciful in victory.

That is a very good ethos for litigation.

It also emphasises that winning the battle is not the same as winning the war. A victory at an interlocutory stage, at trial or on appeal is not a win unless the objective is achieved. So if a successful trial results in the failure of the business that was ordered to pay damages and so the damages remain unpaid, that is not a win.

2.20. Thus it may be known that the leader of armies is the arbiter of the people's fate, the man on whom it depends whether the nation shall be in peace or in peril.

It is very poor form to boast of individual successes and, in so doing, give away information relating to clients. But even without such self-promotion, word soon gets around when one wins.

And word of mouth is a strong form of persuasion when someone is looking for a champion.

In these days of reduced professionalism - where many lawyers behave is if they are in trade rather than in a profession, it is good to know that some lawyers still believe in the power of a satisfied client and a recommendation as a way to good quality business.

This principle supports the idea that by delivering the highest quality service (and, of course, ideally a win), litigators will gain a good reputation in the community they serve.

And that reputation leads to good quality business.

This is not to say that lawyers should not make themselves known, using a wide variety of media, only that such promotions should be moderated.

If lawyers behave like they are in trade, then clients will treat them that way.

Yet in order to properly advise a client, it is necessary to maintain a distance. And the lawyer's professional standing (not arrogance or disassociation from the community) helps in so doing.

It is very difficult to deliver bad news to a friend.

It is also difficult to deliver bad news to someone who has come to your door because of your self-proclaimed ability to win the most difficult cases.

Long term reputation, as Sun Tzu says in this principle, comes from the knowledge that he is ready, willing and able to take on challenges.

Reputations are gained by what other people think, not what the litigator thinks of himself.

It is necessary to relax your muscles when you can.
Relaxing your brain is fatal.

- Sir Stirling Moss
Racing Driver

3. Attack by Stratagem

3. Attack by Stratagem

3.1. Sun Tzu said: in the practical art of war, the best thing of all is to take the enemy's country whole and intact; to shatter and destroy it is not so good. So, too, it is better to recapture an army entire than to destroy it, to capture a regiment, a detachment or a company entire than to destroy them.

If a case can be won without the legal equivalent of bloodshed, that is by far the best result.

Yes, there are clients who want to see their opponents ground to dust. Whether you, as a litigator, wish to act where that is the motive is a matter for you and your conscience.

A good litigator considers ending up in Court as a form of loss in itself. And that is how Sun Tzu sees war as the second principle in this section makes clear:

3.2. Hence to fight and conquer in all your battles is not supreme excellence; supreme excellence consists in breaking the enemy' resistance without fighting.

Some litigators believe that they should keep their evidence until a time as close to trial as they can manage. They fight applications for discovery, they release only that which they are ordered to release and nothing more, even if what they hold back is evidence that would be sufficient to kill their opponent's case.

But that is not a good strategy.

To return to the question of the Letter Before Action: if it makes clear that there is a case to be answered and that there is no good defence, then the litigator who issues it is in a strong position.

If he goes on to demand the decision which, after hearing and testing the evidence, a Court is likely to make, then he can, even in that earliest piece of correspondence, begin to protect his client's position as to costs.

If his demands are reasonable, or unarguable, then he may be able to secure his victory at minimal expense - and stress - to his client.

But there is another chance to kill a case and that comes along almost as soon as the litigation commences.

As soon as a claim is filed, a defendant may - instead of filing a defence - issue an application to strike out the claim as failing to disclose any cause of action.

It is surprising how often a slapdash litigator produces a statement of claim that fails to make the case either in fact or, even more remarkably, in law.

It is the defence litigator's duty to make such an application.

In a class action suit brought against the Bank of New York, the lawyers bringing the action solicited instructions from persons who claimed they had lost value in their shares due to the actions of the bank and its directors. One of those who replied and put himself forward to be "lead plaintiff" was selected.

Incredibly, it was more that two years before the Court considered an application to strike out the action on the basis that the lead plaintiff was not a member of the class. Indeed, he had not been a shareholder at the time of the events complained of.

Aside from the possible failure to check such a fundamental point by the plaintiff's lawyers it is astonishing that, immediately the statement of claim was served, the bank's lawyers appear to have not cross-referenced the list of plaintiffs and, in particular, the lead plaintiff, to the share register.

Under the various principles set out by Sun Tzu, that was a fundamental failure to prepare at the earliest stages.

But equally surprising is that it took so long for the application to be made. If the position was known earlier, then it is difficult to understand what benefit was gained by delaying the making of the application.

The only thought that comes to mind is that, by letting the plaintiff's lawyers - who were working on a contingency fee - run the case and disclose their evidence then there was a double benefit.

First, the plaintiff's lawyers resources would have been depleted, putting them into a weakened financial position if they had to start all over again.

Second, if they did start all over again, then the case would have been, in effect, substantially disclosed.

It is therefore not here alleged that the defence lawyers were negligent in failing to make the application earlier: it is possible that they were applying a strategy to play the man not the ball and / or to ensure full preparedness for any action to come by letting the action run far enough for a full, or nearly full, disclosure of the Plaintiffs' case before killing the action.

For the sake of completeness, it should be noted that the Court dismissed an application for an alternate lead plaintiff to be substituted, saying that the failure was so fundamental and of such magnitude that it was not capable of being remedied.

There are those that argue that battles should not be won in such a way. In 1863, the New York Times carried an article about the Battle of Charleston Harbour. The New York Times, being a Union supporter was extraordinarily biased in its reporting of the attack by Union ships on the Confederate (it calls them "rebels") fleet in its harbour.

The report says "*The rebels in the late fight fired over 3,500 rounds of ponderous shot at our iron-clads; and the latter threw 151 balls at the rebel works. The firing was hot and continuous for two hours and at short range -- some of it as close as 500 yards. And yet the loss of life was no greater than often takes place in duels between two men! There is nothing like this in the previous annals of war.* "

It goes on "*We suppose it must be called a triumph of science. It is conceived by some, that as soon as the nations of the world are blessed with invulnerable ships and impregnable forts, wars will necessarily come to an end, as it would only be a waste of lead and saltpetre to attempt to reduce or capture either. A battle would merely be a contest of forces, each powerless as regards the other; and as each of the contestants could sit down and demonstrate one to the other, by science* and mathematics, the fact of his unconquerability before the proposed contest was opened, it would hardly be worth while to open it at all.

"It may be doubted, however, whether mankind will ever allow such a state of things to be brought about. When a great crime against justice has been committed, it can only be expiated by blood. When passion rules, foemen will somehow or other get at each other's throats."

The report says that, if soldiers were armoured, they would remove their armour so as to better take part in hand-to-hand combat "that they might meet on a fair field and slaughter each other with the "big knives" which have never been out of use since the days before the Flood."

Ignoring the trend towards military hardware that is specifically designed to engage an enemy without putting one's own personnel at risk, it is startling to imagine that anyone would actually prefer to see widespread loss of life rather than a bloodless win.

Not that it was, in fact, bloodless. One man was killed on either side.

The full NYT report "Battle without bloodshed" is at

http://www.nytimes.com/1863/04/06/news/battle-without-bloodshed.html

3.3. Thus the highest form of generalship is to frustrate the enemy's plans; the next best is to prevent the junction of the enemy's forces; the next in order is to attack the enemy's army in the field; and the worst policy of all is to besiege walled cities.

Simply preventing one's opponent from gaining strategic advantage is, according to Sun Tzu, the optimum strategy.

Sun Tzu says that it is best to prevent one's opponent from marshalling his troops, the second best is to attack them in open ground and the tactic least likely to result in success is to lay siege to his walled cities.

In litigation terms, this translates to making interlocutory applications, or defending them, so as to make it difficult for one's opponent to build his case, the second is making applications to strike out evidence or remove witnesses and the third - as has been said several times above, is to go to trial with all the uncertainties that that entails.

Interlocutory applications can take many forms. They are applications for orders before trial. That might seem an obvious statement but it is simplistic because it implies, to some, that they are late-stage applications.

However, they are not.

One of the first interlocutory applications that can be made is an application for summary judgment either in default of the filing or service of a defence or on the grounds that the defence filed does not disclose a defence.

A common practice of defence litigators is to file a "holding defence" which says nothing more than "The defendant denies each and every allegation in the Statement of Claim as if each were here set forth and traversed seriatim." It means "denied one after the other." And, despite the insistence of legislators in some jurisdictions, it's nice to see a bit of Latin from time to time. It reminds us lawyers that we are educated beyond kindergarten. And there's nothing wrong with a bit of mystery: after all, every other skill and trade uses its own argot so why should lawyers be singled out for criticism?

For example: what's a "perk test?" No, it's not a measure of how perky something is, conducted in a bar after a few shots.

It's a mistaken spelling (thanks to plumbers in the USA) of "perc test" which is a test for the rate at which water percolates through e.g. ground. See: it's not only lawyers that have industry specific terms. And isn't it much nicer to have "in camera" instead of "in private" and "forthwith" instead of "straight away?" It makes us feel all growed up.

Rant over. What's wrong with a holding defence?

In principle, nothing. It says what it means - that the Defendant denies all claims made by the Plaintiff.

But a holding defence is not a "pleading" in that it does not plead the grounds of the defence.

There are different views of the merits of a holding defence.

Under the Rules of Court in England and Wales, for example, a holding defence may be permitted simply to prevent the filing of a default judgment.

But it will not stand up to an application for summary judgment based on non-disclosure of defence.

That might, on the face of it, seem ridiculous. What more effective defence can there be than to say "I deny everything" with the implication that, if the plaintiff is to succeed, he must prove his case? That, surely, is the essence of litigation.

But set into the context of litigation where disclosure of relevant facts and law is a pre-requisite to allowing them to be put in at trial, it makes sense to demand that the case is properly pleaded at the outset.

Is this useful to the plaintiff? Yes. Very. It means that the chances of his being taken by surprise are reduced.

Let's look at what the pleadings are for:

a statement of claim is to set out the plaintiff's case. It is not a full statement of facts. However, it was my usual practice to load the Statement of Claim with facts to establish the strength of the case then to use interlocutory applications to force admissions as to fact.

Where it is claimed that the cause of action arises from breach of an obligation or duty imposed by law, then the law should be pleaded.

Where it arises from an obligation created by contract, then both the fact and the relevant content of the contract must be pleaded.

Where the cause of action arises under custom and practice or the common law, then the custom and practice or common law must be pleaded.

Increasingly, courts will allow a holding defence where there is a complex claim, in effect allowing more time for the filing of a full defence. But in simple claims, e.g. for the payment of a debt, courts are seeing holding defences as a device with no purpose other than to delay the inevitable. Therefore, while a holding defence would defeat an automatic entry of a judgment in default of filing a defence, a holding defence is, in many cases, unlikely to survive a hearing to strike it out.

However, from the defendant's point of view, the holding defence will have served at least some of its purpose in that it will have delayed the entry of judgment for as long as it takes for the plaintiff's application to strike it out takes to come to hearing.

Just as holding defences are devoid of detail, some plaintiffs file what amount to holding writs or other commencement documents.

A vague claim is not a valid claim: unless it is clear what harm has been caused and what remedy is required, then a statement of claim is likely to be struck out and, in many cases, the entire action along with it.

Vague claims are often the result of a failure to prepare properly even before the Letter Before Action (have you noticed this recurring theme?) In many jurisdictions (and in the English courts until relatively recently) there was a culture that the pleadings were not especially important, that they could be added to or amended at any future date.

That was a ridiculous culture: it increased costs (generally for the Plaintiff who had to pay for his own lawyers to amend the pleadings and then, often, would be found liable for the defendant's costs in consequence) and delay (an amended pleading is, in effect, a return to the stage of proceedings at that point so an amended statement of claim is, to all intents and purposes, to restart the action).

Of course, minor amendments as to typographical errors, or perhaps a date, will not carry such severe consequences.

Interlocutory applications can be made for many purposes. And they can be extremely powerful.

In a case involving a firm instructed by a financial services business brought against an individual who was in straightened circumstances, the individual engaged the only lawyer she could afford - a sole practitioner who normally handled matrimonial cases. Somehow, the case had been rumbling on for three years and had generated a pile of paper more than a metre high. The individual asked her lawyer if she would mind me taking a look at the papers, even though I was not qualified in that jurisdiction.

I sat in the lawyer's office and read the pleadings. I drafted twelve questions and told the lawyer to serve them under cover of a letter I drafted saying that an application to compel the answers would be filed if a full response was not received by a specific time and date. It was only seven days away, with the time in the mid morning. I told the lawyer to have her clerk waiting at court when the deadline expired (which, if the large firm continued to conduct the litigation to form, it would), to issue the application then and there and to immediately take it to the other side's lawyers and serve it before 4pm.

Less than a week after the application was served, the plaintiffs withdrew the action and agreed to pay the client's costs.

Why was this such a powerful weapon? It was because I was able, by the phrasing of the questions, to make a strong implication of fraud by the financial institution's representative. By bringing those questions before a Judge, to make him order the other side to answer the questions, would mean that the other side would have to admit to conduct that, if not fraudulent, was certainly dubious.

Pleading fraud is a minefield and should be done only when there is an exceptionally strong case for it. In this case, the financial institution did not, itself, commit the fraud - a self-employed representative did - and so to allege fraud on the part of the financial institution (which had lost money as a result) would be more difficult than usual. Adding the self-employed representative as a third party would have only complicated the action and made it last even longer - and deplete the individual's resources even more.

To reduce questions of management, lack of supervision and failure to identify rogue activities by representatives would have fallen short of proving fraud but it would prove, at the very least, a contributory behaviour. And that's before questions of vicarious liability were considered.

3.4. The rule is, not to besiege walled cities if it can possibly be avoided. The preparation of mantlets, movable shelters and various implements of war, will take up three whole months; and the piling up of mounds over against the walls will take three months more.

The question of siege was raised in the commentary on Principle 2.4. Basically, it's a really bad idea. Sun Tzu spells out that the building up of the infrastructure for a siege takes significant time and resources. And a siege has to have an end game: simply waiting until everyone inside dies of starvation, dehydration or old age is not a viable option.

So there must be the tools of war in readiness, partly to keep up the pressure on those inside, so they don't become rested and/or complacent. Fear and loathing are valuable weapons which the target wields against himself while imagining that his real target is the forces outside. By making those under siege feel helpless, as if they have no control over their future, they become frustrated and reckless.

And there must also be a plan for the final invasion: Sun Tzu talks about building up mounds so that the attacking force can over-run the walls.

But in all of this time, the attacking forces have to be fed and otherwise provisioned, their moral has to be kept up and while skirmishes prevent people falling to sleep, they do nothing to let the troops think the end is near and they will soon be able to go home.

That is the debilitating effect of a siege on the attacking forces and it is one of the reasons why a good litigator will not want to delay cases - he wants to clear the case off his desk either to move onto something fresh or, simply, to go home.

Sun Tzu's comments as to the equipment are enlightening: the "moveable shelters" were huts on wheels that could be pushed into place to protect those who were working under the walls or filling in moats and therefore at risk of attack from above. In the West, we tend to think of the Roman "turtle" (more prosaically but more properly called a "Testudo") made up of shields as a great military invention but, in truth, it was primitive compared to the machines of Sun Tzu's day which, historians have learned, were not pushed or pulled from outside: even those making it move were protected by it.

3.5. The general, unable to control his irritation, will launch his men to the assault like swarming ants with the result that one-third of his men are slain while the town still remains untaken. Such are the disastrous effects of a siege.

Sun Tzu confirms that boredom with the wait is a danger for those who try to mount a siege. While bored, while frustrated at the delay in setting up and winning a siege, a commander will be tempted to rush in, resulting in massive casualties.

In litigation, then, the equivalent is in trying to surround one's opponent with obstacles while not actually making progress with the case. While frustrating one's opponent's attempts to move the case forward, care must be taken not to allow one's own case to stagnate.

3.6. Therefore the skilful leader subdues the enemy's troops without any fighting; he captures their cities without laying siege to them; he overthrows their kingdom without lengthy operations in the field.

3.7. With his forces intact he will dispute the mastery of the Empire and thus, without losing a man, his triumph will be complete. This is the method of attacking by stratagem.

As a litigator, the last place one wants to end up is in Court. In court, one loses control of the conduct of the case and it becomes unpredictable. An alternative translation of this principle says that it means that the soldier's weapons remain in perfect order if they have not been blunted in battle. Reading principles 6 and 7 together, it's clear that Sun Tzu remains faithful to the ideas he has espoused before: use strength and strategy to bring about a quick kill.

In our terms, then, the good litigator will, always, be looking to bring the case to a satisfactory conclusion before trial.

It avoids expense but most of all it reduces the risks inherent in a trial.

Witnesses may prove unbelievable even though they are telling the truth; untruthful witnesses may be believable, the Judge or Jury may have unknown specific views (here we are charitable and do not call them "prejudices") or, just to make life difficult, a snow storm may prevent the trial starting on time or a power cut might shut it down at a critical moment during a cross-examination, a crucial participant might be taken ill or, as has happened on many occasions, come back from lunch a little the worse for wear.

We can never predict what will go wrong outside the strict conduct of the case.

I once lost an application in London's High Court because I missed the hearing. The reason that I was not in the hearing was because I got lost in the labyrinthine Royal Courts of Justice and ended up in a lift in a part of the building reserved for Judges. Even that might not have made me too late but the lift broke down and I was trapped. Luckily, someone came and found me. Unluckily, it was a senior Judge who was was not entirely pleased to find a young lawyer in the Judges' private lift. But he turned out to be a nice man who, once he heard that I was about to miss my hearing - and therefore face my case being struck out in my absence - went to his room, telephoned the Master I was supposed to be before and explained what had happened. But it was too late. However, Masters tend to do more or less as senior Judges "suggest" so the Master called his clerk who called my opponent's law firm and told them that the Master was, in effect, cancelling the order he had just made and that the case was to be brought back before him in a couple of hours.

That, it was hoped, would be long enough for me to be res-cued and to find my way to where I should have been all along.

We went back and I got my order as asked, but despite my win, was ordered to pay the cost of the application anyway for the inconvenience I had caused my opponent. That seemed fair to me although my opponent was disgruntled as he had already told his firm he had been successful and now had to admit to a failure.

How much better it would have been if my opponent and I had agreed an Order before hand and we had not had to go to Court to fight out over an administrative matter where the res-ult was, almost, a foregone conclusion anyway.

3.8. It is the rule in war, if our forces are ten to the enemy's one, to surround him; if five to one, to attack him; if twice as numerous, to divide our army into two.

It's logical to say that if one has overwhelming strength, then there are more options than if the parties are evenly matched.

There is an apparent conflict between this principle and others put forward by Sun Tzu.

Here, he appears to suggest that, if there are overwhelming numbers, the stronger force should create a siege.

But that is not what he is actually proposing. He is saying that a significant show of force can intimidate one's opponent, to make him consider either settling or avoiding litigation.

That is entirely in accordance with the over-riding principle that a fight-less win is always better than a hard fought and costly battle.

But, where there is not a totally dominant force of such strength that its mere existence will make one's opposition surrender rather than face certain defeat, then a sudden, surprise and hard attack will often achieve a similar result - or at least make one's opponent realise that he is facing a hard fight and that he should prepare properly and not expect to be given quarter.

But where forces are more equally matched, such a course of action is likely to lead to substantial losses without much chance of success.

Sun Tzu says that in that case, forces should be divided in two, preparing for attacks on two different fronts, so as to force the other side to divide his resources.

It might seem as if such a strategy cannot work in litigation but in fact it can, depending on the case.

For example, in a case where an employee has stolen money, there are three things that can be done: first, attack the funds, secondly, attack the individual, third report the theft to the police.

Attacking the money is essential - once it is frozen in the hands of the bank where it was transferred to, it is secure. It cannot be used by the defendant for fight or flight. Also, it can't be moved out of reach. This action must be taken very, very quickly after the discovery of the theft.

It is in this case that action is taken without first issuing a Letter Before Action.

Attacking the individual is in many cases a diversion: the client doesn't care about the individual - what the client cares about is the money.

Reporting to the police is a highly effective way of augmenting one's resources - and the police will attack the individual, so depleting his resources and diverting his attention from your primary objective.

In some cases there is a fourth option: where the thief exercised a regulated or licensed function, report him to his regulator. Again, this will lead to an augmentation of your own resources and will, once more, deplete his resources.

Using the power of outside enforcement / regulatory bodies can be frustrating - often they are not permitted to share information with you. Also, the police will, in almost all countries, also want to freeze the money (it counts towards their proceeds of crime targets). That's the last thing your client wants: he does not want the money, the absence of which is depleting his cash-flow or capital position, to be locked away until the end of a criminal investigation and trial. Therefore, a good litigator will always seek to freeze the assets for his client's benefit before reporting the theft to the police - even if that report is made only a matter of minutes after a Court freezes the assets.

There is also, in some jurisdictions and in some cases (and generally I regard this course of action as unprofessional and generally dishonourable but there are times that it does have its place) the prospect of using media publicity. Again, it diverts one's opponent's attention and depletes his resources.

3.9. If equally matched, we can offer battle; if slightly inferior in numbers, we can avoid the enemy; if quite unequal in every way, we can flee from him.

It is, generally, not a great idea to get involved in litigation if the two sides, in terms of the strength of the case, are evenly matched. In practice, to take account of litigation risk, I would usually advise clients against starting an action unless there was at least a 70% chance of success. There are always surprises, no matter how well one prepares and no matter how well one conducts the action. In the first part of this principle, Sun Tzu may have got things wrong when it comes to litigation.

A tit-for-tat fight results in costly losses on both sides with the outcome uncertain.

But the second and third parts are sound: if you already know - or have a good reason to expect - that you will lose, it is not sensible to get involved in a fight.

Clients often have a hidden agenda. They may consider that they can afford to lose whereas their opponent cannot afford to win. They may therefore want to pursue a strategy that has, ultimately, nothing to do with the instant case - it may be a step in a long game in which a commercial stratagem is being played out.

In such cases, the litigator can do little other then make the risks and costs clear and to act in accordance with instructions.

In other cases, however, the sensible thing to do is to find a way to avoid conflict.

There are many conflict resolution schemes available, including arbitration. If a client, despite being advised that his prospects of success are slim, persists in litigating because he is convinced he is right and that right always wins, then arbitration can prove to be a quicker, simpler and cheaper way of reaching the end but still allow the client to have, as he sees it, his day in Court.

Negotiated settlements are to be preferred if at all possible, provided neither side takes a firmly entrenched position.

It is a truth that in the vast majority of cases, there is no clear cut case. Obviously, if someone has stolen money from a company's accounts, then that's pretty easy to determine.

But commercial disputes are rarely that simple: the subject matter is frequently open to multiple interpretations.

Also, actions between individuals (and small businesses which are, often, an extension of their owners) are frequently even more complicated, often due to poor record keeping (including notes as to meetings, etc.) and the emotional involvement of the parties.

It is because of this that, in many cases, there is a much more equal position that clients like to believe, or have convinced themselves or are so angry they cannot contemplate the possibility of failure.

3.10. Hence, though an obstinate fight may be made by a small force, in the end it must be captured by the larger force.

Here, we should think of the "force" discussed by Sun Tzu as the evidence, not the teams involved. In the end, a weak case will (almost) always lose and a strong case will (almost) always win.

3.11. Now the general is the bulwark of the State; if the bulwark is complete at all points; the State will be strong; if the bulwark is defective, the State will be weak.

Following on from principle 10, principle 11 relates to the capability of the litigator.

There is always the possibility that a litigator will fail to maximise his advantage, or will fail to properly pursue his case, with the result that a strong case will be defeated, even if only on technical grounds.

3.12. There are three ways in which a ruler can bring misfortune upon his army:—

3.13. By commanding the army to advance or to retreat, being ignorant of the fact that it cannot obey. This is called hobbling the army.

3.14. By attempting to govern an army in the same way as he administers a kingdom, being ignorant of the conditions which obtain in an army. This causes restlessness in the soldier's minds.

3.15. By employing the officers of his army without discrimination, through ignorance of the military principle of adaptation to circumstances. This shakes the confidence of the soldiers.

Principles 12 - 15 sit together as a neat combination.

Sun Tzu points out that the client is king and that his instructions must be followed. But clients may issue instructions that undermine the conduct of their case and may, ultimately, lead to failure.

The client may insist on issuing a Letter Before Action or even commencing an action before full preparation has been made.

Another Chinese military master, T`ai Kung, who, in broad terms was a contemporary of Sun Tzu, said "a kingdom should not be governed from without, nor an army from within." The second part of that statement is completely at odds with the general principle that a client should state the objective and the litigator should form and execute the strategy to achieve that objective.

It is generally undesirable, as Sun Tzu says, for clients to dictate the tactics: if he does so, then the litigator's skill and judgement are undermined (hobbled) and, ultimately, may count for nothing.

Moreover, principle 14 demonstrates that, if a litigator is prevented from the practise of his art, he soon loses his edge, he becomes uncertain of his role and function and the extent of his authority. It is undesirable for a client to manage the litigation.

But the choice of litigator is also important: a poor decision as to the leader will undermine the confidence of the whole team.

Remembering that Sun Tzu wrote *The Art of War* as a guide for both rulers and commanders, these three principles together are directed to the rulers. They are saying, bluntly, "choose the right man for the job, tell him what the job is and let him get on with it."

It's a sensible strategy for business as well as for management generally.

But clients often choose their litigators for the wrong reasons. They may have a long association with a particular firm and even though the case is outside that firm's usual area of expertise, appoint that firm to handle it.

They may choose a friend: perhaps someone who is merely an acquaintance, met in a social environment. I have often heard of clients who appointed a lawyer on the basis that they liked him and decided to "give him a go."

That is an irresponsible course of action.

And it is just as irresponsible for a litigator to take on work which is outside his competence or expertise.

It is not right to say that all litigation is the same. There are material differences between different types of case.

It is incumbent on the client to make the correct choice of litigator, just as it is upon the litigator to make the correct decision as to whether he has the skill, knowledge and capability (including resources) to properly protect his client's interests and achieve the required result.

3.16. But when the army is restless and distrustful, trouble is sure to come from the other feudal princes. This is simply bringing anarchy into the army and flinging victory away.

There are few secrets in litigation!

If a client or a litigator is involved in case that is not going well, others will know. And they will seek to capitalise on it.

So, if other parties, entirely unrelated to the action in hand, are thinking of commencing litigation or, even, trying to gain some commercial advantage, they will take the opportunity when the client is already engaged.

Fighting multiple claims on multiple fronts is debilitating. But commercial opponents are like sharks - they can sense the distress and join in the feeding frenzy.

If the relationship between a client and his litigators is already strained, then this can prove the final undoing - not only for this case but for others.

If we consider a side-ways leap: it is common practice for trades unions to gang up on a company. For example, in the airline industry, often the pilots, aircrew, ground crew, baggage handlers and catering staff (even if they are engaged by sub-contractors) unions co-ordinate their actions.

In the financial services industry, especially in the USA, it is common for multiple regulators and enforcement agencies to take simultaneous action against a particular company or individual: sometimes, as in the 2012 case involving Standard Chartered Bank in New York, a regulator will break ranks with those with whom they had been coordinating forcing the bank to divert its attention from the negotiations that it had been conducting with what had, until then, appeared to be a body of enforcement agencies / regulators acting as one.

It is self-evident that, when a client is already weakened by litigation, that others will try to take advantage of that situation.

In the USA that often means that the class-action sharks start to circle, often within hours and without having first stating an effective case, and often in number.

But this principle also highlights another issue: if it is known that there is dissent between a person giving instructions and the litigator, others within the client organisation may try to jockey for position.

Therefore they may interfere with the conduct of litigation, giving instructions which may be contradictory or at least that require clarification.

To avoid this, it is necessary to ensure that the person giving instructions has full and proper authority and that it is agreed, within the client organisation, that all instructions are channelled through that person. If there is an in-house legal counsel, that that is the obvious channel but if not, then the prudent litigator will ensure that there is a board resolution to commence litigation and that the resolution specifies the company's representative who is authorised to give instructions.

In short, litigation cannot be properly conducted when instructions are coming from diverse people in diverse roles.

It is, in some countries, matter of professional conduct to ensure that a person purporting to represent a company has the actual (not merely implied) authority to instruct the litigator on behalf of the company.

3.17. Thus we may know that there are five essentials for victory:

a) he will win who knows when to fight and when not to fight.

Choosing those fights we can win and avoiding those we cannot is a sensible course of action.

In his book "F**k It," John Parkin espouses a straightforward philosophy. It can be summarised as

- there are things you can control, so control them.

- There are things you can't control, so don't try.

- There are things you want to control, but can't and that will frustrate you and make you unhappy.

-There are things you can control but don't want to and exercising that control will make you stressed and unhappy.

- If there are things that make you unhappy, unless you really, really must (for example, filing tax returns), don't do them.

It's almost a blueprint for litigation and more than a little Sun Tzu-like, again demonstrating the agelessness of his ideas.

b) he will win who knows how to handle both superior and inferior forces.

Here the term "forces" refers to the opposing client, the opposing litigator and his team and the evidence.

Later, Sun Tzu talks of the use of "spies" but he is really discussing intelligence gathering.

Sun Tzu here means that preparation involves being fully familiar with all aspects of the litigation - and what can go wrong as well as what can go wrong.

c) he will win whose army is animated by the same spirit throughout all its ranks.

Sun Tzu returns to this theme often, but usually obliquely. He talks of dividing the forces either physically or by demoralising parts of them.

By keeping all the team singing from the same hymn sheet, they are easier to manage. A team member wandering off and doing things on his own can prove disastrous at worst and expensive at least. After all, his time is being spent unproductively and lawyers' time is expensive.

But Sun Tzu also frequently talks about morale and here he touches on the same subject. Put simply, if a part of the team is disaffected, then they will under-perform and, at worst, accidentally, recklessly or deliberately undermine the case in some way.

d) he will win who, prepared himself, waits to take the enemy unprepared.

Prepare, watch and wait. A general who gets up his force and rushes to meet the enemy puts his men at risk. It's much better to ensure, through the use of intelligence, that your opponent is unprepared.

So, for example, you may know that your opponent is engaged on a large, complex case. The time to strike is when that case is called for trial because, at that point, his resources are fully committed, perhaps even over-committed. He will have to re-order his priorities and even the decision making process in that action is, itself, disruptive.

Therefore, consider filing in your case a very demanding interlocutory application and serving it about half-an-hour before his trial in the other case is due to start. He will be in Court and his staff will have to decide whether to interrupt him with the news. Most likely they will send him a brief message. He will be worried not by your case but that the action in your case has unsettled him for his trial.

And, ruthlessly, worry is worry and who cares which case or what he is worried about? The important thing is that he cannot give full attention to both the trial and the interlocutory application you have served.

Therefore, someone has to take over at least part of one of the cases and that leaves him concerned as to whether the job will be done properly.

e) he will win who has military capacity and is not interfered with by the sovereign.

'nuff said!

3.18. Hence the saying: if you know the enemy and know yourself, you need not fear the result of a hundred battles. If you know yourself but not the enemy, for every victory gained you will also suffer a defeat. If you know neither the enemy nor yourself, you will succumb in every battle.

Quite where Sun Tzu would claim to have found this "saying" is unknown.

But it is one of the most salient truths of litigation.

Of course there are moments that
you wonder how long you should be
doing it because there are aspects
of this lifestyle which are not nice,

But I just love winning.

Ayrton Senna
Racing Driver

4. Tactical Dispositions

4. Tactical Dispositions

4.1. Sun Tzu said: The good fighters of old first put them-selves beyond the possibility of defeat and then waited for an opportunity of defeating the enemy.

A good soldier is mentally and physically prepared for battle. He is armed, armoured and has a plan and knows how to implement it. He has chosen his ground and gathered all available intelligence.

In short, he has done everything he can to repel any assault and to succeed in any attack.

This principle may suggest that he should delay his attack, which is in conflict with principles discussed earlier but this principle can be taken as meaning something different: the idea of avoiding full frontal attack and waiting for one's opponent to expose a weakness.

In litigation there are always weaknesses in the case and its conduct. It is a major part of the function of a litigator to identify those weaknesses in his own case and remedy them and to identify them in his opponent's case and exploit them.

A litigator does not have unlimited resources and a full frontal attack requires that considerable resources are dedicated to it. What this principle says is that there are merits in ensuring that there are resources available, in hand, to make a quick, decisive, incisive, targeted attack on those weaknesses.

Often a litigator's greatest weakness is that which he considers his greatest strength. An over-confident, an arrogant litigator one who has a belief in his own infallibility will risk failure when a more modest approach would be safer and may result in a better result for his client.

4.2. To secure ourselves against defeat lies in our own hands, but the opportunity of defeating the enemy is provided by the enemy himself.

This reinforces the first principle and endorses the explanation of it given above.

4.3. Thus the good fighter is able to secure himself against defeat but cannot make certain of defeating the enemy.

4.4. Hence the saying: One may KNOW how to conquer without being able to do it.

A plan is useless if it cannot be, successfully, put into effect.

4.5. Security against defeat implies defensive tactics; ability to defeat the enemy means taking the offensive.

"Attack is the best form of defence." How often have we heard that? It is a modern version of this principle. Sun Tzu says that while an effective defence is essential, one does not win by defending alone. It is necessary to take the offensive.

Some commentators have taken the view that this principle suggests that, of one cannot win, then not losing is an acceptable result.

That is not a terrible strategy: after all, a negotiated withdrawal of both sides can reduce the adverse effects of costly litigation.

However, if that is the plan, then it is better not to become embroiled in litigation in the first place. It is better to seek a negotiated settlement at the outset.

Despite the good sense in this argument, when embarking on the campaign, each party needs to make the other side realise that they are serious. They need to posture, to rattle their sabres.

But now is also, one might argue, a time to keep at least something in reserve, to avoid showing one's hand entirely.

Again, this is where the Letter Before Action comes in. It should make the broad position clear but not make disclose the full case.

The Australian humorist David Thorne reproduces, in his book "The Internet is a Playground" an excellent example of how not to write a Letter Before Action.

He received the letter from a law firm (which will not be identified here but is named in his book) that reads:

"Dear Mr Thorne

I am writing to you on behalf of our client [x]. I am under instruction to give you 48 hours in which to remove all references to Mr X from your website [address] or we will begin legal proceedings against you. Should you have any questions or response to this request, please call during office hours or e-mail me at [address].

Sincerely

[name]

It is difficult to imagine a more weak Letter Before Action.

First, never, ever, address an opponent by name. Litigation is a form of hostility. Why would you, in aiming to compel someone to do something, water down the message by being friendly?

Secondly, do not ever use the personal pronoun "I" - it personalises the correspondence. The whole point is to make it clear that the recipient is about to be assaulted. A warrior does not face his opponent with a smile. Use "we": make it clear that the whole weight of the firm and, by implication the Court and the law, stands behind the letter - and the threat it contains.

Third, do not, ever, include pointless words and phrases. The letter is supposed to be the equivalent of launching oneself across the room and kicking one's opponent in the teeth before he has time to realise what is happening. It is supposed to frighten him. So "I am writing..." yes, obviously. A waste of ink, paper and impact. Maybe Mr Thorne has a bit more patience, but reading the letter, this author was bored within the first three words. And bored isn't frightened.

"on behalf of..." - yawns. Who cares?

"I am under instruction.... " Yes. That's already implied by the previous few words.

"to give you..." Who does the lawyer think he is? He has no standing to give the recipient anything. There is total weakness in this phrasing.

"48 hours... " from when? Any deadline should be clearly set out. An LBA is no place for uncertainty: how can a threat be carried out in default of compliance if the terms of compliance are not known?

"in which to remove all references to Mr X from your website [address]..." Why? Because he doesn't like it?

"or..." Oh, at last. Something with teeth. A threat is on the way.

"we will begin legal proceedings against you." For what? Exactly what is it alleged has caused an actionable harm and what harm has it caused? What remedy will be sought? This is no different to saying "if you don't do what we want, we'll throw a pillow at you."

"Should you have any questions or response to this request, please call during office hours or e-mail me at [address]."

In litigation, it is a serious error of judgment to invite one's opponent to use e-mail. It is unreliable and has evidential problems. Indeed, it is desirable to specifically exclude service of documents by e-mail or fax when issuing proceedings and specifying an address for service. Because of that, it makes no sense to invite, even at the initial stage, e-mail correspondence and risk an argument over service later. Further, why invite a telephone call? If the demand is just, there is no need for discussion: the litigator just wants the recipient to comply. Again, why would one want to adopt an informal stance in an LBA? It's a threat, not an invitation for coffee and a chat.

"Sincerely," Oh, by omitting the "Yours" does this make it feel like the letter has ended with a strong punch? No, it does not.

And how nice: he's signed it personally. Friendly chap.

Two more criticisms, in this case of form. First, the body of the letter is all in one paragraph. That denies the opportunity for emphasis. Secondly, there is no heading. The heading is the war cry before landing that kick to the teeth.

So, how could the letter have been improved?

Dear Sir

Injunction: content of [website]

We are instructed by Mr X who informs us that you are the owner and publisher of [website] upon which derogatory and defamatory statements relating to him appear.

We are instructed that

a) unless all references (graphical and textual) to our client are removed from the said website no later than 2:30 pm on [date] and

b) no later than that time we receive from you a signed and dated undertaking in the form attached in which you agree not to post further references to our client

we are to commence proceedings against you as defendant and your web hosting company as third party for an injunction requiring the suspension of your website and for damages and legal costs without further notice.

Save for receiving your undertaking, no further correspondence will be entered into.

Yours faithfully
[firm's name]

In the David Thorne's case, the ensuing e-mail correspondence did not improve matters, except in one respect: a clear deadline was set in one e-mail.

But the following phrases also appeared:

a) "we will file a complaint with the courts pending instructions from Mr X"

Let's get this clear: the firm (at least now it's "we") will issue proceedings (although quite where is not clear: courts? With an "s"?) is planning to issue proceedings while it is waiting for instructions? Was this not thought through and all necessary instructions taken before writing the LBA? Clearly, then, the firm is not in a position to actually issue immediately the deadline expired. So the threat is empty and empty threats are weaknesses.

"please just remove the references to Mr X from your website. He has not given you permission to use his image or name."

Oh, go on. Do as we ask. Please. Pretty please. With knobs on. And strawberries and cream.

Aside from the fact that becoming involved in correspond-ence was a waste of resources and a sign of weakness, it also failed to add any pressure.

And if the comments were not derogatory and defamatory, exactly what cause of action is alleged?

Was a breach of copyright alleged? If so, it should have been specified.

Here's the kicker, as some people say. If there is no cause of action and the letter is just a threatening letter without sub-stance, then that is an unwarranted demand with menaces. The common name for that is "blackmail." If there is no basis for bringing an action, it is both unprofessional and, arguably, criminal to issue a Letter Before Action.

Even when a client says "it's just a letter."

When it appears on the litigator's letterhead, it is never "just a letter." It is a preliminary step towards legal action. The firm and its reputation stand behind it.

As a connected aside, there is an increasing tendency for lawyers to write to each other, addressing them by their Chris-tian (or whatever) names. Are they fighting for their clients or arranging a date?

Litigation is confrontational. It is not a gentle chat between pals. It does nothing for the client's confidence in his lawyer to know that the lawyer is not, right from the beginning, ready to (metaphorically) take a baseball bat to his opponent.

People are not horrible to their friends and by definition a friendly approach means they are likely to fail to deliver the full weight available to them. Being overtly friendly towards one's professional opponent runs the not insubstantial risk that clients suspect and fear that their case is being carved up between the lawyers. When, if the lawyers are doing their jobs properly, a proposed compromise is presented clients will be concerned that their champion has not fought as hard for that compromise as expected, almost as if the client suspects that the lawyers have sat down over dinner (perhaps even at the client's expense) and traded out a deal.

Of course, that is exactly what happens in many cases - but clients do not need to know that nor do they need to be put in a position where they feel that their champion is not as strong as they thought.

The "Dear Sirs" approach is designed for the precise purpose of de-personalising the relationship between the champions. It's like two gladiators fighting in masks: they know who they are fighting but the mask allows them to maintain a distance, to be more brutal than they could be if they see their friend's face.

There is, in litigation (conciliation is, by definition, different) no room for being nice. It's stamp or be stamped on.

Unlike negotiating contracts or conveyancing, in litigation clients do not have a shared objective. They aim to destroy or at least cause considerable harm to their opponent. They expect their lawyers to be in the same frame of mind.

"Dear Sirs" is a battle cry, yelled whether on the attack or on the defence. It is a statement of intent. The use of "we" instead of "I" is a statement of force standing behind the correspondence.

"Dear Andrew" or "Dear Steve," for example, is a sign of weakness, not of professionalism and certainly not of strength. And it undermines the lawyer / client relationship.

But we should not think that only practitioners write stupid phrases in their letters. Lord Woolf, invited to review civil procedure in England and Wales, is largely responsible for the dumbing down of the legal system but he had several good ideas, the best of which was "pre-action protocols" of which much more later. But much of the credit has been given to Lord Irvine.

The Department of Justice has issued a draft Letter Before Action (in the brave new world of nu-speak that permeated the government during the Blair/Brown years and changed the ancient office of "The Lord Chancellor's Department" to the USA-aping "Department of Justice," it not called a Letter Before Action: in the words of the Manic Street Preachers - everything must go, including long standing descriptive expressions. It was renamed a "Letter of Claim.") in several types of claim including personal injury claims.

It is headed "Claimant's full name."

It says "please confirm the identity of your insurers." Confirm what? That implies that the information has previously been provided. The letter means to say "please inform us of the identity of your insurers." It should also ask for a policy number but it doesn't.

The "Letter of Claim" goes on:

"a description of our clients' injuries are as follows." Oh, look. In the heading it's a single claimant (the nu-speak word for plaintiff) but in the body of the letter, it becomes plural. Where did the others come from? No one knows. And it should be "is as follows" because it relates to "description" not "injuries." Perhaps someone wrote, more sensibly, "our clients injuries are" then someone decided it needed a nice, warm, cuddly edge and added "a description of...."

And these nice soft words mean "our client suffered the following injuries." It's litigation not social work. It should be treated as such.

"The reason we are alleging fault is..." Means "he was injured as a result of [e.g. a defective guard on a sausage making machine and, therefore his tie got caught and the little pigs that were pictured on it were chopped up into teeny-weeny pieces]. "

"Finally we expect an acknowledgment (sic) of this letter within 21 days by yourselves or your insurers. " It's supposed to be spelt "acknowledgement." If the government department that is in control of the conduct of litigation can't even employ people that can spell in a document that they are publishing as a template, what hope is there for the rest of the profession? There should be a comma after "Finally,..." And, just to be picky, aren't the words in the sentence in the wrong order? Even if we don't change the words or correct the spelling, surely the sentence should read "Finally, we expect an acknowledgment (sic) of this letter by yourselves or your insurers within 21 days." But we do need to change the words because the same issues apply here as in the previous letter: there is no set deadline and no consequences set out for failure.

The pre-action protocol calls for pre-issue pre-discovery i.e. putting the defendant on notice of what documents will be required in discovery. This is a good thing because it oils the later movement of the action. But it is not exclusive and therefore there is still room for additional discovery later.

In essence, the pre-action protocol is to disclose the strength of the claim and give the defendant an opportunity to admit in full or in part or to deny the claim and, if he is to admit it, to enter into settlement negotiations without proceedings being commenced.

While the approach has it merits, it is also open to abuse where defendants pretend to negotiate only to pull back at a later time having secured a delay.

The pre-action protocol for personal injury cases is at http://www.justice.gov.uk/courts/procedure-rules/civil/protocol/prot_pic. The page is several years old but is maintained (indeed, at the time of writing the most recent update is less than a month earlier) and yet even the grammatical and spelling errors have not been spotted and corrected.

The pre-action protocols have their place and perhaps their biggest advantage is that they compel the parties to properly formulate their case before issuing proceedings. They are extended by a system, introduced at the same time, of allowing the Court to take control of the time frames under which steps must be taken, so removing many of the opportunities for interlocutory applications, at least on the face of it. Where a party fails to comply with the protocol, there are no automatic sanctions, rendering the making of applications just as necessary as previously.

Where the pre-action protocol operates most successfully (in principle - practice may be different) is in giving, at a very early stage, outline details of the claim (which is what a good Letter Before Action always should do anyway) and requiring a considered response from the defendant - which is, again, what a good Letter Before Action should demand and which a properly advised defendant should give.

Therefore, the pre-action protocols do not - in most cases - militate against effective litigation but rather compel the principles described in this work into a wide range of litigation options ranging from personal injury to defamation.

However, there is one area where political considerations have been allowed to interfere - or so it seems. Actually, it's common sense and good practice.

In relation to mortgage repossession cases, there is a requirement for a plaintiff to consider any offer put forward for a rescheduling of the debt. This is because there is, on paper, an absolute right to repossession where the mortgage interest is more than two months in arrear. There have long been practice notes requiring courts to consider offers made to mitigate against this harsh contractual position (which is the traditional base-line set by legislation) . The inclusion in the pre-action protocol merely puts the burden on the lender to consider the offer and, if it is not acceptable, to give full justification for it.

When the purpose of pre-action protocols is worked out, i.e. to ensure that the parties are prepared before proceedings are issued, it can be seen that in that respect, at least, they support the ideas of Sun Tzu.

4.6. Standing on the defensive indicates insufficient strength; attacking, a superabundance of strength.

Point made.

But it is not entirely so. One of the first lessons taught to UK Special Forces in hand to hand combat is to put the weight on the back foot, not to lead with the front. It's to draw in one's opponent, to make him charge. Then, shifting one's weight backwards, to twist or sidestep, making his charge miss its target and then to attack *en passant*.

A skilled litigator may allow his opponent to charge, knowing all the time that he has the power to disarm him or deliver a knock-out blow. Sun Tzu encapsulates this concept elsewhere and but chooses not to juxtapose them here, presumably so as not to dilute the impact of this Principle.

4.7. The general who is skilled in defence hides in the most secret recesses of the earth; he who is skilled in attack flashes forth from the topmost heights of heaven. Thus on the one hand we have ability to protect ourselves; on the other, a victory that is complete.

Some litigators defend well and others attack well. This reflects that the world is made up of different personalities.

Those naturally suited to defence will hide everything he can until he must apply himself and his resources.

Earlier, reference was made to those litigators who seek to delay litigation, either in the hope of wearing down their opponent or exhausting his resources.

Those naturally suited to attack will - subject to the overriding principle not to commit all resources in an all or nothing first attack - attack from a position of strength.

Therefore, again, considering the Letter Before Action it is imperative to know exactly what one's client's rights are, exactly how they have been breached and exactly what remedies are available and - equally importantly - are achievable.

A litigator, or a litigation team, that can manage both positions will be strong, provided that there is no dispute as to when to adopt each position.

And when the decision is made to attack, do it from a position of strength, swiftly, decisively, aggressively.

4.8. To see victory only when it is within the ken of the common herd is not the acme of excellence.

This principle is almost a joke. Almost but not quite. Translation: if everyone, including non-litigators, could see how to win that battle then winning it is not something worthy of great praise.

In short, don't become too proud of yourself just because you had an easy win.

It's an important lesson to learn: it is easy to become arrogant or complacent merely because one wins a case. And arrogance and complacency, plays on the mind and when the next case comes along, one might feel that one can win with less effort or attention than the case deserves. And that may well lead to failure.

In litigation, as in many other things, one's reputation tends to be based on one's most recent work. A long history of wins counts for little if one loses a big case today.

4.9. Neither is it the acme of excellence if you fight and conquer and the whole Empire says, "Well done!"

The usual interpretation of this principle is that a good victory comes by surreptitious means. I am not so sure. Sun Tzu was a warrior first and an adviser to kings second. Although he sometimes stood up to the kings as near-equals, he nevertheless adopted a position of humility. For Sun Tzu, the victory and the credit of his king was enough. He did not think it appropriate to be lauded in the streets for his victory.

Therefore, I think that Sun Tzu was actually proposing that the victor should be quietly thanked and humbly go into the background until he is needed again. He may have led heroically but that does not make him a hero.

And that humility and grace in victory, it is here argued, is a significant part of the behaviour of a true professional.

After all, at the end of a war, at the end of litigation, people have been hurt, perhaps destroyed. That is not a cause for celebration but rather for quiet reflection and thanks.

Better to leave the back-slapping, high-fiving, fist bumping and partying to those engaged in less harmful sports than to seek glory for having delivered suffering to another.

4.10. To lift an autumn hair is no sign of great strength; to see the sun and moon is no sign of sharp sight; to hear the noise of thunder is no sign of a quick ear.

Sun Tzu returns to the theme of principle 8, that an easy win is nothing to be proud of. Pleased with, yes; proud of, no.

4.11. What the ancients called a clever fighter is one who not only wins but excels in winning with ease.

At the risk of being repetitious, Sun Tzu re-emphasises that every fighter should seek to out-think his opponent, to look beyond the easy and the obvious and to endeavour to win as economically as possible.

4.12. Hence his victories bring him neither reputation for wisdom nor credit for courage.

When a battle is won but the circumstances that led to the win are not widely known, then the commander gains credit for either his cleverness or his courage.

And so it is with litigation.

Where a settlement is reached but the terms of the deal are to be kept secret, then the litigator cannot claim a great victory. Private settlements (and that often includes arbitration) do not bring the litigators on either side publicity. That benefits the winner and the loser equally.

A bald statement that an action has been compromised on confidential terms agreed between the parties is, therefore, no use as a publicity tool.

But litigators who are authorised to publicise their involvement in the case may find that the secret leaks out anyway, particularly for public companies in jurisdictions were there is a requirement to include in annual reports or regulatory filings anything that has a material impact on the company, its management, its profits or its balance sheet.

Also, one of the commentators, Tu Mu, wrote "inasmuch as the hostile state submits before there has been any bloodshed, [the commander] received no credit for courage.

Lesson to learn? Say after me: get the Letter Before Action right.

4.13. He wins his battles by making no mistakes. Making no mistakes is what establishes the certainty of victory, for it means conquering an enemy that is already defeated.

It might seem a somewhat sideways leap, but for a moment think away from the battlefield and towards a different kind of test - motor racing.

Motor racing is one of the least forgiving forms of sport (except, perhaps, racquet sports where line decisions are critical). Motor racing requires the delivery of a perfect lap time after time after time.....

Some races last for several hundred laps and there is no room for error.

A mechanic that lets a wheel roll away so it is out of reach when it comes to putting in on the car, a driver who stalls the engine in the pits, a wheel nut that gets stuck because different materials expand at different rates and someone got their sums wrong at the design stage, the bodywork comes loose after a small "off" because a clip wasn't fitted properly, the driver runs up the back of a car that brakes into a corner because he failed to calculate his closing speed correctly, the driver spins off in a corner because he wasn't looking where he was going.

There are some basic rules on corners:

first, slow in, fast out.

Secondly, look where you want to go and that's where the car will go.

OK, so now the motor racing analogy becomes clear.

Slow in, fast out: prepare properly, execute effectively and exit safely and quickly.

If you look where you want to go, that's where the car will go: in a race, other cars, flying birds, morons wandering onto the track in the middle of a race are just hazards that are seen with the eyes then the eyes move on: they don't focus on the hazard. The brain deals with the hazard and tells the body what to do to limit or avoid the harm that that risk poses. The eyes are already looking beyond the hazard, deciding where the next braking or turning point is. The most important point for focus is the apex of the next bend. Although racing drivers have famously wide peripheral vision which allows them to *see* a great deal, the point they *look* at is the next apex and, as they approach that one, knowing that the car is already set up for it, they focus on the next braking and turning point which is where the car is set up (prepared) for the corner and the apex after that.

So, what is the apex of the corner? It's that point where the car is perfectly balanced, ready to accelerate out of the bend, the point where everything seems calm, for a split second, almost serene, the point where, for smooth drivers, the power is just feeding back in. It's also the point where, if the driver gets it wrong, the car suddenly breaks away and flies off the track. By stringing together apex after apex, a driver reduces the lateral movements of the car, reducing wear on mechanicals, tyres and the driver. And if he gets each corner right, one after another, it's the fastest, safest and most satisfying way around the track.

Mess up an apex and you're probably going to end up in barrier. I know. I've hit plenty of barriers. Hard. And it hurts.

That's just like litigation: as each step is approached, the good litigator is already preparing for the next, looking through the current activity and on to the next. The direction his case takes is the direction that he is looking in. He *sees* all kinds of other things, he, notices the peripheral issues and hazards and deals with them almost subconsciously. But he *looks* at the next activity to be performed, prepares for it and focusses on that as an interim objective.

And as one activity is at its crucial point, he is already preparing for the next, similar to positioning the car on the racing line, the shortest, most economical, most efficient distance, the least stressful line.

And where a driver successfully does those things, corner after corner, lap after lap, with no other failures in the mechanicals or pits, he knows that it is extremely difficult for anyone to beat him.

And so does the successful litigator.

That is at the heart of Sun Tzu's principle. If he performs perfectly, his opponent cannot do so. And because his opponent cannot perform perfectly, his opponent will lose.

4.14. Hence the skilful fighter puts himself into a position which makes defeat impossible and does not miss the moment for defeating the enemy.

Squash. The game, not the drink or that silly thing we used to do to see how many people we could get into a Morris Mini.

The successful squash player dominates the T in the centre of the court. He puts himself into a position where his opponent has to go around him, has to use more energy, to be off-balance when he connects with the ball, therefore preventing the playing of an optimum shot.

To continue the motor racing analogy: where an opportunity to overtake comes, it must be taken quickly and decisively. And then the overtaker puts his car on the very place on the track where the overtaken driver needs to be to secure an optimum entry to or exit from a corner, or has to go wide and onto the dirty part of the track so compromising grip. In this way, he tries to prevent a counter-attack.

That is what Sun Tzu says here.

Having created the circumstances where one is performing perfectly, the only thing between the litigator and success is the performance of his opponent. He must, in motor racing terms, force a mistake by his opponent, force him to run wide on a corner, to brake too early and compromise his approach, to box him in behind a slower moving car.

In litigation, he must be looking for any opportunity to take his opponent by surprise, to find the weak spot described earlier.

In this principle, "position" does not mean the geographical location (although that is relevant). It means the state of preparation.

But more than that, he is also looking for an opportunity to "feint," to mislead his opponent into thinking he is going to focus on one aspect of the case and in doing so divert attention from the actual point of attack. Or from a weak-spot in his own case.

4.15. Thus it is that in war the victorious strategist only seeks battle after the victory has been won, whereas he who is destined to defeat first fights and afterwards looks for victory.

This is a strange principle. There are many different interpretations of it but the most viable is that it reinforces earlier principles that say that one should be fully prepared and that the fully prepared will win. Once a winning strategy has been settled on and fully prepared for, then and only then should battle be joined.

This is consistent with the argument repeatedly put forward in this book: even before writing a Letter Before Action, the case should be fully assessed and action fully prepared for.

But to lunge forwards, unprepared, not having a properly formed plan and not knowing one's opponent's strengths and weaknesses almost guarantees that one will lose.

This is applicable to more than the Letter Before Action: it applies to the whole conduct of proceedings including all interlocutory applications and all hearings.

This author has seen many cases lost by litigators who, too lazy to properly conduct their case, would brief a barrister to appear with the briefest of briefs - and no, this does not mean a posing pouch or a G-string.

One such was a solicitor in England who, habitually, would send a brief to counsel (barristers or advocates) consisting of a photocopy of his entire file with the "instructions" being "See the enclosed documents."

He employed competent barristers but because he did not provide proper instructions as to the objectives and the evidence, leaving the barrister to try to read and understand what was going on and what he had to do, the conduct of hearings was seriously compromised.

As a result, the barristers were not properly prepared and were constantly taken by surprise.

Worse, he kept poor file records and so attendance notes were sketchy and did not make clear what had been discussed with clients, only a brief note of the instructions received - often something as nebulous as "issue writ." Therefore barristers at court would not know what advice had been tendered orally. He did not follow the safe practice of confirming the full contents of a telephone call or meeting in correspondence.

But the solicitor compounded his poor instructions by not going to court himself: he would send a junior clerk to "attend on Counsel." In England and Wales, in most cases, barristers are required to be supported by the solicitor or a representative of his firm. The representative is supposed to be of sufficient standing and authority to instruct counsel and to obtain instructions from the client; he is also supposed to be familiar with the case.

The solicitor did not ensure any of those requirements were met, indeed, he would send the most junior person he thought he could get away with and who was available at the time.

He would instruct barristers to attend even the simplest interrogatory applications, generally choosing not to attend court himself and no engaging any competent advocates in his firm.

But he would offer tiny fees - often using pupils from chambers hoping for bigger cases from him - to attend applications. The pupils were paid either nothing or little more than travelling expenses.

And yet his fees, it was later found out, would include a charge for the barrister's attendance as if the barrister were a member of the firm. This was fraudulent.

He had a terrible success record. He was, so far as most of the litigators in the town where he operated were concerned, regarded as a remarkably easy opponent. And he was.

4.16. The consummate leader cultivates the moral law and strictly adheres to method and discipline; thus it is in his power to control success.

For Sun Tzu, "the moral law" has nothing to do with morality. It means the will of the leader, emphasising that the commander is the delegated representative of the king and the king, as in so many cultures, is hand-picked by God and therefore stands in the stead of God. Therefore his will must be obeyed as if it is the word of God.

And that is, as noted earlier, the essence of litigation: the litigator strives to achieve the client's objectives, albeit tempered with good counsel on what is achievable either in absolute or economic terms.

But the Principle goes further: it is in this Principle that so many management consultants find inspiration.

Sun Tzu says that a good leader will set out systems and processes and be able to rely on his support team to follow those processes.

In other worlds, this is known as "compliance."

It is essential that a well-formed plan is adhered to (subject to the demands of flexibility discussed earlier).

A basic principle is that, if a member of the team considers a plan to have a weakness, that he discusses it with his leader, not goes off on his own and modifies the plan without authority.

One of the reasons for this is that, even if a plan is flawed, it at least has the advantage of being a plan that everyone is working to. Deviation from the plan undermines the broader strategy and also morale.

No one wants his own team shot by friendly fire because they were not where they were supposed to be, or finds that a weakness is exploited by the other side because someone had left his post to focus on something he had decided, on his own, was more important.

Thus Sun Tzu says that success is more likely where the plan is followed than when the support team make unilateral decisions to break formation.

4.17. In respect of military method, we have,

first, Measurement;

secondly, Estimation of quantity;

third, Calculation;

fourth, Balancing of chances;

fifthly, Victory.

This is simply a summary of the previous principles. It's bullet points. A presentation slide. And a simple, one-side-of-a-page reminder of how to develop a game plan. But there is some small explanation offered in the following principle.

4.18. Measurement owes its existence to Earth; Estimation of quantity to Measurement; Calculation to Estimation of quantity; Balancing of chances to Calculation; and Victory to Balancing of chances.

This sounds almost like the work of a quantity surveyor. What Sun Tzu is getting at is much more prosaic. He says that the second to fifth elements in principle 17 are each dependent on the previous one.

Back to basics: measure everything as a part of the initial preparation process. Do not rely on the client's (understandably) biased interpretation of facts. And measure as much of one's opponents case as can be identified.

Once everything is measured, assess it for veracity. In short, test the evidence. Cases are often lost because something was open to challenge and thereby excluded - or, worse, found to be false.

Based upon the results of testing, work out the prospects for success and develop and compare several strategies. And work out the likely cost of both winning and losing under each.

Fourth, choose the strategy that offers the best prospect of success at the lowest cost. Use what is known of one's opponent's case to assess the strength and weaknesses of each strategy as part of this assessment.

Lastly, if all the preparation has been done right and the strategy executed flawlessly, victory will flow.

Of course, that is not always so because of the inevitable unpredictability of litigation risk but what Sun Tzu counsels is that by managing both the upside and the downside, one is prepared for surprises and the chances of losing are minimised.

4.19. A victorious army as opposed to a routed one is as a pound's weight placed in the scale against a single grain.

A defeated opponent is demoralised. Of course, in litigation, that is not always the case: he may simply be angered into making a (hopefully ill-considered) appeal.

But that, of itself, is a sign of desperation. After all, an appeal should not be necessary if the case has been properly fought.

4.20. The onrush of a conquering force is like the bursting of pent-up waters into a chasm a thousand fathoms deep.

This is rhetoric to boost the king's opinion of Sun Tzu. No comment needed here.

No one is so brave that he is not
disturbed by something unexpected.

Julius Caesar

5. Energy

5. Energy

5.1. Sun Tzu said: the control of a large force is the same principle as the control of a few men: it is merely a question of dividing up their numbers.

A large force requires considerable management time. Sun Tzu recommends dividing the force into smaller units, each with its own commander and the General having direct contact with the commanders rather than the whole force.

This makes sense.

There is a general rule in problem solving: a shoal of piranha pick bones cleaner than a shark - hence big problems are best solved by dividing them into manageable chunks and allowing each group to deal with each area according to their specific skill sets.

Perhaps we should look at this as saying that a full team is made up of smaller teams.

When planning a campaign, one looks at the available resources and allocates them to the required tasks.

Therefore the general sits atop the management structure and makes strategic decisions, developing the plan and giving orders to his divisional commanders who, knowing the systems and controls (see above) know how the general wants his orders carried out.

It is the responsibility of the divisional commanders to ensure that happens.

But it is also their job to be the general's eyes and ears, noticing and reporting back factors that might influence the decisions already made, perhaps even requiring the modification of a plan.

5.2. Fighting with a large army under your command is no different from fighting with a small one: it is merely a question of instituting signs and signals.

Systems. Controls. Compliance. Sun Tzu understood the importance of these and the principles are as valuable today as they were then, even if the field of battle is differently defined.

It is amazing how, in an industry that is rules driven, litigators do not see the benefits of systems such as ISO9002.

Often, it seems that litigators think they are above the need for routines, which is all that ISO9002 is about.

However, seen as the equivalent of railway tracks, the importance of routines is clear: they allow for progress without thought as to direction, allowing the litigator to concentrate on the material aspects of the conduct of the case.

Compare that to roads, where there are constant decisions to be made as to speed, lane control, other road-users and a host of other distractions.

Simply, the more precise the systems, the more they become habit, the more litigators keep their eye on the objectives and the execution of the plan.

5.3. To ensure that your whole host may withstand the brunt of the enemy's attack and remain unshaken - this is effected by manœuvres direct and indirect.

Sun Tzu was an ancient Chinese and so his work was influenced by ancient Chinese culture. There are elements of this that have come to the attention of "the West" such as Ying and Yang - the concept of balance in all things.

Another pair of elements, less well known, is the "Cheng" and the "Ch'i"

These two elements are also in balance. Some ancient commentators on Sun Tzu's work say that facing down or making a direct attack on one's opponent is Cheng while using diversions is Ch'i. Others take the view that Ch'i is active while Cheng is passive. Ho Shih said (in modern terms) "we should make a frontal attack but convince the enemy that it is a subterfuge and convince him that a diversionary attack is a frontal attack: in this way, Cheng and Ch'i are the same, interchangeable."

The ancient commentators argue that a surprise attack from an unexpected direction is Ch'i while to march directly on one's opponent is Cheng.

The lessons of history are clear: a well-formed strategy allows for multiple forms of attack, always ready for action when a weak-spot opens up on one's opponent's flank or rear but also allows for the making of an attack to distract from the true target.

The balance between these two courses of action will increase the chances of success. Of course, Sun Tzu, writing to impress, suggests that success will, in this way, be guaranteed which is never the case.

5.4. That the impact of your army may be like a grindstone dashed against an egg - this is effected by the science of weak points and strong.

Sun Tzu seems to be running out of ideas. Here, he repeats the same concepts as previously: that victory is planned for and the chances increased by identifying and exploiting one's opponent's weak spots while protecting one's own. And of using ultimate force in the initial stages - in modern pop-warfare terms, delivering shock and awe.

5.5. In all fighting, the direct method may be used for joining battle but indirect methods will be needed in order to secure victory.

And, again, Sun Tzu repeats himself, emphasising the importance of always keeping a surprise ready for deployment at an opportune moment. But in this case, there is more that can be squeezed out of the principle.

In every case, there are twists and turns. There are open attacks, subterfuges and diversions. It is these latter, indirect, methods that destabilise one's opponent, making success more likely.

However, modern litigation is, in many countries, bound by rules that are designed to prevent surprises. Therefore the litigator must be especially careful when planning them.

In many jurisdictions, for example, he cannot, without the risk of penalty, spring a witness on his opponent during the trial. Witness lists and even witness statements are to be exchanged, leaving examination in chief to be something of a recitation and giving the other side ample opportunity to prepare cross-examination. But there is no requirement for the disclosure of what that cross-examination will focus on.

The nett effect of this is that cross-examination has now become a much more vicious and highly targeted affair and the witness is exposed to a much brighter light than if his evidence is not fully disclosed in advance.

Of course, generally nothing should be left out of a witness statement on the grounds that it might be harmful to the case but it can be carefully phrased so that it is true and full but not blatant or patent.

For example, a red light is a red light. There is no dispute. But the witness might be able to say, truthfully, that the light was not green. Cross-examination is designed to get behind such weasel words, to get to the bald truth. Ambiguity is generally undesirable but, in a witness statement, carefully calculated ambiguity can provide the opportunity for uncertainty regarding one's opponent's case.

Re-examination (which in some countries is called "redirection") does not allow for the introduction of new evidence but it is specifically designed for clarification of matters raised in cross-examination.

As a result, where the cross-examination seeks to put an unfavourable interpretation on that ambiguity, then re-examination can be used to forcefully put the correct interpretation with no opportunity for come-back.

But even more important, cross-examination is not limited to the evidence that the witness provides in his statement or in his examination in chief. Cross-examination is supposed to be a forceful (not brutal) testing of the evidence and in order to do so, external matters can be introduced.

Where those matters require reference to exhibits, there is a requirement that they be disclosed in advance. However, where it relates to exhibits that have been disclosed, albeit in a different context, then witnesses (and the litigators whose case they are supporting) are taken by surprise.

Indeed, re-examination is, at trial, an exceptionally powerful device which many advocates overlook. Whenever one hears an advocate say "no questions" after cross-examination, he is gambling on his ability to explain away any holes in the story in his closing argument. That is, generally, not to be recommended. Whether the case appears before a Judge alone or a Judge and jury, to leave an open wound seeping throughout the conduct of the case in the hope that a sticking plaster can be applied later is, often, reckless.

However, there may be other reasons for leaving a point open: as noted later, it may be that the advocate knows that he has strong evidence that will contradict, even completely knock out, the issue that is causing concern. If that point comes up in cross-examination (as distinct from re-examination) then to press for an admission that the witness is wrong (or some lesser word such as "mistaken) will invite reinforcement which would be more difficult to counter later.

5.6. Indirect tactics, efficiently applied, are inexhaustible (without boundaries) as Heaven and Earth, unending as the flow of rivers and streams; like the sun and moon, they end but to begin anew; like the four seasons, they pass away to return once more.

For much of this work so far, I have concentrated on overall strategies and preparation and on the early knock out. But now we are looking at the trial itself, the final (at least subject to the risk of appeal) battle - but, as noted elsewhere, not the final victory.

When battle is joined, subject to the Rules of Court and professional honour and duty, there are no holds barred. All out war is not pretty. Today, war is conducted by drones and long-distance weapons but litigation is more like hand-to-hand combat. As ammunition runs out, bayonets are drawn. The trial becomes a battle with swords, clubs and mace (the spiked ball on a stick, not the anti-assault spray).

It's bloody. It's emotional. If an advocate is not drained at the end of a day in court, he's not been trying hard enough.

He must pay attention to every word, cross-referencing it to the weight of the evidence, looking at how every comment affects his case.

From the opening speech - in which the advocates present, often, a version of events that is not supported by the evidence, trying to sway the court by creating pre-conceived notions of what the evidence will show (even if the evidence, ultimately, does not actually support the version put forward) - through the giving of evidence to the final closing speeches, every single word, every inflection, every gesture should be calculated for effect - or to undo the effect that the opposing advocate has sought to create.

It is no accident that so many advocates are frustrated performers: actors or musicians. Appearing in court is a performance. Advocates use props to make their point, sometimes even without introducing them into evidence.

In practice, I began my career in high street practice and continued to deal with cases where individuals needed help even though at the end of my career my clients were mainly multinational corporations and financial institutions. I never forgot my roots helping people who could not help themselves. I therefore kept a small part of my practice dealing with, inter alia, domestic violence cases.

Domestic violence is not funny but some of the cases are.

One day, a clerk from the law firm on the ground floor of the building where I had my office telephoned and said she was sending a man up in a domestic violence case because they did not deal with that kind of work. Natural prejudice told me that his wife was applying for an injunction and I therefore prepared to tell him that the rights and wrongs were - in the great scheme of things - irrelevant and that the correct course of action was to go to court, say he didn't do it if he did not or admit to it if he did and say he was sorry. Whichever was the case, he should offer to the Court an undertaking - a promise - that he would not hit her (for the first time or again, depending on the circumstances). So long as he followed the advice, there would be no need for me to appear.

I waited. And waited. And waited. He did not arrive. I wandered into the waiting room to look for him and then I heard bumping on the stairs.

When he came through the door at the top of the stairs, he had a plaster on his leg and one on his arm.

A cup of tea and a rest later (amid my apologies that he had had to climb the stairs when, if the firm downstairs had told me his condition, I could have seen him in their interview room instead of his having to struggle up the steep and narrow staircase) he told me the story. His wife beat him. Often. But as a rough, tough man he never fought back (except to push her away) and never complained. Until this assault, he had never consulted a doctor. How, I asked, had she caused such serious injury?

It turned out that he had been sitting watching TV. His wife had flown into one of her rages and begun to slap him. He had tried to ignore her, tried to reason with her and eventually sworn at her. She had then picked up a dining chair - the heavy kind with arms, called a "carver," - and smashed it down on him. He put up his arm to defend himself and that's how his arm was broken. Then as he escaped from the sofa, he fell over and she again wielded the chair, this time breaking his leg.

We had two options: go to Court without notice or wait a few hours and give the wife notice of the hearing. I chose the second course and asked the client to meet me at Court with the chair.

We trooped into Court, the wife with her solcitor and me with my client and, behind him, his brother with the large, heavy chair that he clearly had some difficulty carrying around. As we walked into Court, I watched the Judge who was paying close attention to the chair.

The affidavit in support of the application explained the circumstances.

The Judge read the papers and looked at the wife. "Did you hit him with the chair?" he asked. She said she had and launched into a justification for her actions. The Judge told her to be quiet. "Is that the chair?" he asked. "It looks like it," she said. "We have two of them." "I don't care what you think he did wrong, you were not defending yourself and so I'm ordering you not to assault him again."

The wife's solicitor was flabbergasted. He had not even spoken (and nor, incidentally, had I). We had secured the injunction by properly presented affidavit evidence - and the presence of a piece of furniture which had not even been introduced as an exhibit.

As we turned to leave, I said loud enough for the Judge to hear but speaking to my client's brother "take up thy chair and walk." I heard the Judge laughing behind me.

Making the Judge laugh is a good investment for future cases where one might need a little goodwill.

And the presence of the chair, being carried, with obvious difficulty, into Court by a large man, blind-sided my opponent who had been so fascinated by its arrival that he did not think through its implications and how to challenge its presence.

The following four principles can be grouped together:

5.7. There are not more than five musical notes, yet the combinations of these five give rise to more melodies than can ever be heard.

5.8. There are not more than five primary colours (blue, yellow, red, white and black), yet in combination they produce more hues than can ever been seen.

5.9. There are not more than five cardinal tastes (sour, acrid, salt, sweet, bitter), yet combinations of them yield more flavours than can ever be tasted.

5.10. In battle, there are not more than two methods of attack - the direct and the indirect; yet these two in combination give rise to an endless series of manœuvres.

Of course, there are more than five musical notes. Clearly Sun Tzu did not consider the ehru which has an infinite variety notes of haunting beauty within its range and came from the Silk Road area of Northern China although its original age is, it seems, not known. Nor the Tibetan dizi, a bamboo flute with six finger holes (rather like a modern recorder) popular more than 2,000 years ago.

He really should have known about the Gu Zheng. That's upturned-boat shaped instrument with 21 strings and a wide range that one often sees in (generally expensive) Chinese restaurants. It was already 400 years old when Sun Tzu wrote his treatise and in widespread use during the Qin Dynasty and the Warring States period.

But his comments as to colour are correct and his analysis of tastes still informs oriental cooking (which balances sweet and sour, salty with sweet, hot with sweet) in a dazzling array of tastes many of which are regarded as specialities of specific regions across south east Asia.

In Principles 7 - 9, Sun Tzu was using a technique used today by teachers and politicians: to take something that his audience would already be familiar with and to use that to illustrate his specific point.

The point made in Principle 10 is that one does not need an infinite variety of basics: it is the combination of them that produces the magical music, colour schemes and tastes that delight.

And so he uses this to reinforce the simple message that one should not rely on just one plan of attack and that a mix of full frontal and surprise, diversionary or with subterfuge is likely to increase the chances of success.

5.11. The direct and the indirect lead on to each other in turn. It is like moving in a circle - you never come to an end. Who can exhaust the possibilities of their combination?

Sun Tzu returns to the Cheng and Ch'i idea and points out that they are not only complimentary, but they lead one into the other. They are not two sides of the same coin, but each is an extension of the other, like a rubber band: no visible join.

He emphasises that the two approaches are intertwined. That the surprise, separate attack is as important as the direct approach, that linking the two are complimentary not divisive.

Tying this back to Principles 1 and 2, on the use of large forces, it can be seen that the prospects of success are enhanced by specialist teams doing their area of work and co-ordinating at the moment of battle.

But, as Principle 12 shows, Sun Tzu recognises that the main thrust of battle will always be with the larger force in full frontal attack, seeking to overwhelm the opposing force.

5.12. The onset of troops is like the rush of a torrent which will even roll stones along in its course.

In short, Sun Tzu is saying "don't try to be too clever." He is recommending that there are primary and secondary attacks and that the diversionary or secondary attacks should not take up too great a share of resources or time.

He is right. A favourite comment of Judges, irritated that the case has not been properly prepared, is that litigators should "get their tackle in order." Sometimes Judges say that litigators should "get all their ducks in a row."

These phrases are taken from "gentlemen's pursuits" - huntin', fishin', shootin'.

It is not a co-incidence that these phrases have passed into common use: they indicate that one cannot hope to be success-ful even in field pursuits, if one is not prepared.

This theme, again hinted at here by Sun Tzu, is recurrent. As supported by Principle 13.

5.13. The quality of decision is like the well-timed swoop of a falcon which enables it to strike and destroy its victim.

5.14. Therefore the good fighter will be terrible in his onset and prompt in his decision.

Forget modern warfare: for true shock and awe look at the animal kingdom. A falcon flies slowly over its territory looking for prey and, when it sees it, it does not hesitate, folds its wings and turns its body into a missile, pulling up its head, opening its wings and extending its talons milliseconds before they clamp onto its prey.

But the prey rarely dies from the talon cutting into it: it is the physical shock of the impact and the emotional shock (awe) of the sudden thud.

Here Sun Tzu draws that parallel: attack without warning, hard, fast and with commitment.

It gives a psychological advantage and a broken or worried opponent does not fight effectively.

Mind games have their place but there is nothing as effective as taking out, right before or at the commencement of a trial, a piece of evidence or a witness that is key to one's opponent's case.

Therefore, a well-timed application in relation to evidence or a witness that is due to be introduced later can be a devastating tactic.

Of course, such an application could be made in the run-up to the trial but to do so provides one's opponent with an opportunity to find a new way to introduce the same or similar evidence or otherwise plug the hole in his case.

To make an application returnable immediately before trial or even on the morning the trial is due to begin (in effect, then, before the opening speeches are made) is a seriously hostile step. Some Judges may refuse to hear it, saying that as the trial is about to begin, the appropriate time for such an application is when the evidence is about to be introduced or the witness called.

However, that means that one's opponent will be able to make reference to it, without complaint, during his scene-setting. By removing it prior to that there are two consequences: first he cannot make any reference to it and secondly it means his opening speech is in disarray.

5.15. Energy may be likened to the bending of a crossbow; decision, to the releasing of a trigger.

Sun Tzu says that there should be stored energy, waiting to be released. And that, when the decision is made to release it, that is like the trigger on a primed cross-bow.

Think about it: when the trigger is pulled, the energy is instantly and devastatingly released.

Here, then, Sun Tzu is saying that - once a decision is made - it is generally best to act on it immediately.

The preparation for trial is the priming of the crossbow; the trigger is the unleashing of the full force of advocacy and evidence.

5.16. Amid the turmoil and tumult of battle, there may be
seeming disorder and yet no real disorder at all; amid confu-
sion and chaos, your array may be without head or tail yet it
will be proof against defeat.

Sun Tzu does not say that an army in battle is like a headless chicken, running around the yard because it doesn't realise
it's dead.

Far from it.

In fact, he says that, once the battle plan is formulated and
the forces properly marshalled and briefed, that - if they stick
to the plan - the plan should work as expected even if the leaders are killed or busy elsewhere.

He recognises that battles are untidy - and one only has to
look at the amount of paper that is generated in courtrooms
that do not have electronic documents systems to understand
that - and yet everything has a place and it should be in its
place, however chaotic that seems from outside.

In short, out of chaos comes organisation and the best
organised stands the best chance of success.

Some of that - on a purely physical level - is true in a
court-room.

Judges and, especially, juries are prone to making assess-
ments not just on the evidence but also on the demeanour of
the advocate and witnesses. No matter how often they are told
that it is the evidence that decides a case, research after
research shows that juries pay great (if unrecognised) attention
to body language.

A witness that stutters out his answers or who overtly tries to phrase them carefully appears uncertain of his ground. And in the minds of those assessing evidence, that translates to not being convinced of the accuracy of their evidence - and inaccurate evidence is seen as, at least in part, untrue.

Where an advocate stumbles over finding documents, it has a devastating impact on a jury - and irritates the hell out of Judges.

Let's return to the idea that advocates are performers. If a person goes to the theatre and the actors stumble over their lines, he is viewed as not performing adequately.

It is instructive to sit at the back of lower courts and watch advocates perform. Some are, simply hilarious as they struggle to present even a simple case. Sometimes this is due to lack of skill, sometimes due to lack of preparation and sometimes due to (bizarrely) shyness. The polished performers are able to rise above adversity, to use a strong voice when things are going wrong, to use strong terms (e.g. I'll have it for you in a moment Your Honour. Bear with me while I find it").

Weaker advocates say things like "I'm sure it's here somewhere Your Honour. Can I have a few moments to look for it?"

Judges are like elephants and hawks - a dangerous combination. They do not forget and even if that first delay is tolerated, they bank that event for later criticism when similar circumstances arise. And they pounce hard when they decide they have had enough. And for the more cantankerous judges, that will not be long.

As it should not be: an advocate who does not know his way around his papers is not prepared. He has not got his tackle in order or his ducks in a row.

A strong advocate gives the Court the respect it deserves but does not grovel, does not display weakness. For if he does, then there is an implication that he is not sure of the strength of his case and that means that he has doubts as to its "winnability."

And if he isn't sure he's going to win, a Judge or jury won't be sure either.

5.17. Simulated disorder postulates perfect discipline, simulated fear postulates courage; simulated weakness postulates strength.

Sun Tzu says, simply, feign weakness or confusion to lull one's opponent into a false sense of security.

And there are times for that, but very rarely at trial.

Earlier, mention was made of the concept of apparent bumbling in order to make a witness repeat evidence that militated against his own case ("I'm sorry, I didn't get that, can you repeat it for me") for reinforcement.

Or to ask a witness to clarify something they have said ("I'm sorry, I didn't quite understand that. Are you saying......")

That is not so difficult to pull off.

But it is inherently undesirable at trial to appear weak and confused for the reasons described in the commentary to Principle 16.

It takes bravery to fake timidity in order to bring the witness nearer to the point you want. It's like in tennis, suckering one's opponent nearer to the net, thinking you have lost the power in your shot so that you can lob the ball over his head into the back of the court. But sometimes it goes wrong, your opponent spots the trap and flicks the ball just out of your reach.

And then you have to go and search for it.

5.18. Hiding order beneath the cloak of disorder is simply a question of subdivision; concealing courage under a show of timidity presupposes a fund of latent energy masking strength with weakness is to be effected by tactical disposi-tions.

Sun Tzu says that, if you are going to be brave enough to pretend weakness, you must back it up with exceptional strength. When the opponent flicks that ball, you must have reserves of skill and energy - and probably spider-like jumping and co-ordination levels - to avoid losing the point.

5.19. Thus one who is skilful at keeping the enemy on the move maintains deceitful appearances, according to which the enemy will act.

Just as in squash, keeping one's opponent moving to defend so as to make it difficult for him to formulate and execute his strategy is a recipe for successful litigation, both in pre-trial stages and in court.

Constantly wrong-footing one's opponent, even in the robing room or in the court's ante-room is a good start.

In a domestic violence case, Mr X was a frequent visitor to my office. The first time he came, we ended up with me enjoying his company so much I did that rare thing of taking a client out for a drink.

Mr X was a really nice man and his wife, when she was in a good mood was, he said, a really nice woman.

But she had a tendency to lash out.

"She hit me. She's always hitting me," he said. "These are my best glasses. And they are made up of spare parts."

I looked at his spectacles and they were, indeed, a composite of three different pairs: the arms did not match each other and neither matched the frame. I couldn't help laughing and, thankfully, nor could he.

We prepared his affidavit in support of his application and I quoted his plaintive way of explaining the plight of his eyewear.

We sat in front of the Judge and I handed over the affidavit. Knowing that I would have a fit of the giggles if I read it out, as was the custom for that Judge, I invited him to read it for himself. As he got to to the part about being hit and the glasses, the Judge looked up at me, then at my client, back to the affidavit then to my client, peering at his face, then looking to the left and right of his head.

"She broke your glasses?" He asked my client, trying to choke back giggles, clearly thinking that speaking might distract him from the laughter he was trying to control.

"Yes, sir. Many times."

The Judge tried and failed. He started to smile, then chuckle.

Mr X, so nice that he didn't think the whole legal profession was full of nut-cases who laugh at his misfortune, took it all in good part.

Mrs X and her solicitor did not. The solicitor humphed. Mrs X got cross.

The Judge asked how she hit him and she said "with me fists, Your Honour."

We would learn over time that, no matter how many times the Judge told her to call him "Judge" or "sir," she would persist in calling him "Your Honour." And every time she did, the humour levels rose.

"How did you break his glasses?"

"He wasn't wearing them when they broke this last time, Your Honour."

"What happened?"

"We was driving and I smacked him in the face. His glasses flew off and landed on the floor."

"Yes?"

"And I stamped on them, Your Honour."

The Judge and I stared at each other, daring the other to be the first to laugh.

We left court, her undertaking "not to hit him like that in future" was recorded.

The next time we arrived in court after she threw an ashtray at him, lacerating his forehead but, thankfully, missing his glasses. I sat down in front of the Judge and plonked a piece of thick blue glass on his table.

"You promised me you wouldn't hit him again," the Judge said.

Mrs X said "no, Your Honour. I said I wouldn't hit him like that again." She triumphantly emphasised "like that."

Again, my side of the room struggled with the giggles. The Judge looked incredulous and stared at her solicitor.

"Yes, sir. That's exactly what she said. I have it in my notes."

The Judge looked at me. Unable to speak without laughing, I just smiled and shrugged. The Judge fought a losing battle with a face that was determined to smile.

"What's that?" he asked me, pointing to the piece of thick glass.

"That's what's left of the ash tray."

"How big was it?"

Mr X made a circle with his hands, roughly the size of a tea plate.

Suddenly not laughing, the Judge said "you could have done serious injury. Why did you do that?"

"I wanted to go to bed and he wanted to watch TV."

No one asked the obvious question as to why any man in his right mind would want to go to bed with this (not a clinical diagnosis) crazy woman.

Another undertaking was given. She would not hit him or throw things at him.

A few weeks later, Mr X and I were sitting in the ante room waiting for another case to come out of the Judge's chambers. He had brought with him a Galliano bottle with a dancing ballerina in the bottom. When it was wound up, the ballerina twirled and a painful version of music from Swan Lake jangled out. Bored, I wound it up. Then the door to chambers opened. Heart sinking, I picked up the bottle with the little figure spinning round and the noise still permeating the whole room and walked towards the door. It stopped as I walked into Chambers and I put it on the corner of the Judge's table.

We weren't there because of the bottle. We were there because she had thumped him again, this time injuring his arm so he could not drive. To a van driver, this was a handicap. Now things were serious.

The Judge took none of Mrs X's nonsense. There was no laughing. He gave her a strong dressing down and made it plain to her solicitor that he considered the solicitor had failed in his duty to make his client understand the seriousness of the situation. He made it plain that, even though Mr X was not asking for his wife's committal that, if she ended up before him again, he would not hesitate to send her to jail for contempt in breaking her undertaking. Except this time he would not accept an undertaking. He issued an injunction. He ordered the solicitor and Mrs X to wait in the precincts of the Court until the order was drawn up and served on her.

As we left chambers, I picked up the bottle.

"What's the bottle for?" he asked me.

"She hits him with it," I said.

No one laughed.

I saw them once more, several months later. He was driving his van. He was wearing new glasses. She was in the passenger seat. They were both smiling.

Even today, I am not sure who was most wrong footed in our encounters. Mrs X seemed to have a degree of control over proceedings that she should not have had. Her solicitor was weak and dominated by his client and confused to the point of fascination with the props I carried into the ante-room, totally uncertain as to what I intended to do with them: he was to all intents and purposes lost before we walked through the door of the Judge's chambers. And that was made worse by the Judge's efforts to study the evidence of the piecemeal spectacles without making it obvious he was staring at my client. The Judge had no defence to the ludicrousness of the situation until driven to distraction by Mrs X. I know I had total control over whether we won - there was no chance we would lose - but in the actual hearings I had no control over what was happening.

But I do know I won the battle over gaining recognition from the Judge. Several months later, I heard a story about a solicitor who had carried a large bottle into the Judge's chambers with the thing playing music from Swan Lake and with a little dancing ballerina in it. The Judge had told the story at a dinner so now dozens of people knew.

5.20. By holding out baits, he keeps him on the march; then with a body of picked men he lies in wait for him.

Sun Tzu says to use crumbs to suck one's opponent in, then pounce on him, not with full force but with a carefully selected specialist team.

This is a valuable tactic in hearings.

In cross-examination, leading the witness is permitted, indeed it is a valid tactic.

When leading a witness, it is perfectly acceptable to mis-lead him into thinking that one is addressing one issue while obtaining an admission to another point. It might be regarded as a little unfair - after all, lawyers are supposed to be good with words and witnesses are - in many cases - not expected to perform as well under pressure.

But all's fair in love and litigation. Well, kind of. Subject to the Rules, professional behaviour and what the Judge will allow.

Diversionary questioning is a good tactic. Taking a witness through a series of documents securing a "yes" answer to a number of questions and then asking about an entry to which a "no" answer, or a qualified answer is expected will often result in a "yes."

Lawyers are, too often, elitist: many do not realise that lit-igation is in fact a form of sales and once in court, the tricks used by salesmen can often result in admissions. Lawyers often think that to take sales training is beneath them. It is not: learning to get to "yes" is the essence of good cross-examination.

And it is also the essence of a good opening and closing argument. Outside the court-room, such presentations are sales pitches. It is the arrogance of lawyers that makes them feel that the techniques of trade are somehow beneath them. Yet the lessons of traders are invaluable in a court room.

Market traders know how to set out their stall. They know to put the nice fruit at the front but fill customers' bags from the back. They know that customers accept what they are told and are rarely sceptical. They know how to attract the customer's attention and to steer them to the purchases that the trader wants them to make.

Insurance salesmen - even burger bar staff - know how to cross-sell or up-sell: "You want fries with that?"

Waiters steer diners to the specials - which are often the dishes with the highest margins for that day - or using product that is reaching the end of its shelf-life.

Techniques of persuasion are all around us: but lawyers often don't learn from them.

This is what Sun Tzu is aiming to overcome. Hold out little treats, sell the benefit, then when the target (be it witness, Judge or jury) is softened up, use carefully selected points to push home an advantage.

5.21. The clever combatant looks to the effect of combined energy and does not require too much from individuals.

No one man can win a war, but one man can lose it. Therefore, says Sun Tzu, one should not rely on a single person to win but rather make sure that the whole team is working together.

This recalls the previous arguments that a team should be made up of a range of specialists, each doing what they do best.

And a commander should not expect foot-soldiers to excel nor should he expect excellent performance from those that he demands operate outside their sphere of expertise.

The clever commander chooses his team carefully and makes sure they work together effectively without overlap (wasted energy and, worse, the risk of conflict within the team) and without gaps through which an opponent may drive a wedge.

5.22. When he utilizes combined energy, his fighting men become as it were like unto rolling logs or stones. For it is the nature of a log or stone to remain motionless on level ground and to move when on a slope; if four-cornered, to come to a standstill, but if round-shaped, to go rolling down.

5.23. Thus the energy developed by good fighting men is as the momentum of a round stone rolled down a mountain thousands of feet in height. So much on the subject of energy.

Ah, inertia. It's a wonderful thing. And the enemy of successful litigation. A case that is in hover-mode is wasting everyone's time and money and - from the client's point of view - emotional and even commercial cost.

It follows that energy is actually created not wasted by movement. A log or stone rolling downhill gains speed.

In England, a peculiar form of sport is the annual Running of the Cheese competition. A wheel of hand-made Double Gloucester cheese from the farm of Mrs. Diana Smart of Churcham (www.smartsgloucestercheese.com) is taken to the top of a 100 foot hill and rolled down. Entrants chase after it, the winner being the person who is first to reach the cheese. Being a wheel, when it hits a bump, it launches into the air and in this way accelerates rather than being slowed. Runners, on the other hand, fall over and injuries are common.

And so it is with litigation: it takes on a momentum of its own and proceeds, inexorably, towards trial. But sometimes, unlike the cheese, it stalls. When that happens, it atrophies. Once a case stops, inertia sets in. Often neither litigator has much enthusiasm for kick-starting it.

There's an old adage: justice delayed is justice denied.

Therefore, for a plaintiff a stalled action is as good as a loss.

After all, the plaintiff began the action to achieve an objective and he, rightly, expects progress to be made towards that objective whenever possible.

But more than that, if a plaintiff's litigator fails to prosecute the claim forcefully, then he allows the defence team time to better prepare and therefore actually increases his own chance of losing.

It is fatal to enter any war
without the will to win it.

Douglas MacArther,
General, US Army

6. Weaknesses and Strengths

6 Weaknesses and strengths

6.1. Sun Tzu said: Whoever is first in the field and awaits the coming of the enemy, will be fresh for the fight; whoever is second in the field and has to hasten to battle will arrive exhausted.

Sun Tzu spells out a self-evident truth. Sometimes one hears people say "being on time is being late."

The simple reality is this: by being well prepared, in advance and arriving early so as to be refreshed in time for the battle is always likely to result in a better performance than someone who dashes out of his office, to court or a meeting and arrives breathless and has to calm himself down before he becomes effective.

Some people think that rushing makes them look busy and important. As a practitioner, I knew that anyone who arrived looking flustered was going to be easy meat.

Much better to be early, calm down and to be able to make a suitable entrance.

Being late, or nearly late, is to have already entered the mindset that things are not within one's control.

But for a successful litigator, control is at least as important as knowledge and skill.

If one is sitting, calmly, almost looking bored when one's opponent arrives, especially if he arrives right as a hearing is due to be called, one exudes confidence. It says "I'm not worried."

It is the simplest - and one of the most effective - mind games an advocate can play.

And the amazing thing is that even though one's opponent is aware that the image is an illusion, it almost always has a negative impact on his confidence. And Sun Tzu knew this and emphasised it in the next principle.

But there's more. If an advocate has rushed to Court, there will always be, in the back of his mind, the feeling that he might have left something behind.

Because he will have been, right before starting his case, focussing on the logistics (everything from remembering to fill up his car, through finding a parking space to having to take a second lift because the first one was full), he will not have tuned-in to his case. And no matter how well he knows his case, he will under-perform if it is not front and centre in his thoughts.

To take a lesson from sports, his head will not be "in the game."

To perform well, the litigator and in particular the advocate must disassociate himself from external distractions. Being uncertain as to whether the Court might start without him is a major distraction during his last-minute preparation time.

6.2. Therefore the clever combatant imposes his will on the enemy, but does not allow the enemy's will to be imposed on him.

Incredibly, as shown in the narrative to the previous principle, this can be achieved without saying even one word. If one's opponent is late, or just on time, he will, almost always, open with an apology, even to an advocate who is sitting outside Court obviously waiting.

The one who is waiting knows that his opponent, for all his bluster, will not be fully concentrating at the beginning. And therefore he knows that, if he has an aspect of his case which is less strong than the rest, that may be the best time to deal with it.

Or he may know that there is an aspect of his opponent's case that can be damaging but not have much probative value. Therefore an early attack on that aspect might be worthwhile.

It could be something as simple as a piece of evidence that is open to challenge for some reason. Or it might be someone on the witness list, for example, an expert who it has been discovered does not have the credentials claimed. The Judge may take the view that an application in relation to either would be best taken when it is sought to introduce it.

6.3. By holding out advantages to him, he can cause the enemy to approach of his own accord; or, by inflicting damage, he can make it impossible for the enemy to draw near.

In cross-examination, it is acceptable to lead the witness, including to lead him into making a mistake. It is not acceptable to mislead by untruth, but it is acceptable to create an impression in the mind of the witness so long as it is done with reference to the truth. Sun Tzu emphasises that a person may be led into thinking one thing when another is actually happening.

The second part of this principle emphasises that, once one's opponent begins to charge, a sudden and forceful counter-attack can wrong-foot him and make his continued progress impossible.

By combining both parts, Sun Tzu demonstrates that by encouraging one's opponent (in the context of this explanation a witness) to make an ill-considered rush, it is then easy to trip him up.

So, by creating either intellectual or emotional confusion, a witness can be put off his stride and distracted from his prepared answers.

6.4. If the enemy is taking his ease, harass him; if well supplied with food, starve him out; if quietly encamped, force him to move.

On the face of it, this might appear to be encouraging siege, which Sun Tzu elsewhere cautions against.

But this principle is dealing with a different situation: siege relates to a city or other permanent establishment. Here, Sun Tzu is talking about a mobile force that has set up camp. Never let the enemy rest - a rested army is a strong army. It has also had time to plan and re-plan. So it's important that there is constant harassment of an opponent, preventing rest. It is important to disrupt his supply lines.

In the context of litigation, this is has no obvious equivalent: it is, obviously, not acceptable to try to disrupt communications, etc. But, to force him to move is directly applicable in
litigation: the making of applications, the demands for information and so on prevent a party from settling and, therefore,
disrupt his opportunity to prepare.

6.5. Appear at points which the enemy must hasten to de-fend; march swiftly to places where you are not expected.

Let's think about sports, again. A great tennis player is
constantly thinking about where the ball is coming from and
where it is aimed and how to get there, where his opponent
will run to after hitting a shot and how well he will be able to
change direction and get somewhere else, how to place the
returned ball into a place on the court that his opponent will
struggle to reach and as soon as it is hit on return, to try to get
back into a position from which the whole of the court can be
reached quickly. Like in chess, a good tennis player is not only
thinking about the ball he is about to hit: he is thinking about
the one that will be hit back and how he will respond to that
and so on.

Virginia Wade, a Wimbledon champion, said "It's difficult
for most people to imagine the creative process in tennis.
Seemingly it's just an athletic matter of hitting the ball consist-
ently well within the boundaries of the court. That analysis is
just as specious as thinking that the difficulty in portraying
King Lear on stage is learning all the lines."

The same goes for litigation. Learning and applying the rules is easy. It's the strategy, the action and reaction that is difficult.

It follows, then, that here Sun Tzu is likening the battle to tennis: when one's opponent is running one way, hit the ball the other and, working out where his response is likely to go, be there before he hits it, ready for a return and to make him run, again, to a place on the court he did not expect to be.

6.6. An army may march great distances without distress, if it marches through country where the enemy is not.

This principle is the opposite of that shown at principle 4. Here, Sun Tzu says that a good leader will ensure that he is not intercepted nor meet the opponent's battle force and therefore not subject himself to the risks that an opponent giving effect to principle 4 would create.

6.7. You can be sure of succeeding in your attacks if you only attack places which are undefended. You can ensure the safety of your defence if you only hold positions that cannot be attacked.

Some commentators e.g. Wang Hsi regards "undefended" as meaning areas where defence is weak either because of lack of resources or because there is some lack of will on the part of the defenders or a failure of leadership. That makes a great deal of sense - it would be difficult to imagine a complete lack of any defensive force: after all, that's why each party has instructed lawyers.

How else can a defence be weakened? Earlier, reference was made to playing the man not the ball, to identify personal traits or weaknesses in one's opponent and exploit them.

For example, an opposing litigator may have recently lost a high profile case. Reminding him of that at a strategic moment may unsettle him. Or he may have recently lost a valuable member of his team to a rival firm - questions as to why someone would jump ship may distract one's opponent.

Commentators say that this principle contains a sub-meaning, that a good defence includes ensuring security at points that are unlikely to be attacked.

6.9. O divine art of subtlety and secrecy! Through you we learn to be invisible, through you inaudible; and hence we can hold the enemy's fate in our hands.

Sun Tzu again emphasises the importance of surprise, of playing one's cards close to one's chest. Of course, the Rules of Court require the disclosure of material facts and law but they do not require the disclosure of a strategy or a line of questioning. Sun Tzu says that the application of an unexpected stratagem will increase the chances of success.

6.10. You may advance and be absolutely irresistible, if you make for the enemy's weak points; you may retire and be safe from pursuit if your movements are more rapid than those of the enemy.

Are there opportunities in litigation for what amount to a rush in to attack a weak spot, then withdraw rapidly before one's opponent has a chance to regroup and chase?

Yes, there are. Again, this is a place where interrogatories have a place but there is another technique which is more subtle and can have an even more devastating effect because it adopts a strategy that divides one's opponent from his client.

Reference was made earlier to the strategic advantage of making an offer that would make the opposing client think hard about accepting it, even if his lawyer's advice is to refuse.

The offer may, on the face of it appear to be generous - and it should be sufficiently attractive that it will not be dismissed out of hand.

But the offer might be accompanied, at the same time, by a form of attack. This may be interrogatories or it may be by something more direct: the disclosure of a key fact that makes one's opponent recognise an increased prospect of defeat.

Take, for example, a case involving a defective motor vehicle as a result of which a person is injured. The defendant company will not, generally wish to settle early - to do so might invite a flood of cases or, at least, a flood of demands for that model to be subject to a recall.

Where an expert's report shows that there was, indeed, a defective component, either by design or in the manufacturing process, then an offer to settle upon payment of x can be accompanied by additional pressure.

There are two ways of creating this pressure. The first is to make the report available to the defendant.

But there is another tactic: the report can be made available to safety regulators or, even, consumer groups in the markets where the car is sold.

There is nothing improper about revealing a report in this way: indeed, it may be seen as socially responsible.

The additional pressure that suddenly lands on the car company, either through regulators demanding more information or by consumer groups creating media pressure, is considerable.

The car company is likely, therefore, to want the existing case out of the way as soon as possible. Moreover, if there is a public outcry then damages awards may increase. Therefore a settlement can ensure that there is a base-line should there be any further actions.

These are the weak points where pressure can be brought to bear.

The defence have no answer to such a tactic: the plaintiff has done nothing wrong by revealing the information.

What must not be done is to say "if the defendant does not accept this offer of settlement, we will release the report to...." That is blackmail.

If the defendant decides to tough it out, not to accept the offer, then the plaintiff need do nothing further.

Most likely is that a lower counter-offer will be made. This is how defendants chase plaintiffs: hoping that the plaintiff will accept rather than continue. But in these circumstances, the plaintiff has already delivered his blow and run back for cover.

A well prepared litigator will have prepared the plaintiff for the likely response and have an answer to the counter-offer: if below y, then reject, if above y, either hold out or accept. But, whatever the counter-offer, he will not respond immediately but, instead to wait and see if his opponent is made nervous by delay.

In some ways, we can see that the idea of dividing the lawyer from the client is similar to the Roman tactic called "The Wedge." A body of men formed a triangular formation and the pointed end moved forward, protected by shields on either side and overhead, into the opposing forces. The use of the shields made their formation difficult to attack and, as the wedge moved forward, it forced the opposing forces apart, so dividing and weakening them.

But more than that, the wedge was self-sustaining: the men in the middle of the triangle filled in if one of those on the edge fell but also, as the wedge moved forward, the men in the middle moved to the end of the sides of the triangle, so extending it, ultimately creating a much greater division between the two halves of the defending force than its original size would have suggested. This technique also reduced the opportunity for the defending forces to rush around behind the wedge where it may have been more exposed.

The wedge was most often used to break long battle lines and several used together could break a long line into much smaller, manageable sections.

We can see that this tactic can be used to separate issues, enabling them to be put before the arbiters of fact as separate matters that are joined up to make a compelling case but also allowing the case to stand if one of those issues falls.

6.11. If we wish to fight, the enemy can be forced to an engagement even though he be sheltered behind a high rampart and a deep ditch. All we need do is attack some other place that he will be obliged to relieve.

This principle seems to be in contrast to others - but it is, in effect, an extension of the insistence that a siege is undesirable. Viewed as a continuation of principle 10, it can be seen that the defendant may think he is secure even after such an attack but that a second attack, on a different weak spot, will spread his resources - and divert his attention. Sun Tzu says that an enemy that wishes to avoid a battle can be made to engage by frequent attacks.

Sun Tzu is not a fan of frontal attack: he sees it as a waste of men and equipment. That is why he developed his strategies: to find ways of deploying his resources most effectively while seeking to limit loses.

The Romans were fully aware of the risk of weak-spots and they had a tactic called "The Saw." This was to hold, in reserve, small, highly trained units - today we would consider them tactical support units - which were able to move at high speed behind the lines to plug any weak spots, regardless of the reason they appeared.

6.12. If we do not wish to fight, we can prevent the enemy from engaging us even though the lines of our encampment be merely traced out on the ground. All we need do is to throw something odd and unaccountable in his way.

This is a strange principle, on the face of it. Sun Tzu says that a force may be as yet unprepared for battle when it is engaged. He suggests that one way of dealing with this is to pretend not to be a battle force. Li Ch'uan, another Chinese general, says that he found that, by striking his colours (i.e. taking down his battle standard) and pretending to be settlers, his opponent withdrew, thinking that it must be a trick and that an ambush was imminent.

6.13. By discovering the enemy's dispositions and remaining invisible ourselves we can keep our forces concentrated while the enemy's must be divided.

Sun Tzu returns to the idea that a general should keep his strategies close to his chest. By having a single large force in place, then one's opponents know exactly what they are dealing with. Far better, he says, to find out how one's opponent's forces are deployed while keeping one's own strength and resources secret. In this way, the enemy will be compelled to set up defences against all possibilities rather than against a definable and predictable force.

6.14. We can form a single united body while the enemy must split up into fractions. Hence there will be a whole pitted against separate parts of a whole which means that we shall be many to the enemy's few.

Sun Tzu discusses a concept that is clearly similar to The Wedge. Keeping a strong central force and dividing the opposing forces will mean that one's opponent's efforts are fragmented and more easily defeated. Of course, this does not always work: it was the basic idea behind circling the wagons but in that case the attacking force was operating in a much greater arena and the circle created what amounts to a killing ground. Even so, it was probably a better tactic than trying to outrun a fast group on horseback.

How can we use this idea in litigation? Again, it comes to the old phrase "divide and conquer." By one team remaining united while trying to cause dissent in the other team, one firm can cause both cost and disruption to the way the other party conducts the case.

6.15. And if we are able thus to attack an inferior force with a superior one our opponents will be in dire straits.

Again, Sun Tzu says that a superior force will defeat an inferior force. This is not just about numbers and fire-power, it is also about intellect. But we should focus on the fire-power: in this context, the evidence. If there is overwhelming evidence, then use it, both before trial to compel, or try to compel, a settlement or at the beginning of the trial.

Sometimes, instead of using early witnesses to scene-set, it can be valuable to use them to deliver strong evidence. For example, if there is clear and incontrovertible evidence that the CEO of a company signed off on false accounts, then instead of first calling witnesses who have lost money, call evidence that the accounts were in fact filed, were in fact signed off on by the CEO and that the CEO was or should have been aware that they were false. Once the arbiters of fact have those points, everything else is, basically, a question of quantum.

6.16. The spot where we intend to fight must not be made known; for then the enemy will have to prepare against a possible attack at several different points; and his forces being thus distributed in many directions, the numbers we shall have to face at any given point will be proportionately few.

6.17. For should the enemy strengthen his vanguard, he will weaken his rear; should he strengthen his rear, he will weaken his vanguard; should he strengthen his left, he will weaken his right; should he strengthen his right, he will weaken his left. If he sends reinforcements everywhere, he will everywhere be weak.

16 should be read in conjunction with 17.

Thus, except in cases where the order of witnesses must be disclosed, an advocate should not give notice of when individuals will give evidence.

That means that the other side has to be prepared, every day, for each and every witness that might be called. That costs time and resources and, as Sun Tzu says, preparing for many possible points of attack means that the other side's preparations are spread more thinly.

6.18. Numerical weakness comes from having to prepare against possible attacks; numerical strength, from compelling our adversary to make these preparations against us.

A Yankee general in the American Civil War, Philip Henry Sheridan, once said of his mentor Ulyssees S Grant that he won because while the enemy were trying to work out what Grant would do next, they could not because Grant was still working out his own plan.

This is not, in its literal sense, to be recommended. The story is told by some commentators on Sun Tzu to support principles 16 - 18 but, in fact, it does the opposite.

Sun Tzu is in fact saying that an attacking force should ensure that they are in a position to attack in several places at once, so making the defendants - for want of a better phrase - run around like headless chickens. Simply, if they do not know where the attack will come, they will rush around trying to bolster all possible points and, as a result, become weakened in numbers, so making their defeat more achievable than if they were fully prepared and in unity.

6.19. Knowing the place and the time of the coming battle, we may concentrate from the greatest distances in order to fight.

If the witness list and order is known, then an advocate has time to prepare in advance. If it is not, then he must expect to deal with situations as they arise.

6.20. But if neither time nor place be known, then the left wing will be impotent to succour the right, the right equally impotent to succour the left, the vanguard unable to relieve the rear, or the rear to support the van vanguard. How much more so if the furthest portions of the army are anything under a hundred Li apart and even the nearest are separated by several Li!

Where is the battleground? After all the skirmishes, the guerilla attacks, the raiding parties and ambushes, the intelligence gathering and the spreading of dis-information, where does the final battle take place?

Sun Tzu appears to say that once the time and place is known, then a good general will keep his forces back until they are needed, resting, preparing and then swoop into the battleground ready for a fight.

This is, seemingly, contrary to his previous ideas which seemed to suggest that a battle force should arrive at the battle ground early so as to be refreshed and ready for their opponents.

However, what Sun Tzu really means in principles 19 and 20 is that the full battle plans should be fully ready and communicated to the commanders who will implement them, that the general should be preparing in the calm of (as he said earlier) his temple. And that, when the battle is about to be joined, his forces should be united.

6.21. Though according to my estimate the soldiers of Yueh exceed our own in number, that shall advantage them noth-ing in the matter of victory. I say then that victory can be achieved.

This principle is part of Sun Tzu's sales pitch to his boss, the King. The war between Wu and Yueh went on for centuries - ending in about 473 B.C. which is long after Sun Tzu's death. Wu lost and the kingdom was subsumed into Yueh. By my reading, the principle is simply rhetoric, telling the King what he wants to hear - that the opposing forces are larger but that guile and skill will defeat them.

Some commentators say that this passage refers to Sun Tzu's presumption that Yueh's soldiers were not kept informed of strategy and, therefore, would not know where or when battle was to be joined and therefore, being mentally unpre-pared for battle, they would lose.

Although I cannot see that the principle says that, the concept has merit: after all, earlier I said that one should serve notice of interlocutory hearings as close to the hearing as pos-sible (where service is within one's own control), but generally, at least for large trials, the final hearing date is known well in advance. Smaller trials are, of course, subject to being planted in a "warned list" which means the court sets a period during which, if time becomes available, a trial may be called on at short notice.

It is difficult to see how this principle relates to the ignorance of the foot soldiers, even if what the commentators said is valuable.

6.22. Though the enemy be stronger in numbers, we may prevent him from fighting. Scheme so as to discover his plans and the likelihood of their success.

In the final chapter, Sun Tzu talks of the use of spies. Although actual espionage is not part of the repertoire of most litigators, information gathering is. Here Sun Tzu encourages the engaging of the other side in conversation and trying to elicit information as to what they intend to do.

However, it is always important to realise that their plans today may not be the same as their plans tomorrow and that the information they give may be, deliberately or not, false.

6.23. Rouse him and learn the principle of his activity or inactivity. Force him to reveal himself so as to find out his vulnerable spots.

Again, in our context, this can be seen as interrogatories or offers in settlement. They prevent one's opponent resting and the way he responds can give clues as to his strategy, strenghts and weaknesses.

6.24. Carefully compare the opposing army with your own so that you may know where strength is superabundant and where it is deficient.

This is a common theme: know your enemy and avoid his strengths and exploit his weaknesses.

Of course, this can relate to the people involved, particularly with regard to the skill of the advocate, but we will find it more useful to relate it to the evidence.

And in doing so, it reinforces the point that there must be total preparation right from the outset, gaining full intelligence as to the evidence available to both sides and testing that evidence. But here Sun Tzu says that such intelligence gathering and testing must be a continuous process, continuing right up to and throughout the trial.

6.25. *In making tactical dispositions, the highest pitch you can attain is to conceal them; conceal your plans and you will be safe from the prying of the subtlest spies, from the machinations of the wisest brains.*

Sun Tzu says that it is essential to avoid the plan becoming known for, if it does, then the opposing generals will be able to work out how to prepare and therefore defeat it.

Again, with the effective ban on surprise witnesses and the general rule that evidence is disclosed in advance of trial, surprises are quite difficult to set up and, if they are, they will often appear contrived with the risk of penalty from the Judge.

But while facts are put in evidence, interpretations are not. Ordinary witnesses are supposed to be witnesses as to fact but in many cases, their personal reaction to those facts is an integral part of the case.

While the "how does that make you feel?" line of questioning should be challenged and should be disallowed unless it is directly relevant to the question of damages (it is generally designed to create an emotional response in the arbiters of fact, not a response based purely on fact), questions such as "what was the effect of the crash" are acceptable in order to demonstrate the severity of an impact and the resulting injury.

6.26. How victory may be produced for them out of the enemy's own tactics - that is what the multitude cannot comprehend.

If the other side can be tripped up by their own evidence, that is a good result, in part because the opportunity for appeal is reduced. Also, if the other side's own evidence is demonstrated to be false, then that will have an impact on the quantum of general damages.

6.27. All men can see the tactics whereby I conquer but what none can see is the strategy out of which victory is evolved.

When all is done and the parties leave Court, the tactics that the litigator used have been laid out for all to see. But, says Sun Tzu, the strategies that were developed to win remain secret. The tips and tricks that make the victor strong are not visible even during battle.

6.28. Do not repeat the tactics which have gained you one victory, but let your methods be regulated by the infinite variety of circumstances.

Sun Tzu reminds us that from one battle to the next a good general must remain unpredictable. Therefore he should not take one tactic and use it in each battle.

What he does not say is to carry forward from the previous principle the idea that a stratagem can be re-applied, even though the tactics and execution are different.

In short, Sun Tzu is making sure his book become a best seller and is read down the generations: he proposes a system of strategies that is long on ideas but short on detail.

The details are the tactics that forces will adopt in each battle while the strategies are common to all (or most) forms of warfare.

Given that his ideas have been adopted by military leaders for longer than we have had The Bible, he seems to have had the right approach. No doubt, wherever he is, he is wishing he was still collecting royalties.

6.29. Military tactics are like unto water; for water in its natural course runs away from high places and hastens downwards.

6.30. So in war, the way is to avoid what is strong and to strike at what is weak.

6.31. Water shapes its course according to the nature of the ground over which it flows; the soldier works out his victory in relation to the foe whom he is facing.

6.32. Therefore, just as water retains no constant shape, so in warfare there are no constant conditions.

6.33. He who can modify his tactics in relation to his opponent and thereby succeed in winning, may be called a heaven-born captain.

6.34. The five elements (water, fire, wood, metal, earth) are not always equally predominant; the four seasons make way for each other in turn. There are short days and long; the moon has its periods of waning and waxing.

Sun Tzu's ability to rephrase the same few principles and to push them out again later is rather like the litigators' saying that one tells the facts so that the court has some idea what's going on, then repeats the facts so they can understand them, then repeats them again so they can remember them.

Principles 29 - 34 are repeats of principles that have been discussed at length, phrased in a slightly different way.

If there is anything fresh to be gleaned from these principles, it's that the five elements are not in balance and that, from time to time one will be more important than the others.

In reality, though, these principles reinforce what has gone before.

Sometimes life is like a horror movie.
You know what you are seeing isn't real
but still you are scared.

Jefferson Galt
Author

7. Manœuvring

---

7. Manœuvring

7.1. Sun Tzu said: in war, the general receives his commands from the sovereign.

The client is king.

7.2. Having collected an army and concentrated his forces, he must blend and harmonise the different elements thereof before pitching his camp.

This principle relates to team building: in the introduction, Isaid that a litigator will have many skill-sets at his disposal. As in war, a litigator must choose his support people carefully, ensuring that they gel as a unit. This, Sun Tzu emphasises is an absolute priority, even before anyone pitches his tent or, in our terms, snatches the corner office or the cubicle with the best view of the girls-walking-by corridor.

7.3. After that comes tactical manœuvring, than which there is nothing more difficult. The difficulty of tactical manœuvring consists in turning the devious into the direct and misfortune into gain.

We can see Sun Tzu's tactical manœuvring as ensuring that the arbiters of fact are presented with the case in the way that will most aid them to remember and understand it.

The use of graphics in a trial, where the technology is available is useful. But even if there is no, or insufficient, technology, a laptop and a colour printer can prove just as effective.

In fact, I prefer to use printed documents: the jury can take them away, instead of having to try to copy them from a screen. And very few courts have display technology in the jury room.

In the mid-1990s, when I first took a portable computer into court, the term "laptop" did not exist. My first laptop, as we would come to recognise it, did not arrive until the late 1990s. And notebooks (except the amazing and sadly ill-fated Psion MC series which was so far ahead of its time that it was like science fiction), tablets (except those in the film *2001: A Space Odyssey*) and phones capable of taking notes were not even on the horizon. I used the computer to help me sort through documents: it was faster than reading - and it allowed me to make notes in the documents. But colour coding? Not a hope: the best I could do on the monochrome screen on a machine running DOS (which, in my case, was DR-DOS) was bold, italic and underline.

I found that using a spreadsheet (thanks to Framework, the forerunner of all those "office" packages) allowed me to take notes during evidence and then cross-reference them.

Today, life is much easier but the spreadsheet remains a useful tool for comparing evidence given by witnesses.

For example,

- Officer Smith approached the Defendant as he came out of a shop

- Officer Smith approached the Defendant who was standing on the kerb trying to hail a taxi

- I did not see Officer Smith approach the Defendant but I saw them talking in front of Bill's Bar and Grill.

Once statements are compared, then they can be printed out in colour: the similarities in black and the differences in red. Printed aids can assist a jury to remember exactly what was said. And if anything turns on exactly where Officer Smith encountered the Defendant, then the point is difficult to miss.

Flow charts are also extremely useful. They can be prepared in advance of the hearing for use during evidence or during the hearing to demonstrate the evidence given. Again, they can be printed out.

A flow-chart (or an organisational chart) can show

- consistency between the timelines of events
- inconsistency between the timelines of events
- relationships between witnesses and parties and, of course, third parties
- how information flowed e.g. how a report found its way from Officer Smith to Detective Jones who acted on it later, along with the graphical representation of how time was lost at a critical stage of the investigation

A simplified flow-chart can graphically demonstrate a sequence of events. E.g.

- Peter James phoned John Paul at 13:12 The call lasted 25 seconds
- John Paul phoned Abel Matthews at 13.13. The call lasted three seconds

Abel Matthews phoned Judas Fisher at 13:13. The call lasted three seconds.

Mary Joseph was shot at 13:14

Judas Fisher phoned Abel Matthews at 13:15. The call lasted two seconds

Abel Matthews phoned John Paul at 13:15. The call lasted two seconds.

John Paul phoned Peter James at 13:15. The call lasted two seconds.

There were no other calls between those numbers that day.

Scattergrams are invaluable for demonstrating links between parties. They can demonstrate links between addresses, telephone numbers, telephone calls made, the places they frequent and so on. They can demonstrate indirect links between persons that may claim to know nothing of each other.

Bar charts can demonstrate, in a memorable fashion, how often one person calls another, or visits a particular place. A clear inference can be demonstrated that, if two people visit a particular bar or club each weekend, and have done so for several months, that they are likely to have at least bumped into each other, so undermining a claim that they do not know each other.

By adding that to other affiliations - e.g. support the same soccer team, share a religion or special interest - and a picture of two people who are likely to know each other is built. Add that to their apparently studious attempts to avoid each other raises suspicions that may turn into fact.

But graphics alone are not enough, even when they show how the bits fit together. For the jury to be able to relate to that information, they have to understand it, understand what it does, how it works. That's where the oratory skill of the advocate comes in. And so does the way he interacts with the jury as a body and as individuals.

Rapport with a jury is an essential part of advocacy. But the jury is not the advocate's friend: in a subtle, gentle way, the jury is as much an adversary as the opposing advocate. Juries are supposed to be sceptical but they can't ask questions for clarification, at least not during the conduct of the trial. And when they go to the jury room, if they have unanswered questions, they are more likely than not to discuss it between themselves.

Juries are not instructed on what they can and cannot do. They are not told if it's OK to take notes. They do not come equipped with notepads and pens/pencils and many courts do not provide them unless requested to do so. Juries are not told whether then can ask questions during the trial (of course, they are told they cannot speak during the trial).

In fact juries are told only what they cannot do: do not discuss the case with anyone outside this room, do not read the newspapers, do not watch TV, do not tweet or post on Facebook (actually, they are rarely told this and some do, which has led to some trials being abandoned and started all over again). They are told they will have to put their lives on hold for the duration of the trial (defendants in criminal cases sometimes try to make trials long so that jurors are inconvenienced and have to ask to be excused) , that they will be sequestered in a hotel when what they really need to do is get to the first night of their child's nativity play.

They may be self-employed and therefore a long trial may cause them serious financial hardship. Or they may be a single parent in a city where there is no family and therefore need to do the school runs and all the other stuff that looking after a child entails. Not all judges are sympathetic to such difficulties.

And so jurors are, often, resentful. They don't want to be there. And it doesn't matter whether an advocate is for the prosecution / plaintiff or the defendant, he is still the reason that the juror is living in a period of suspended animation, expected to deal with - in some cases - complex issues of which they have no prior knowledge, feeling inadequate, confused and worried whether they will be able to make the right decision at the end of the trial.

Juries are not predictable or, at least, not reliably so. Juries are, generally, responsible and do decide according to the evidence.

But juries do make decisions that, if not flying in the face of the evidence, seem to be against its general weight.

This is because juries are not a cohesive, single-minded body. Juries are made up of people and each one is different. While jury selection (in whatever form it takes) may be intended to produce a jury that is as close to homogenised as possible, differences in the ways that people think, the ways they absorb information, the reaction they have to the way witnesses speak or hold themselves will result in a different way that one juror views the evidence compared to another.

How do juries make their decision as to what is right and what is wrong?

In my world of counter-money laundering strategies, we need to know how people assess suspicion because, if they are suspicious that a transaction is or may be related to money laundering or providing support for terrorism, or if they believe that a person might be involved in such conduct, they must make a suspicious transaction (or activity) report.

Thus the whole question of the effect of laws to counter these offences turns on the question of how people decide what is suspicious. But the question of suspicion is actually not the most basic question: that is "what is right, and what is wrong?"

At The Anti Money Laundering Network, we've been doing this a long time: since the early 1990s, in fact. And we have some interesting data. For the purposes of this book, though, we are going to look at just one thing because it's the thing that most closely relates to how a jury thinks.

The basic truth is this: people consider right and wrong with reference to their own morality. In my world, then, if someone's personal morality does not see conduct as immoral, then - unless they have some very specific information that turns that conduct into a crime - then they will not be suspicious that an offence has been committed and, therefore, will not make a report.

We found an example that gives a very clear indication of how most people think: in Bangkok, a girl who is from the countryside has a job as a hairdresser. It's not very well paid but it's enough to pay for her single rented room and for her to send money to her home to support her elderly parents. On Friday nights, only, she goes to Sukumvit, a district popular with visiting business men and she waits to be picked up, taken back to a hotel room and paid for sex. Her Friday nights pay for her clothes and most of her food and when she goes, with friends to coffee shops where many people congregate for a natter.

In London, a woman working in a shop and living with her parents out of town, Her salary pays for all her living expenses and her season ticket and, even for nights out with friends. But she wants to go to expensive restaurants and clubs. So after work she goes into the shop toilets, changes and does her make-up and heads to the City bars hoping to find a lawyer or banker that will take her to the sort of places she wants to go. After midnight, her season ticket is useless and it will cost her a huge amount to get home in a taxi. She either spends the night with her target or hopes he will get her home, the price for which, along with the night out, is sex.

So, accepting that both are immoral, which is more immoral? Almost everyone says the girl in London. But they say that the one in Bangkok is committing an offence. Actually, unless she asks for payment, she does not commit the offence of soliciting. But the girl in London, because she might ask for a benefit that is not money, does not commit an offence either. Her conduct, arguably, is much closer to soliciting.

We know that suspicion of tax evasion is rarely reported but that suspicion of benefits fraud is. The reason, it seems, is that most people regard the tax man as an imposition while benefits are something from which society gains. There is also an element that many people enjoy seeing the taxman beaten, with a grudging admiration for the small-time cheat but they see benefits fraud as taking their own money, albeit having been passed through government on its way.

It can be seen, then, that the views of a jury are influenced by their own morals and mores. Even though juries are, for the most part, very responsible, nevertheless, advocates must be aware of the foundations upon which their decision making process is based.

People listen at different speeds. For some, the Bloomberg TV style of breathless presentation is not actually fast, but annoying in its approach, others like it; for some the BBC's measured presentation is fast, but staid, others like it. In fact, the words per minute count are remarkably similar: the difference lies not in the speed of the words but in the heavy use of buzzwords and trendy phrases and the (ab)use of emphasis in the Bloomberg presentation compared to the more straightforward BBC style. There is more on emphasis below.

Jurors may or may not understand word plays. Out of a dozen people, at least some will not understand a pun, sarcasm or irony. They will not see the fun in making up words, stretching and twisting the language just because we can. They are in a stressful environment while we, as advocates, are in our element. The good advocate must accept the limitations of the jury, not because jurors are stupid but because they have a completely different mindset to that of the advocate. The advocate is (albeit for great stakes) playing a game; for a jury, there is nothing fun about their situation. They take things much more literally than they would in their ordinary lives. As a result, they become unpredictable when the advocate thinks he's drawing them in by clever use of language.

The advocate must keep it simple, both in terms of language and in terms of how his speeches are presented. And he must make certain that his examination of witnesses is tailored not only to the witness but also to the arbiters of fact.

Elsewhere, jury selection is considered. But once the trial starts, we need to look beyond that; we have the jury we have. And we must therefore play to its strengths and weaknesses, its fears and its favours. And we must help the jury to understand which means giving it information in ways that do not bore, irritate, confuse or tire it.

And, despite what many would argue, exactly the same applies where a case is heard by a Judge alone or in a panel.

When Sun Tzu talks about preparing the battle ground, this is how it translates to litigation. The battleground is not the few metres in front of the advocates, between them and the Judge or jury, it is not the press-box nor any media scrum on the steps of the Court but, rather, it is few centimetres between the ears of the arbiters of fact.

The advocate must make sure that the 20% of information that juries get from aural reception counts as much as possible. Note that I talk of aural not oral. That's because, I estimate, 80% of the presentation made by advocates and witnesses is oral - even though only 20% of the jury's absorption is aural. In short, advocates rely mostly on the spoken word, juries rely mostly on something else.

It is emphasis that actually makes more difference than anything else. Emphasis is generated by putting weight on different words in a sentence.

To emphasise that a word is the most important in a sentence, it is said in a slightly different way, a way that creates importance for it.

News reporting tends to put the emphasis in the correct place in a sentence. Current affairs and entertainment broadcasting have an increasing tendency to put the emphasis on the wrong word. They do it so that the overall sound pattern is more modulated, so that it sounds almost like the beat of a song or poem. But it makes it difficult to understand although it's perhaps easier to hear everything on a purely superficial level.

How do we know what is important in a sentence or phrase? Actually, it's pretty simple.

Where two things are compared, the emphasis is on the difference;

- She was wearing a blue coat

- She was wearing a red coat.

The sing-along style of presentation would put the emphasis on "wear" in "wearing.

Putting the emphasis on "she" makes the person the most important aspect of the sentence, diminishing the impact of the difference in colour. But it can also have another effect, depending on exactly how the word is pronounced, it can imply either approval or disapproval. For example: "*She* is a good mother" compared with "She is a bad mother." It can also imply a comment on a person who is not specifically referenced in the sentence, to imply that someone other than the person specifically mentioned is not a good mother.

The emphasis we are looking for in this evidence puts the stress on the colour of the coat.

But now to complicate things: what if there were two women?

Then there would be stress on both "she" and the colour.

Speech mannerisms are important in many other ways, too.

I am not, here, talking about accents nor, even dialects or languages. Those are fine, so long as the jury understands them. Here I am assuming that an advocate is sufficiently educated to speak what amounts to national language in a standard form.

And for the avoidance of doubt, American and English may have the same root but, today, they are, in many ways, different languages with common words. Other variants of English have different differences.

While media may have created a homogenisation of some of these differences across borders, they have not created a homogenisation across generations, even within countries.

An elderly, well-educated, North Bostonian knows that "I protested the behaviour" is the opposite of "I protested against the behaviour." But Americans across the country of middle age and below fail to make that distinction. Similarly, the relatively recent development of phrases such as "First of all,.... second of all"... and "I could care less," (by which the user means "I could *not* care less") are problematic across generations.

In the UK, the 1980s trend amongst the young (who are now not so young) to "yoof-speak" became a source of irritation to many, in part because it eroded regional accents and dialect. A witness who uses the glottal stop, a feature of so-called Estuary English, a particularly lazy form of speech that often seems as if the speaker did not bother to learn to speak properly and, therefore, is either a bit thick or is uneducated, causes irritation for middle aged and older jurors.

In the vast majority of cases it is not true that the speaker is a bit thick or uneducated: it was simply a fashion where youth all over the UK tried to sound as if they were from a somewhat nebulous region to the east of London.

It follows, then, that an advocate who speaks in such a way is perceived as being less able, or less educated (and therefore less likely to be right) than one who speaks clearly, enunciates properly and whose grammar and vocal emphasis are structured to make his presentation easier to listen to, to absorb, to comprehend and to retain.

Once people start on the second half of their lives, they start to become more pedantic: many don't like change unless they can see a positive result. Change is destabilising. It reminds them (us) of how much time has passed. A slower pace of change means more time left.

It is important to avoid fashionable use of language. "It's like a dog" is not the same as "it's, like, a dog." Similarly, fashionable inflection must be avoided: statements should not end with a lift in the tone: that implies a question and, therefore, uncertainty.

It follows, then, that a presentation must be tailored to the style of speech that the jury is most likely to understand and, more importantly, be comfortable with.

Today, outside the confines of a courtroom, I start presentations with a disclaimer: "I am paid to be a communicator. If I speak too fast - which I will, if I use terms that you are not familiar with - which is likely, if I go off on a tangent because something more interesting has suddenly occurred to me - which happens a lot, tell me. Tell me then and there, do not wait until the end of the presentation to tell me because, by then, the point will have been lost and anything that was based on it will not have been understood. If you do not understand something, it's my fault not yours. My job is to impart not just knowledge - you can get that for yourselves - but to create awareness and understanding so that you are able to use that in your everyday lives. So don't be embarrassed to say you don't understand something: blame me not yourself and speak up, wave a hand, send me an SMS but do it right then. Don't complain at the end of the course that it didn't make sense."

During that little speech, which I deliver on autopilot, I am searching the faces around the room, looking to see who understood everything, who is a bit puzzled, who is shy, who nods in agreement and who looks startled that they might be expected to speak up.

It's exactly the same in court, although my speech isn't applicable there. Or at least not in the same terms.

Many advocates turn to the jury with a stare, almost daring them not to register a point made in evidence. It's a one-way stare, an attempt to impose the advocate's will on the jury. This is a serious mistake.

Sun Tzu emphasises the need for constant intelligence gathering: instead of a hard stare at the jury, a benign (friendly might be asking a bit much) look will pay dividends. First, it will not alienate those who think (either because he is or because of a general prejudice) that the advocate is an arrogant prig.

Secondly, it will not shock the more gentle members of the jury who may be a little nervous and nervous people do unpredictable things).

Third - and most importantly - it allows the advocate to pick up on non-verbal communication. A confused juror will (unless his primary emotion is boredom) look confused.

A hard stare makes people turn away or become confrontational. Both undermine the empathy that the advocate needs from the jury.

Overdone theatrics really, really piss jurors off: so arm waving and other demonstrative behaviour including shouting at a witness actually have a negative impact on the way jurors perceive an advocate.

And so does the use of bad language. Did the first sentence in the previous paragraph jar with you? Probably. But it would probably not have done so in a novel or on a TV drama. It's all to do with context.

The reason is simple: the jury has been taken out of their ordinary lives and while some might like that, seeing jury service as a paid break from an otherwise mundane and pointless existence, they take their duties seriously. They do not want to be treated as if they are in an audience at a play that is so far off-Broadway it's in the back room of a bar in a one-horse town in Arizona.

How do people assess information? There are lots of schools of thought. Picking between them, I find a truth about juries in particular. First, ability to gather and repeat knowledge is not the same as intelligence.

Intelligence is about gathering, filing, cross-referencing and recovering information and being able to comprehend and communicate the findings.

Knowledge is not the same as intelligence. Someone is not "smart" just because he can remember and recite, regardless of how much he remembers or how accurately it is recited

It follows, then, that dogmatising is not a demonstration of intelligence.

Secondly, the brain files and organises and builds links between data while a person sleeps, not while they are awake. Therefore an advocate must make those links apparent because jurors don't get as much sleep as they are used to, often because they go home and then have to do the things they would normally have done during the day and, of course, because they are unsettled because they are not allowed to talk about their day.

Third, this filing and cross-referencing is a form of pattern-recognition and that is informed not only by the evidence but by everything that happens in Court and by their own life experience. For jurors, pattern recognition is how they set context, how they make the pieces of the puzzle fit together and how they identify anomalies or what they think are anomalies.

Fourthly: some people deal in logic, some in the abstract. Imagine a square, rotate it 90 degrees. Is it the same as before? Would someone seeing that square for the first time after it was rotated know it had been rotated? Would someone seeing the square before it was rotated, then after it was rotated but not seeing the actual rotation know that it had been rotated? Some will argue that it is the same, some would argue that the square has been fundamentally altered and some would say "who cares? It's a square."

The answer to that question is that we should care because a square is actually a rectangle: it just that all the sides happen to be the same length and so it's been given a specific name to differentiate its specific properties. In fact, giving it that name goes against one of the basic principles of language in law: when laws are drafted, when judgments are given, the basic rule is that if it's called something different, it's because it is different. Worse, to call it a square is misleading: the term square comes not from the length of the sides but from the fact that all four corners are right angles. Technically, linguistically, then, all rectangles are squares. But mathematicians, perhaps more properly geometrists, have reversed that to make a square a sub-set of rectangle rather than the other way around.

If a rectangle is rotated through 90 degrees, then there would be a visible difference. The measurements for height and width would be transposed: a 100x50 rectangle would become a 50x100. Would it then be different?

It depends on one's use of linguistic perspective: some may see a rectangle. Some would see a slab in one case and a column in another.

Moreover, people see and hear what they expect or want to see or hear.

Fraudsters make use of this in creating the impression they want to create - they already know how people will react to certain phrases so they can say one thing, making prosecution difficult, knowing that the person they are dealing with will register something different.

A simple example that I use in training for money launder-ing risk management is to put up a slide of photographs of three oranges. Actually, even that is an illusion: it's really one photograph of one orange, replicated three times across the screen. Above the oranges is the phrase "Make a choice." As I put up the slide, I say, clearly, make a choice."

In well over 95% of cases, each person chooses one of the three oranges. When asked why, they say "you said to choose one." When I remind them of exactly what I said, and point out that the phrase is actually written right in front of them in close proximity to the photographs, the mix of reactions is interest-ing.

Some are angry that they have been tricked - some with me, some with themselves; some are self-conscious because they did not pay sufficient attention to what was said and what was written, having made assumptions; some are disbelieving that such a trick would work even though they have fallen for it.

The best answer ever was "orange juice." That wasn't on my list of possible answers. It is now and I thank the person who said that for reminding me that there are no limits to thought, only to how we, as individuals, think.

And it's the same for juries and judges. The advocate must move their mindset to where he needs it to be. In the vernacu-lar, he has to make sure that everyone is on the same page, singing from the same hymn sheet, etc.

Each advocate is trying to do the same: although a Court is supposed to be finding the truth, the definition of truth depends on who tells it.

Real evidence is rarely open to interpretation. But it may be.

A hole in a wall with a bullet embedded in it is a hole in a wall with a bullet embedded in it. It is an inference, albeit a strong one, that the bullet was shot into the wall. However, there is no real evidence to prove it. Even though unlikely it is possible that a different bullet or even a drill or something else made the hole, was removed and the bullet found in the hole inserted.

The arbiters of fact must believe the witnesses but must also understand and retain what they learn.

Witness coaches (don't huff: everyone coaches in one way or another) will advise witnesses what to wear, how to speak, how to stand or sit, where to look. That is not the same as telling a witness what to say, which is not permissible - although is widely done by implication for example during the taking of a witness statement where phrasing might be subtly altered to vary its impact. "Would you say...." is a clear invitation to phrase a response in a particular way.

Regardless of what TV cop shows insist on saying, means, motive and opportunity are not *evidence* of the commission of a crime. They are merely *circumstances* that create a picture into which prosecutors hope to insert the defendant. It's like those boards painted with funny bodies in a cowboy suit, a fat

farmer's wife or Napoleon that you put your face in to be photographed at a fun fair or school fête.

Fictional example:

Prosecutor: "The State will prove that the defendant had
the means, motive and opportunity to murder the defendant.
"The evidence will show:
"The means: the Defendant had access to the kitchen
knife that was used to murder Mr X.
"The motive: the Defendant had been in an argument
with Mr X because Mr X had stolen money from him
"The opportunity: the Defendant was at a party where
Mr X was also present when he was murdered."

Defence: "The State says that it can prove three things:
means, motive and opportunity. What it does not say, what it
cannot say, is that it can prove that he did in fact commit the
crime.
"A jury must consider the evidence, not the editorialising
of a prosecution advocate.
"Did my client have the means to commit the crime? It is
accepted that there was a party at the house that evening
and that my client went into the kitchen. There is, Indeed,
evidence that my client touched the knife. And my client
admits that he did. There is no need for the state to lead
evidence on that point but they will because they need to
make you believe they have fully investigated the case. But
what they will not tell you, unless pushed into doing so, is
that the knife had been on the counter-top in the kitchen
throughout the party, alongside a bowl of lemons so that
people could slice their own for their drinks. What the prosec-

ution will not tell you , unless pushed, is that there is evidence that dozens of people touched the knife.

"Did my client have motive? Yes. Mr X stole more than a million dollars from him. And another 2,000 odd people Mr X scammed in a hedge fund ponzi scheme had the same motive for the same reason. We've all been wronged, tricked into making a loss of something that was important to us. We've all wanted to do the culprit some harm. But we don't, because we are civilised. To suggest that my client is the one person in 2,000 who would harm the culprit is not evidence. And, one has to remember, that once this so-called "motive" was found, investigators no longer looked for another explanation or motive. What about a cuckolded husband? A business partner whose reputation was destroyed by Mr X's actions? A father angry that Mr X had made his teenage daughter pregnant and then left her with no further word? People just like all of these also had the motive to commit the crime.

"Motive" is not the same as "intention" - merely having a reason to commit an offence does not prove that a person did it nor, even, intended to do it. "Motive" is not about the state of mind when the offence is committed: it is merely a matter of background.

"It is true that my client had an argument with Mr X at the party. The prosecution will lead evidence that it was not the first confrontation between them and invite you to infer that there was an underlying threat of violence. What the prosecution will not say, unless pushed, is that Mr X had been abused and, in some cases, actually assaulted by many people - even at the doors of the courthouse where his trial took place when he was in the custody of the police.

"If motive were enough, then all of those 2,000 odd people or those that champion them such as children who now have to support elderly parents who lost their life savings would be standing alongside my client. And so would dozens if not hundreds of people who have confronted Mr X.

"What the prosecution will not tell you, unless pushed, is how many others at that party were victims of Mr X's fraud or were the cuckolded husbands or the father of a pregnant teenage girl or had some other motive.

"Did my client have opportunity? Yes. He was at the party and so was Mr X. So were more than 100 other people.

"Prosecutions should not be about choosing the most likely suspect and relying on you believing their advocate. They should be about facts and law. And no matter what the prosecution lawyers and their witnesses will tell you their case lacks one vital ingredient.

"Evidence.

"And without evidence, you cannot find a person guilty. Supposition is not enough. When you listen to the prosecution case, think as much about what they are not telling you as what they are telling you. Because what they are not telling you is that they have no provable case against my client. "

"And, lastly, and most importantly, they will keep using the word "murder."

"In fact, it took my learned friend only 15 words to first use it. Then he used it twice more in the next three sentences. You have to understand that his use of the word "murder" is a trap. It's not a trap for the judge or my client or even me: it's a trap for you. When we come to the end of the trial, you will be asked if my client committed murder. And for however long this trial has continued, you will have heard that word over and over again. You may even have heard my client described as a murderer. He is not. He is innocent unless proved guilty. It is true that a person died in suspicious circumstances: but it has not been established in a Court that he was murdered. Whether a person is murdered is not a decision made by prosecutors - it's made by you. And it is therefore important that you pay no attention to the prosecutor's repetitive use of such an emotive word. It's a form of almost subliminal persuasion to convince you that an offence has been committed even before it is proved. And you should be aware of such tricks and traps."

It follows, then, that the basic principle right from the very beginning of this book remains valid at each stage of the litigation. Preparation, laying the ground work, heading off one's opponent before he is able to fully settle into his battle positions are as important in the opening minutes of a trial as they are when a client first gives instructions.

And as soon as battle is joined, with the first intake of breath by the plaintiff's or prosecution advocate, the defence team is exactly that - defending. The opening speech is as they run up the hill towards the defending force's position. The defence opening speech is as they run down the hill, the advantage being with them because by then the initial strategy has been disclosed.

Quick thinking and rapid responses are vital. A skirmish lost at this stage may not be the ultimate cause of a final loss but it will make a win more difficult.

7.4. Thus, to take a long and circuitous route, after enticing the enemy out of the way and though starting after him, to contrive to reach the goal before him, shows knowledge of the artifice of devious plans.

In this context, Sun Tzu says that deviousness is simply that of appearing to be doing one thing while actually doing another, for example, making a great play that securing a copy of a particular document is an objective while in fact the plan is to find an expert witness able to support one's case.

Long after Sun Tzu's death Choa SHE, in 270 B.C. had to undertake a long, fast march towards the Chin forces. But for the first several days, She (who was, of course, a "he" and not in any trans-gender or cross-dressing sense) marched a relatively short march then built trenches and fortifications. Then, for a month, She continued to strengthen the fortifications. Once She was satisfied that Chin's spies had reported back that She had travelled a short distance and dug in, She started a fast forced march, arriving unexpectedly, able to take control of strategic ground and to defeat the Chin army.

By the way, "She" is pronounced "shuh." Of course, I could have told you earlier but, in the immortal words of Roger Rabbit, I could tell you "only when it was funny," proving another aspect of advocacy: timing is an essential part of the presentation.

7.5. Manoeuvring with an army is advantageous; with an undisciplined multitude, most dangerous.

Sun Tzu says that an orderly force can be properly managed. A disorderly force cannot be managed and is likely to result in loss.

7.6. If you set a fully equipped army in march in order to snatch an advantage, the chances are that you will be too late. On the other hand, to detach a flying column for the purpose involves abandoning its baggage and stores.

Sun Tzu refers to the inertia and complications of moving a large body of men, preferring to use smaller bodies operating in a co-ordinated manner. He says that a small force, moving fast, may have to abandon its support structure. What he implies but does not say is that the support will come up behind as the larger force catches up.

This makes sense. There is no need to deploy all resources at all times during the conduct of a case. Often, one aspect of the case can be properly and effectively dealt with by a specialist unit. That unit may operate relatively independently of the main body working on the case but, when tactical or other support is needed, it can be moved into position easily.

Therefore, Sun Tzu's principle is applied to the division of labour according to skills, but subject to proper supervision and management.

7. Thus, if you order your men to roll up their buff-coats and make forced marches without halting day or night, covering double the usual distance at a stretch, doing a hundred LI in order to wrest an advantage, the leaders of all your three divisions will fall into the hands of the enemy.

It would be possible to place all kinds of explanation onto this principle but the simplest is the best: pulling an all-nighter or a series of them may seem macho but it is counter-productive because the person who has not rested does not operate at his peak of performance or intellect.

8. The stronger men will be in front, the jaded ones will fall behind and on this plan only one-tenth of your army will reach its destination.

Just because some of the team are strong and can work for long hours for days at at a time it does not mean that they all can. People have different physiologies and by pushing someone beyond their tolerance levels, the whole team is weakened.

Everything from colds and stomach upsets, general lethargy and difficulty concentrating to simply not being able to focus on the task in hand are the results of trying to work too much for too long.

And that's just having regard to physical stamina. Mental stamina suffers through lack of sleep and lack of routine. There are dozens of studies of the effect on one's ability to function with ever-changing shift patterns, for example.

In addition there are stresses placed on home and social life by the demands of a case, families become disjointed, spouses feel neglected, children - who have a much nearer horizon - feel abandoned, sports teams drop players who miss practice or, worse, games, dinner party invitations dry up after missing one or more, dates walk away after cancellations or no-shows.

It's not weak to take a break: it's good sense.

The next three principles while having no direct equivalent in litigation underline the point made in this principle.

7.9. If you march fifty LI in order to out-manœuvre the enemy, you will lose the leader of your first division and only half your force will reach the goal.

7.10. If you march thirty LI with the same object, two-thirds of your army will arrive.

7.11. We may take it then that an army without its baggage-train is lost; without provisions it is lost; without bases of supply it is lost.

While an advance / raiding party can travel light and fast, the army as a whole needs its full resources and infrastructure. In litigation we can take this as meaning that the team that goes to court might be few, but the team left back at base must be fully prepared and resourced, ready to provide such back-up as the court team requires.

We see this principle at work in Formula One: the track-side team is small compared to the team that remains at the factory. At the factory, they have instant access to all track-side data including that received from the car through its on-board monitoring systems. The factory team has a full range of data-modelling information that enables them to feed advice back to the track-side team and, through them, the driver in real-time.

In today's world of always-on information systems, the court team has access to research and advice capabilities that were unheard of even in the mid 2000s.

In this way, we can see that Sun Tzu's concepts are applicable in ways he could not have imagined and yet, amazingly, in an almost identical way.

7.12. We cannot enter into alliances until we are acquainted with the designs of our neighbours

Where there are others with an interest in the outcome of litigation, the good litigator ascertains what their objectives are. This is prudent because of the risk that, depending on the final order and even upon what evidence is presented, someone with an interest may be able to use that, including admissions made in evidence, against our own client.

Sun Tzu also makes it clear that, if those with interests in the outcome are to work together, their desired outcome must be known. If there is to be any disparity between desired outcomes, they must be negotiated and agreed at the outset, not shortly before trial. The reason for this is simple: where there are multiple plaintiffs, a defendant will always aim to divide them and, if their objectives are different, or cannot be reconciled, then the defendant will find this easy.

Similarly, in a criminal trial, where co-defendants have a conflict, it is always important to discover this at an early stage and, if that conflict cannot be reconciled, separate trials must be sought.

Courts may not wish to hear such an application but a good litigator will impress upon the Court that one or more parties will be prejudiced if a jury hears testimony that relates to one but not directly to another.

This is one reason why prosecutors like to tag on conspiracy charges: it is then open to them to drop a substantive charge in order to keep a trial together. The penalties for conspiracy are generally similar to those for the substantive offence. Conspiracy can be implied in circumstances where there is insufficient evidence for a substantive charge.

7.13. We are not fit to lead an army on the march unless we are familiar with the face of the country—its mountains and forests, its pitfalls and precipices, its marshes and swamps.

How often does it need to be said? Prepare, prepare, prepare. Do not go into any litigation or stage of litigation unless the ground is known and prepared.

Sun Tzu makes it clear that failure to be prepared is the fault of the general, not of the commanders nor of the foot-soldiers.

And if a loss results due to failure to be properly prepared, it is the general - in our terms the litigation partner - who must be prepared for the consequences including the risk of being sued for negligence.

7.14. We shall be unable to turn natural advantage to account unless we make use of local guides.

It is perhaps helpful to see this not in the sense of geography nor even of local practices but of specialist and expert assistance in the preparation and presentation of the case.

Not all experts are equal. An expert is someone that the Court (not the parties) says has the education, skill, knowledge or experience to enable him to analyse relevant facts and explain them to the Court. At least, that's the ideal.

In the USA, at state level, there is a long-standing debate as to how experts should be assessed by a court: there are two standards - the Frye standard and the Daubert standard. Federal courts and a small number of states use the latter. Many states use a modified version of the Daubert standard. A number of states use the Frye standard which many have been trying to discredit since the US Supreme Court adopted the Daubert standard in 1993 in *Daubert* v. Merrell Dow Pharmaceuticals, Inc .

The Frye standard can be summarised as requiring only that expert testimony be generally accepted in its field. In summary, that means so long as it has not been discredited, it should be accepted. Critics say this opens the way to the acceptance of "junk science."

The Daubert standard requires that the expert witness should present established scientific knowledge and that it be relevant and reliable.

Another significant difference is that the parties define their experts under Frye but the Judge has power to accept or reject an expert under Daubert.

In the USA, the general principle is that a party may call anyone as an expert but any other party may issue a "Daubert challenge" which the Judge must consider and then issue a ruling as to whether the person is, indeed, expert in relation to the issues in the case.

The fact that a person has been accepted as an expert in one court, or even a case in the same court, does not mean that he will be automatically accepted in another case in the event that a party can ascertain that his expertise, etc. does not apply in the particular circumstances of the present litigation.

In theory, an expert is non-partisan but that is a vain hope in the real world. This is because experts may be accepted by the court but they are chosen, appointed and paid by the parties.

Parties, of course, choose an expert that they believe will favour an interpretation that benefits their case. As a result, many trials include a "battle of the experts."

Experts, unlike other witnesses, are able to present their opinion. Indeed, that is their function. Thus their evidence is not fact. It follows, then, that where two or more experts differ on the interpretation of facts, their opinions will also differ.

Juries have difficulty understanding the weight to be attributed to an expert. As is noted elsewhere, Juries defer to better educated persons or those with perceived higher social status. Therefore a doctor's expert testimony is likely to be given more weight than the factual testimony of a waiter, even though the waiter's evidence is first hand evidence and, in law, should be given greater weight.

Juries should *believe* or *disbelieve* facts but *accept* or *reject* opinion

There is debate as to whether it is fair to juries to expect them to determine a battle of the experts who may be presenting evidence in a highly technical manner and, ultimately, the decision may come down to personality as much as the evidence they present.

But it may also come down to something as nebulous as the title an expert applies to himself: which sounds more impressive - an auditor or a forensic accountant? But there is sufficient cross-over between the two areas that each may, in particular cases, have equally valid methodologies and conclusions.

7.15. In war, practice dissimulation and you will succeed.

7.16. Whether to concentrate or to divide your troops, must be decided by circumstances.

Sun Tzu says that the size of an army should be disguised: instead of assimilating it for all to see, keeping units in reserve and out of sight will mean that success is more likely, simply because the enemy is unable to assess one's strength.

But frankly, principle 15 is greatly undermined by the general idea which appears both before this principle and in a whole section later; the use of spies to gather intelligence is one of Sun Tzu's favourite themes.

In litigation, the simple reality is that it is not difficult to assess the likely personnel that a law firm can deploy into any action. It follows, then, that principle 16 also falls into the same broad category of principles that do not take us much further forward when considering the conduct of litigation.

7.17. Let your rapidity be that of the wind, your compactness that of the forest.

7.18. In raiding and plundering be like fire, in immovability like a mountain.

7.19. Let your plans be dark and impenetrable as night and when you move, fall like a thunderbolt.

Principles 17, 18 and 19 fit neatly together and have great and obvious lessons for litigators. Move quickly; take one's opponent by surprise; when holding station, stand fast and keep one's plans secret until they are executed with force.

Strike hard and fast and without taking or giving quarter. Right from the moment the opening speeches begin.

7.20. When you plunder a countryside let the spoil be divided amongst your men; when you capture new territory cut it up into allotments for the benefit of the soldiery.

This principle has been foreshadowed earlier but here we can find additional clarity. The concept is simple: that spoils of war should be shared amongst the men. He appears to imply, by the term "allotments" that there should be equal shares but that is unlikely to be so for usually there will be greater shares for the more senior officers.

If we look at this in today's terms, there is another dimension: by properly rewarding the staff who are engaged in litigation, their loyalty is less likely to waver than it would if they feel they have been hard done by.

While the instant case may be concluded, there are others. If someone feels unjustly treated, he becomes corruptible either at his own instigation or at the instigation of others.

7.21. Ponder and deliberate before you make a move.

7.22. He will conquer who has learnt the artifice of deviation. Such is the art of manœuvring.

These two principles round-off the chapter and are repeats of principles found in earlier chapters. However, somewhat surprisingly, Sun Tzu incorporated, after his own principles, a series of principles that he found in a book published before his own. Giles says "The style of this fragment is not noticeably different from that of Sun Tzu himself, but no commentator raises a doubt as to its genuineness." Clearly, then, he intended that these principles be adopted into his concepts but did not intend to be accused of plagiarism.

7.23. The Book of Army Management says: on the field of battle, the spoken word does not carry far enough: hence the institution of gongs and drums. Nor can ordinary objects be seen clearly enough: hence the institution of banners and flags.

7.24. Gongs and drums, banners and flags, are means whereby the ears and eyes of the host may be focused on one particular point.

Bizarre, isn't it, that a book that is thousands of years old and deals with physical warfare should preface the use of visual aids?

The interesting aspect of the addition of these principles is that they are not about preparation, moving into position or skirmishes but they are about the final battle.

For our purposes, the final battle is the trial.

In a trial, the focus of attention changes. Up until the moment the trial starts, the focus of all efforts is on the opposing client and his representation.

In a trial, the focus shifts to the arbiter of fact, be it judge or jury.

In court, impressions matter. From the clothes the advocates and witnesses wear to the way they walk and onto the layout of papers on their benches someone is going to notice.

But what matters more is the way in which the arbiter of fact responds to the presentation of the case.

We will be looking at trial in much more detail in the chapter on Terrain for the terrain that is being fought on and over is the judge and /or jury.

But this section allows a great deal of scene setting.

We all see, on American TV programmes and films, the dramatised version of opening speeches, especially in criminal cases. Regrettably, some of those do represent the way some lawyers behave.

The opening speech is an excellent opportunity to set the scene, to make a jury (where there is one) feel that one's case is going to be something worth listening to, that there is - in fact - a case.

But it is also an opportunity to lose the case even before it gets started.

Several surveys over the years, around the world, have shown that, on average, 80% of jurors are from a blue collar background. So what does that mean?

It means that they are unlikely to be educated beyond whatever their country provides as state-funded (or subsidised) education beyond, say, 18 years and many not beyond, say, 16 years of age. But what that does not mean is that they are stupid. There is a tendency to equate knowledge to intelligence. To do *that* is stupid. We hear the derogatory expression "street smart," meaning lacking in formal education but with a natural capacity to achieve or, in the alternative, having learned from a peer group.

But it does mean that jurors may not fully understand the language used in Court. An advocate who talks down to a jury does his client a disservice. But so does an advocate who is so pompous and prissy with words that the jury cannot follow him. It is not for the jury to have to try to interpret what the advocates are saying: the advocate is supposed to be a communicator *par excellence*, it is his job, his function, to make sure his audience understands him.

He is not a pretentious artist, saying that if someone doesn't understand his art, it's because the other person is lacking in intellect. Anyone who argues that is, himself, lacking in the intellect necessary to be an effective communicator.

Therefore the advocate must ensure that his vocabulary is clear, unambiguous and of a type that the jury can understand.

For sure, there are times when a specific juror will have a specific problem: for example, the language in which proceedings are conducted is not his first language. That is a reason for challenge. It is not a reason for demeaning him and - especially - it is not a reason to prejudice the case by knowingly having a juror who will not keep up.

That is not to say that a case should be presented in kindergarten language: it should not. A court is a grown up, serious place and should be treated as such and, regardless of the trend towards informality, I believe that the pomp and ceremony of a Courtroom has a very valuable, sobering effect on the participants.

What else does the predominance of "blue collars" on the jury mean?

Everyone comes with their own prejudices. Despite the common misconception, these are rarely race, colour or gender related. Jurors dislike defendants and witnesses for all kinds of reasons: their accent, their clothes, their attitude but, more often than not, because of a widely held attitude to their jobs. Jurors don't like people who are in jobs that are widely held to be a bit "roguish." Anyone who has been ripped off - or think they have been ripped off - by a tradesman e.g. a plumber or a builder will almost certainly have a hurdle to jump before believing any other plumber or builder, even on the witness stand.

The general and widespread criticism of lawyers and bankers makes them victims of prejudice.

The opposite is true: people, including jurors, have a soft-spot for teachers, nurses and others in caring professions. But that does not, in many cases, extend to doctors or social workers. Yet the chap who delivers meals on wheels during his office lunchtime and asks for no pay? He's almost a saint in the eyes of many.

So what of the circumstances where a witness of fact is presented with pointed reference to his occupation? I have seen this done so blatantly that the advocate asked "what is your occupation?" and then looked at the jury to make sure that the point had registered. Unless his occupation is directly relevant to the evidence, it should not, in most cases, be left without question.

However, to jump up and object to the question would most likely be seen as ridiculous and desperate by the the jury. Much better, then, to deal with it gently in cross-examination with a question such as "Do you like your job?..... How long have you been working in that job? .... Does your job make you more aware of things around you? ..... " and so on.

There is no need to be unpleasant or accusatorial: the objective is merely to allow him to continue to be seen as a nice chap but to then, in summary or closing, make the point that while he is nice and that it's wonderful that he spends his time looking for new homes for stray rabbits, that has no bearing on his evidence or the weight that should be placed on it.

7.25. The host thus forming a single united body, is it impossible either for the brave to advance alone or for the cowardly to retreat alone. This is the art of handling large masses of men.

7.26. In night-fighting, then, make much use of signal-fires and drums and in fighting by day of flags and banners as a means of influencing the ears and eyes of your army.

7.27. A whole army may be robbed of its spirit; a commander-in-chief may be robbed of his presence of mind.

A show of force is a powerful weapon. Therefore at the commencement of a trial, a well presented group giving the jury or judge the clear impression that they are all fully up to speed, fully able and fully versed in the case or at least those aspects with which they will be called upon to handle will impress, even if they mostly go back to the office in the first break after the opening speeches.

In addition, props that demonstrate a fully connected group will again provide a show of force. Therefore the, in effect, uniformed ranks sitting with their laptops open on their desks will provide an impression of a large group with the necessary technology and effective communications.

Principle 25 has been interpreted by several ancient commentators as meaning that the body of men must move as one: none moving ahead of the rest either in advance or retreat. Indeed, according to Giles, an ancient commentator called Tu

Mu told the story of a soldier in the army of Wh Ch'i . A soldier saw an opportunity for a raid and, all alone, dashed forward, killed two of the opposing force and returned with their heads. He was immediately executed despite his daring and recognition as a good soldier: but he had broken ranks and acted without orders. This is in broad keeping with the approach advocated by Sun Tzu himself in relation to discipline.

There have been several similar cases in the modern, real world: an off-duty life-guard entered the water by someone else's station to effect a rescue and was fired; a bank clerk chased a robber down the road and was sacked by the bank: both employers say that they have policies and procedures in place that are designed for the protection of staff as well as others and that going off-plan is not acceptable.

The lifeguard story is at www.theblaze.com/stories/life-guard-fired-after-violating-policy-to-save-a-drown-ing-mans-life/ and the bank clerk case is at www.foxnews.-com/story /0,2933,536061,00.html.

In litigation, the lesson is simple: if someone goes off on his own he can undermine the whole strategy and risk bringing down the entire case. This is, especially in relation to settlement negotiations. Similarly if, during the conduct of a trial, an advocate goes off-piste, a carefully constructed case can be compromised.

It has been said, in many different ways, that the most valuable asset of any commander is his ability to concentrate on the matters at hand and to revise his plans as and when required. This is what the author of *The Book of Army Management* calls the presence of mind.

Again, to use modern parlance, the good general will not only use force against his opponent but also "psyche him out."

It doesn't make any difference if it's a squash game, a motor race or a trial: the ability to force an error in one's opponent's strategy or execution is vital.

7.28. Now a soldier's spirit is keenest in the morning; by noonday it has begun to flag; and in the evening, his mind is bent only on returning to camp.

7.29. A clever general, therefore, avoids an army when its spirit is keen, but attacks it when it is sluggish and inclined to return. This is the art of studying moods.

The are no lunch breaks in a battle but, in ancient times, dusk was a signal to return to camp, to live to fight another day. For those that still could make the return.

There is an old saw that an army marches on its stomach. It also fights.

Reading these two principles together, they can be read as relating to the need for provisions and shelter.

A trial starts, usually, around 10:00 hours, has a break around 11:30 and then a lunch break about 13:00, restarting about 14:00 and packing up around 16:00. If the court sits later, then there will be a mid-afternoon break, too. So, clearly, there is plenty of opportunity for provisions and, even rest (which is the obvious modern equivalent of shelter).

The question of sustenance and nutrition is vital for all the participants in a trial. But the lawyers often fail to pay sufficient attention to it, fuelling ourselves on quantities of industrial strength coffee and Mars Bars.

In 2008, a study conducted by Cambridge University found that:

- Skipping meals can lead to reduced levels of serotonin, a brain chemical that helps to keep careless and impulsive behaviour in check.

- Equally, a good meal can help prevent people behaving in a cranky, aggressive and unfair way by maintaining levels of serotonin,

- Some foods are particularly rich in the amino acid, notably chicken soup and chocolate. Red meat, dairy products, nuts, seeds, bananas, tuna, shellfish and soya products are also good sources.

- "Our results suggest that serotonin plays a critical role in social decision-making by normally keeping aggressive social responses in check. Changes in diet and stress cause our serotonin levels to fluctuate naturally, so it's important to understand how this might affect our everyday decision-making."

- Serotonin is known to have a significant effect on mood.

So, everyone involved in a trial, advocates, judges, juries and witnesses will have times of the day when their decision making is better than at other times. So are their abilities to interact with others including the ability to be sociable and their tendency to be forceful. The study also demonstrates that the important chemical serotonin affects by stress levels which goes some way to explaining why some people get cranky when they are put under pressure.

Clearly, then, late afternoon is, as Sun Tzu said, the wrong time to be dealing with complex and difficult, including morally difficult decisions. It's much better to to the difficult stuff when people are fresh.

And the Cambridge study shows that litigators should use their breaks wisely to provide proper nutrition and rest and not for example, dash to a room to work on another case or even rush back to the office for a meeting.

There are two groups of principles remaining in this chapter. It is interesting that the first group (30, 31 and 36) are basically re-prints of Sun Tzu's previous principles but the second group (33 - 35) are lessons to defend against the principles outlined by Sun Tzu for attack. The principles stand with the previous notes and require no further comment at this point.

7.30. Disciplined and calm, to await the appearance of disorder and hubbub amongst the enemy:—this is the art of retaining self-possession.

7.31. To be near the goal while the enemy is still far from it, to wait at ease while the enemy is toiling and struggling, to be well-fed while the enemy is famished:—this is the art of husbanding one's strength.

7.32. To refrain from intercepting an enemy whose banners are in perfect order, to refrain from attacking an army drawn up in calm and confident array:—this is the art of studying circumstances.

7.33. It is a military axiom not to advance uphill against the enemy, nor to oppose him when he comes downhill.

7.34. Do not pursue an enemy who simulates flight; do not attack soldiers whose temper is keen.

7.35. Do not swallow bait offered by the enemy. Do not interfere with an army that is returning home.

7.36. When you surround an army, leave an outlet free. Do not press a desperate foe too hard.

7.37. Such is the art of warfare.

In preparing for battle
I have always found that plans are useless,
but planning is indispensable.

Dwight D Eisenhower
US General

8. Variation in Tactics

8. Variation in Tactics

8.1. Sun Tzu said: in war, the general receives his commands from the sovereign, collects his army and concentrates his forces.

This principle is repeated from the previous chapter. Giles suggests that it has been inserted simply as way of starting this series of principles.

I would say that it should be printed on a large poster and given to each client to hang on a wall where he cannot but see it often.

"Dear Client, tell me what you want and leave me to work out how to get it. You just make decisions when I ask for them and pay the bills when I present them."

8.2. When in difficult country, do not encamp. In country where high roads intersect, join hands with your allies. Do not linger in dangerously isolated positions. In hemmed-in situations, you must resort to stratagem. In desperate position, you must fight.

8.3. There are roads which must not be followed, armies which must be not attacked, towns which must not be besieged, positions which must not be contested, commands of the sovereign which must not be obeyed.

The Romans murmured that one should not rest on one's laurels. That's not what Sun Tzu was warning against: he warns that to rest before reaching a place of safety can be very costly. Note that, as in the early part of the work, Sun Tzu recommends fighting only as a last resort.

Sun Tzu says to choose one's route wisely: not through inaccessible places nor places that are vulnerable to attack and not to pick a fight with an army that, at that moment, would not suffer serious defeat as a result of an attack.

In litigation, the principles are the same: during the course of a case, there will be some courses of action that lay the advocate open to easy counter-attack or where his own preparation may become bogged down. And there are attacks that will be costly to mount but will result in little gain.

Surprising, given Sun Tzu's previous comments on discipline and obedience, is the final sentence of principle 3. In the context of litigation, we know that there will, from time to time be instructions that overstep the bounds of legality, rules of court or professional ethics and, sometimes, our own morality. And we will need to tell the client that we will not act on those instructions.

8.4. The general who thoroughly understands the advantages that accompany variation of tactics knows how to handle his troops.

8.5. The general who does not understand these, may be well acquainted with the configuration of the country, yet he will not be able to turn his knowledge to practical account.

Sun Tzu says that the successful commander always works out how to gain the best tactical advantage from the ground on which he fights. But he also needs to know how to manage his troops.

For the litigator, this translates to understanding the dynamics in the Courtroom and how best to manage the presentation of the evidence.

This means understanding how juries relate to evidence as it is presented.

Go and get a big pot of coffee and the biscuit barrel. We're going to get techie.

Understanding juries (and judges) is not easy.

How do people take in information?

Various studies show that only some 20% of the information absorbed is aural. Think about that: more than three-quarters of what influences a jury has nothing to do with what is said. And the research cited by Madge (see below) demonstrates that only about 25% of that 20% is recalled or recalled correctly. So only about 5% of what you say in court is correctly received, remembered and processed.

That, contrary to the thought you are having right now, does not mean it's all about non-verbal communication or body language, although they have their place.

The challenge for an advocate is to engage as much of the remaining 80% as possible, for as much of the time as possible and to improve that 5% ratio.

It is not enough to flood the minds of jurors with information. They have to be told how that information joins up, why it is relevant. To give the jurors all the facts while not linking one to another, or making that links as soon as possible, is no different to throwing them a Meccano set (the original, metal, one) and saying "build me an atomic reactor." All the bits are there, but without detailed instructions, it's not going to work. I know: I was a great disappointment to my engineer father, at least in one respect - no matter how hard I tried, I could never make anything presentable from my Meccano set because it was a box of bits and I had to design and invent to produce anything and that is not how my brain works. Yet I could make Airfix models (when they had words in the instructions - it all ground to a halt when all I got in the box was a diagram in a sad aping of the instructions that came with the USA's Revell models). Why Airfix? Because, when I had words, I learned what the parts were, where they went and what they did. I gained understanding of the model as a working object not just a plastic statute.

That is how jurors think: they need to know what they are supposed to be building and how the parts all fit together. They cannot be expected to be given a box of bits and work it out for themselves.

There is another issue relating to how juries - and Judges take in information. It might be considered a question of attention span but in fact it's much more than that: it relates to the ability of the human brain to absorb information.

There is much research that shows that people absorb information from oral sources much less readily than from other forms of presentation. This does not, however, mean that the use of slides or other visual aids is necessarily beneficial.

One of the most important findings is that, in many tests, the usual time at which brains reach overload is at about two hours.

That does not mean that a person cannot concentrate for more than two hours, it means that a person has difficulty concentrating *on the same thing* for more than two hours.

Therefore, in a case where a witness is on the stand for several days, the jury will have a much harder time dealing with his evidence than they would have dealing with the evidence of several witnesses over the same period.

To be fair, evidence can be extremely boring, especially when the point of the questioning is not immediately apparent. And, where an advocate is circling a witness, preparing for the killer question, then he will be trying to avoid his point being obvious.

This problem is especially severe in the case of technical evidence and even worse where there is numerical data.

In one case I dealt with, we had ten ring-binders full of telephone records and we were proving that the call records, insofar as they had been billed to the customer, were unreliable. After only five minutes and with thousands of incorrect records to go, the Judge - who was at best ill-tempered - insisted we stop putting the records to the witness. And then, at the end of the case, said we had failed to establish that the calls were wrongly billed. Fortunately, for other reasons, we did not need to appeal.

All seasoned litigators will have appeared before Judges who appear to be - or actually are - dozing. Indeed, in February

2012, a retrial was ordered in a case in Gothenburg, Sweden because the Judge fell asleep. Worse, reports suggest he did it twice.

Jurors are no better at staying focussed - even though they risk contempt proceedings. In fact, in a trial that has kept US media busy during much of the early part of 2012, that of Roger Clemens, not one but two jurors fell asleep and were discharged. In December 2011, an American sentenced to death in Arkansas was granted a retrial after it was found that one of the jurors had slept during the trial. And these examples do not include those who fall asleep because they are drunk or hungover - as happened in a drugs trial in the UK in 2012.

8.6. So, the student of war who is unversed in the art of war of varying his plans, even though he be acquainted with the Five Advantages, will fail to make the best use of his men.

8.7. Hence in the wise leader's plans, considerations of advantage and of disadvantage will be blended together.

8.8. If our expectation of advantage be tempered in this way, we may succeed in accomplishing the essential part of our schemes.

Sun Tzu says that an inability to tailor the attack to the circumstances will lead to failure but a wise leader will bear in mind that it is necessary to surrender some advantages in order to gain the greater advantage and ultimate victory. He also recognises that there will be, sometimes, losses on the way to victory.

8.9. If, on the other hand, in the midst of difficulties we are always ready to seize an advantage, we may extricate ourselves from misfortune.

It follows, then, that even when losing, if an opportunity for a gain presents itself, the advocate should take it for that may be the turning point in any war.

Counter-attack, provided it does not guarantee a costly loss should always be considered and, in many cases, taken.

8.10. Reduce the hostile chiefs by inflicting damage on them; and make trouble for them and keep them constantly engaged; hold out specious allurements and make them rush to any given point.

This Principle has been covered earlier, in several parts. In short, take every opportunity to weaken one's opponent, distract one's opponent by constant harrying, appear to be weaker than one really is and encourage an attack in a place where one is confident of success.

8.11. The art of war teaches us to rely not on the likelihood of the enemy's not coming but on our own readiness to receive him; not on the chance of his not attacking but rather on the fact that we have made our position unassailable.

Sun Tzu says that defences should always be prepared, ready for an attack, even if none is considered imminent. He says, simply, that the mere fact that the defences are in place and properly manned and resourced, is itself a deterrent.

Therefore a litigator who has the reputation of always being ready to repel any attack is likely to be an intimidating opponent and therefore, perhaps, suffer less skirmish attacks than a litigator who is known to be rattled by such tactics.

8.12. There are five dangerous faults which may affect a general:

a) Recklessness, which leads to destruction;

In this context, "recklessness" can be translated as the old saying "fools rush in where angels fear to tread." Put simply, being brave and foolhardy produces poor results; being brave and thoughtful produces victory.

b) cowardice, which leads to capture;

A better interpretation of this principle would be to refer to "timidity" rather than cowardice. Sun Tzu is here recommending that there should be bravery coupled with decisive action in order to increase the chances of success.

c) a hasty temper, which can be provoked by insults;

The difference between this and a) is not immediately apparent. In fact, the difference lies in the second part and, like the warnings against allowing oneself to be baited by false offers, this is a warning against being hot-headed and being drawn in by taunts.

The principle speaks of the situation one sometimes sees in a boxing ring where one pugilist dances around, waiting for the other to rush forward to make a wild shot, knowing that it can be easily dodged or deflected and a stronger counter-blow delivered to an off-balance or distracted opponent.

d) a delicacy of honour which is sensitive to shame;

Sun Tzu was a general of considerable honour and so were those he served (at least by the standards of the day). He expected those serving under him to have and operate under a duty of honour. Therefore those who think this principle says, in effect, "check your honour at the door," do not understand its import.

At the beginning of this work, I said that litigation is a matter of honour. And it is and must be conducted as such.

Here Sun Tzu is saying that there is no dishonour in a loss if it has been fought hard, fairly and well. He is saying that a litigator should not be worried about his personal reputation or that of his firm during a trial because, to do so, would distract him from the case and give his opponent an opportunity to attack.

e) over-solicitude for his men, which exposes him to worry and trouble.

Again, there are some who wrongly interpret this is saying that a leader does not need to care for his subordinates. But we know that that is not true: elsewhere, Sun Tzu makes a great (and repeated) point about taking care of his troops. So what was Sun Tzu actually saying?

He is saying that a general needs to keep his eye on the prize, that on the way there will be losses and that he must be prepared for that before commencing his campaign and that, when the losses occur, that he must not dally on thoughts of the men that have lost their lives nor the consequences for them or their families but must press on which his battle plan.

There is a parallel interpretation: that the welfare of the troops is vital but that it is not paramount. He must take reasonable and proper care of them but he must also recognise that they are soldiers and that they will inevitably suffer hardship from marching, poor food, inadequate shelter and so on and that these problems must not be the source of a distraction.

8.13. These are the five besetting sins of a general, ruinous to the conduct of war.

8.14. When an army is overthrown and its leader slain, the cause will surely be found among these five dangerous faults. Let them be a subject of meditation.

Do not fear to be eccentric in opinion,
for every opinion now accepted was once eccentric.

Bertrand Russell
Author

9. The Army on the March

9. The Army on the March

9.1. Sun Tzu said: we come now to the question of encamp-ing the army and observing signs of the enemy. Pass quickly over mountains and keep in the neighbourhood of valleys.

9.2. Camp in high places, facing the sun. Do not climb heights in order to fight. So much for mountain warfare.

Sun Tzu says that the high-ground is an advantage but that if the ground is too high, it creates a disadvantage. This is because mountains present an unassailable position and one from which the enemy can be observed. However, high-mountain positions are at risk of harsh weather and it is difficult to maintain supply lines. In short, by taking a position in the high mountains a force effectively cuts itself off.

We can translate this to litigation by taking this to mean trying to find more than is necessary for victory. There are times when a litigator has to say "enough" and to realise that he has sufficient evidence to ensure that his client's case will prevail. In warfare terms, there is no need for "overkill."

The lesson is straightforward: prepare appropriately, ensure that the case is strong and then attack. Do not delay and do not over-complicate it.

9.3. After crossing a river, you should get far away from it.

9.4. When an invading force crosses a river in its onward march, do not advance to meet it in mid-stream. It will be best to let half the army get across and then deliver your attack.

9.5. If you are anxious to fight, you should not go to meet the invader near a river which he has to cross.

9.6. Moor your craft higher up than the enemy and facing the sun. Do not move up-stream to meet the enemy. So much for river warfare.

Sun Tzu really, really, really does not like water. Everywhere he talks about it, he talks about getting away from it as quickly as possible. And he is especially harsh when it comes to questions of having to fight in water. His principles are curt in the extreme.

Principle 4, however, is actually quite important: what is says is that, if a battle on the banks of a river is unavoidable, by allowing half the force to cross, the full weight of one's own army can be brought to bear upon them. Their retreat will be cut off because they will not be able to turn and run : their own men will be standing behind them, unable to quickly move because they are in the river. Therefore, those on the riverbank can be easily slaughtered while those in the river are at the mercy of the river.

Reading principles 3 - 6 together, there is a clear direction in relation to treacherous terrain.

In litigation terms, treacherous terrain is the trial.

A trial is always uncertain. Even the system of precedent is not a complete guide to what will happen and nor is a clear, documented, breach of e.g. the terms of a contract. In court, everything is open to interpretation.

Sun Tzu has some simple rules: do not tarry once a high-risk point has been proved (principle 3). When an opponent is taking a high-risk strategy, do not intercept immediately: wait until he has passed the point of no return, where he cannot pull back from that strategy, then attack at its weakest point. In this way, the whole strategy can be made to collapse, like a pack of cards (principle 4). Do not meet a high-risk strategy where to do so places your own strategy at risk (principle 5) and remember that water flows downhill: if the attack is coming to you, lie in wait and do not expend energy fighting the current and so be in weakened state when battle is joined.

9.7. In crossing salt-marshes your sole concern should be to get over them quickly, without any delay.

9.8. If forced to fight in a salt-marsh you should have water and grass near you and get your back to a clump of trees. So much for operations in salt-marshes.

Though Sun Tzu hates water, he hates tidal marshes even more. And he is right to do so for the sudden inrush of a tide can easily swamp a team that is struggling through the mud.

It is easy to get bogged down in a part of the case which does not take it significantly further. Therefore where there is a part of the case that does not result in significant gains, deal with it quickly and move on as fast as possible.

9. In dry, level country, take up an easily accessible position with rising ground to your right and on your rear, so that the danger may be in front and safety lie behind. So much for campaigning in flat country.

Sun Tzu says to protect the rear and the flanks with difficult terrain. But it should not be so difficult as to present no room for manoeuvre or retreat. If a strategy, or a line of evidence, becomes problematic, then a withdrawal and an attack from another direction is better than a loss.

9.10. These are the four useful branches of military knowledge which enabled the Yellow Emperor to vanquish four several sovereigns.

9.11. All armies prefer high ground to low and sunny places to dark.

9.12. If you are careful of your men and camp on hard ground, the army will be free from disease of every kind and this will spell victory.

Low ground is often boggy and boggy land often breeds diseases. Sun is a natural antibiotic and most disease-bearing insects prefer to stay out of the sun.

In litigation terms, this means not to become bogged down in detail which does not take the case significantly forward.

It may be sufficient to establish a course of conduct without having to prove each and every incidence of breach. For example, in a spouse-beating case, it may be sufficient to produce medical evidence of two or three events and then to simply confirm with reference to medical or other records the number of occasions on which the injured party sought medical attention without having to produce evidence of each examination individually.

The more evidence that is presented the more the opportunity is created for the other side to sow the seeds of confusion in the minds of the judge or jury. As in all things, simple is best. And so is knowing all the risks associated with the terrain.

In 1303, a mighty English army attacked Scotland in The Battle of Roslin. Greatly outnumbered, the Scots had a tiny but powerful ally: a minute flying insect with a taste for human flesh - the midge or Scots gnat. Midges do not carry disease but they swarm in incalculable numbers and they get everywhere: in the eyes, ears, nostrils and inside clothes. They bite and cause itching that is totally non-threatening but is exceedingly annoying and distracting. It is not true to say that the midges won the battle for Scotland (a series of tactical blunders most of which flew in the face of Sun Tzu's major principles resulted in the English being roundly thrashed) but they did distract the soldiers who, despite being a professional force that outnumbered Scotland's ad hoc army more than three to one, found the onslaught of the tiny creatures a major distraction. Myth - and partisan film-making - often depict the English running down hillsides, thrashing their arms about, throwing off their clothes and generally displaying the signs of idiocy in their attempts to escape the little blighters. The midge is not credited with defeating the English but it is cred-

ited with being something that the English were totally unprepared for and find difficult to contend with.

It is not the only example of how disaster arose out of a
failure to understand the battle arena: after WW1, France built
The Maginot Line, its own version of Hadrian's Wall or The
Great Wall of China, designed to repel invasion from the East.
It was a formidable structure with fortified battle stations. They
are often called "forts" but most people think of a fort as a
mini-castle and in this case they were more like a giant *char
sui bau* (a Chinese roast pork bun) with gun slots sitting atop a
fortified bunker. It was not a continuous structure: the barrier
might be considered, in modern terms, a "virtual barrier"
because the various forms of weaponry - from light machine
guns to (for then) long range Howitzer-type guns and a variety
of anti tank and anti personnel arms and devices overlapped
from fort to fort. With rotating turrets, a line of fire could be
laid down creating a barrier between forts as well as repelling
direct attacks on the forts themselves.

During WWII, as Germany advanced, the commanders
realised that a full frontal assault on The Maginot Line would
prove costly in terms of both casualties and lives so they formulated an alternative strategy: they simply drove their
armoured divisions around the ends of the line, outflanked the
French and began the falling-domino effect that resulted in the
Dunkirk evacuation.

In fact, the Germans never did capture, in battle, more than
a handful of the smaller forts and none of the large ones. Once

the Germans were behind the wall, most of the French defenders either abandoned their posts or surrendered.

But that's not the end of the story. There's a well known phrase that winning a battle is not winning the war. Four years later, Germany had become complacent. By then, it had covered much of Europe with its flag and in 1944 was more concerned with the fighting on the Russian Front and Hitler's ego-centrical obsession with invading and conquering Britain and - equally importantly for him - defeating and humiliating Churchill.

The Maginot Line was in the middle of territory, that German strategists considered safe. They moved the heavy guns to locations where more fighting was going on and to defend against possible attack from the Atlantic Ocean. They allowed the underground tunnels and storage to decay. The forts were empty or undermanned. Ammunition stores were depleted.

Then the Allies came back, pushing hard and fast across France. The German forces retreated - and then found that The Maginot Line was not only understaffed, under-gunned and dilapidated but - crucially, had not been designed to defend against attacks from the west. Suddenly, their fall-back position was hardly any less vulnerable than the places they were leaving.

What lessons do we learn?

First, the French failed to consider that a strong enemy would simply go around their defences. As a result, the Germans had a cheap, quick and easy victory - and it was the proximate cause of the invasion and occupation of France. This supports Sun Tzu's argument that, when developing strategies, one must think of all the possibilities - and then think of more.

Secondly, the Germans won a great victory by planning and subterfuge. Then they lost it by a combination of cockiness, by inappropriate re-allocation of resources and failure to assess risk.

The arrogance was simply that, once the occupation of France was complete, the Germans did not countenance the possibility of a large-scale counter-attack driving them back. Their approach was always one of attack and pushing forwards. If any attack on France did arrive, they decided, it would come from the West, from the Atlantic coast. But the Atlantic is a vicious ocean and the prospects of marshalling and landing a large force in difficult sea conditions was never really likely. Added to that, the Germans controlled the sea lanes and so a long-distance assault from, e.g. the USA, would have been an easy target for their destroyers and U-Boats. The big guns were in the wrong place. And because they did not think they would be driven back, a strong defence of their own back yard was considered unnecessary.

We learn that a win at an interlocutory stage rarely defines the final outcome and that a strategy to handle a counter-attack from a weakened opponent must always be ready.

An aside, having mentioned the Great Wall of China: it was defeated not by force but by bribing the guards.

While bribery is, of course, not acceptable much of what is expressed in this work is about finding pressure points for those who guard your opponent's case.

9.13. When you come to a hill or a bank, occupy the sunny side, with the slope on your right rear. Thus you will at once act for the benefit of your soldiers and utilise the natural advantages of the ground.

Sun Tzu says: don't try to run uphill, Instead prepare in a position where your opponent cannot take you by surprise from behind (hence standing in a position which allows a view both up and down the hill) and where your men keep the benefit of light and warmth.

Sun Tzu says something more: he emphasises that plans must take account of all relevant factors. He chooses the slope of the hill as his example of attention to detail. The reason for the slope being on the "right rear" is because most people are right handed and swing across their body to maximise rotational force with e.g. a sword. To have the slope on the left rear would mean relying on back-handed swings: to try to use a forearm on that slope would mean that the torque of the swing would twist the body, turning it downwards and making the man topple forwards.

9.14. When, in consequence of heavy rains up-country, a river which you wish to ford is swollen and flecked with foam, you must wait until it subsides.

Sun Tzu says to wait until a flooded and fast flowing river subsides. It's the same in litigation. If a litigator's opponent uses the tactic of "death by paper," that is to flood the litigator with a vast number of documents, knowing that somewhere in there is either evidence that will undermine his own case or simply to use up the litigator's resources (either time before a hearing or his clients' funds) then the litigator should wait until he is sure that all the documents have been delivered, not begin work on them piecemeal.

The reason for this is simple: a pile of paper is overwhelming but a large quantity followed by more deliveries is demoralising. And demoralised people do not work well.

If the documents are not listed in a comprehensive schedule (document type, date, parties, box / file / page number) then the sender should be required to produce an accurate schedule. If he does not do so, then an applications should be filed to obtain an order for a schedule.

Further, the sender should be required to state, clearly and unequivocally that the documents submitted include all such that he intends to rely on at trial and that no further deliveries will be made.

If later deliveries are made, then that statement can be relied on in an application for costs.

If new documents are produced at, or right before trial, then the statement can be produced in support of an application for a adjournment if necessary.

And, in the case of a jury trial, the statement can be used to imply that the person producing the document was reckless or deliberately misled in order to gain an advantage.

9.15. Country in which there are precipitous cliffs with tor-rents running between, deep natural hollows, confined places, tangled thickets, quagmires and crevasses, should be left with all possible speed and not approached.

9.16. While we keep away from such places, we should get the enemy to approach them; while we face them, we should let the enemy have them on his rear.

9.17. If in the neighbourhood of your camp there should be any hilly country, ponds surrounded by aquatic grass, hollow basins filled with reeds, or woods with thick undergrowth, they must be carefully routed out and searched; for these are places where men in ambush or insidious spies are likely to be lurking.

Sun Tzu says not to enter or, if there is no choice but to enter, not to delay in terrain of uncertain ground or where ambush might be laid. But, if at all possible, the enemy should be drawn into such terrain. Moreover, if it is possible to squeeze the enemy so that such terrain is behind him, being his only escape route, then that is to be an objective.

The most difficult terrain in litigation is often the media. It is not a relevant issue in the vast majority of cases and it is not a significant problem in most of the others. But in a case that attracts media attention, it is a quagmire of relationships that can look stable but turn to sticky mud at a moment's notice.

These two principles together say that to try to use the media to one's advantage is to be avoided and, if there is media interest, to try to deflect it onto one's opponent, to let him have to field the questions and give answers that might, if he make an error, come back to bit his case on the backside.

Training to handle media is a highly specialised area and very few advocates translate court-room skills to media presentation. For one thing, they don't know when to stop talking. Reporters do try to get admissions, even as to matters that are going to be dealt with in Court. They do say that they will report what they believe to be the case (by which some mean they will make it up). The correct answer is to reply that all evidence in the case will be heard in Court and if they want to know what that evidence is, they must sit in the press box, not to attempt to try the case on the steps of the Court.

Unfortunately, even though the formal media are bound by at least some code of conduct, that is not the case with those who pretend to journalism on "blogs." The growth of what is mistakenly called "citizen journalism" is a blight on true journalism: there are some very good blogs maintained with the integrity that one hopes full newspapers would display. But for every one good one, there are many for which opinion, no matter how ill-founded or however motivated, will always trump facts and evidence.

There are instances of jurors who have posted on social media sites their opinion and decision (one said "he's definitely guilty") long before the evidence is concluded.

It is therefore essential that there is some control over media leakage and, most importantly, that where there is leakage, one's opponent is the one who is tricked into doing it. It is also clear, from principle 17, that one should not talk to anyone who might be a stringer for a media outlet, trying to earn money or kudos from tips or someone who is just looking for something to print on his blog.

In today's weird media-crazy world, that could be pretty much anyone you don't know but who tries to talk to you - or your staff - about the case.

Principles 18 - 45 (that is the remainder of this Chapter) all deal with "the reading of signs." Giles is seriously enamoured with Sun Tzu's remarks on this subject of which he (Giles) says "much of which is so good that it could almost be included in a modern manual like Gen. Baden-Powell's *Aids to Scouting.*

Some of them are repeats of matters dealt with elsewhere. Some are so obscure that it is difficult to see a relevance to litigation. The comments (in some cases the absence of comment) will make clear which it is.

9.18. When the enemy is close at hand and remains quiet he is relying on the natural strength of his position.

Sun Tzu is saying, in other words, "empty vessels make the most noise." A confident commander does not need to puff up himself and his force to make them seem bigger than they are. He knows that, when it is time to join battle, his strength, discipline and skill will be victorious.

9.19. When he keeps aloof and tries to provoke a battle he is anxious for the other side to advance.

A litigator that stands back and taunts his opponent into making the first move is hoping to trick his opponent into making a tactical error. This is advising a defending litigator on dealing with the tactics that were previously advised to an attacking litigator.

20. If his place of encampment is easy of access he is tendering a bait.

Sun Tzu often makes reference to baits - which are traps. Here he says that if an easy target is presented, it is a trap.

9.21. Movement amongst the trees of a forest shows that the
enemy is advancing. The appearance of a number of screens in the midst of thick grass means that the enemy wants to make us suspicious.

Where there is activity but no forward movement, it means that the opposing force is preparing for an assault. But there may be an alternative plan which is to provide some means of hiding the true intent, the building of screens. These are not diversions but they may be designed to make a litigator suspect that an attack is imminent and therefore either use resources, unsettle his men or launch a premature - and therefore probably unsuccessful - attack.

9.22. The rising of birds in their flight is the sign of an ambuscade. Startled beasts indicate that a sudden attack is coming.

Sun Tzu says not to look only in the direction of one's opponent. There may be signs outside the obvious arena that activity is happening.

For example, a potential witness may go on holiday and therefore not be available for the taking of a witness statement or deposition. That may imply that an application is going to be made in which that witness's evidence would be key.

9.23. When there is dust rising in a high column, it is the sign of chariots advancing; when the dust is low, but spread over a wide area, it betokens the approach of infantry. When it branches out in different directions, it shows that parties have been sent to collect firewood. A few clouds of dust moving to and fro signify that the army is encamping.

9.24. Humble words and increased preparations are signs that the enemy is about to advance. Violent language and driving forward as if to the attack are signs that he will retreat.

When a usually belligerent opponent goes quiet, it will often mean that he is in the final stages of preparation.

But when he becomes bellicose, it is often because he real-ises that his assault will fail and he is making a last show of force before ordering a rapid retreat.

25. When the light chariots come out first and take up a position on the wings, it is a sign that the enemy is forming for battle.

At trial, everyone wants to edge in slowly. Everyone wants to appear to be the nice guy. It's the smile on the face of the shark. All the nice soft words and chat are a disguise: the teeth are waiting to bite. The only reason it hasn't happened yet is that the litigator is choosing the moment when he can attack the soft-spot and get a quick kill. Look for the quiet man in the team: he is most likely to be either the strategist or the sniper. It's him you need to focus on because he is the one who will instruct the advocate when to go in for that quick kill. He will not, probably, be the one who stands up, makes speeches and examines witnesses.

9.26. Peace proposals unaccompanied by a sworn covenant indicate a plot.

Consider this principle in the context of "he that doth protest too much."

Basically, when a settlement proposal is tendered, look at the objectives set by the client. Do not become distracted by other considerations. If the client wants a fence restored to its original position, then an offer to put the fence somewhere else and to build a nice new fence, painted to your client's choice and made of your client's choice of material so long as the litigation is withdrawn might on the face of it be attractive. But if the Court is going to order the fence to be re-sited to its original position it must be restored to no worse condition than previously. Therefore the additional clauses may appear generous but they are not.

So, basically, any proposal must meet one's client's objectives but also be capable of being reduced to a compromise agreement which the Court will accept and Order.

In the above example, the offer appears to sugar-coat an unsatisfactory deal - but equally it diverts attention from the making of a Court Order which, if properly made, would include an undertaking not to move or destroy the fence in the future. The lack of the undertaking means that he could simply tear down the fence and move it again.

9.27. When there is much running about and the soldiers fall into rank, it means that the critical moment has come.

Right before an attack, final preparations are seen. In Court, this is often signified by the frantic passing of notes in Court and much urgent discussion, often in the corridor outside Court. Sun Tzu says to expect an attack at such moments.

9.28. When some are seen advancing and some retreating, it is a lure.

Sun Tzu clearly sets out that, in litigation, there is often something similar to the sales tactic of "bait and switch," to hold out one thing but to deliver something different. Litigators must be aware that an apparent backing down on one point may be to encourage an opponent into a false sense of security so as to be vulnerable to a quick and decisive attack.

9.29. When the soldiers stand leaning on their spears, they are faint from want of food.

9.30. If those who are sent to draw water begin by drinking themselves, the army is suffering from thirst.

We should not take these principles literally. Rather, what they mean in the context of litigation is that if an advocate is shuffling his papers or fumbling over his questions, he is out of ideas. He is in a weak position and waiting for something to occur or be presented to him.

If, when information comes in, he pounces on it instead of it being considered by the full team, it shows desperation.

9.31. If the enemy sees an advantage to be gained and makes no effort to secure it, the soldiers are exhausted.

If, during cross examination, an advocate fails to identify and attack a weak point in the witness's answers, that probably means that the advocate is reaching the limit of his concentration or even that he thinks the case is lost and is not enthusiastic any longer.

9.32. If birds gather on any spot, it is unoccupied. Clamour by night betokens nervousness.

9.33. If there is disturbance in the camp, the general's authority is weak. If the banners and flags are shifted about, sedition is afoot. If the officers are angry, it means that the men are weary.

If the advocate's support team are standing around chatting, they have nothing to do. Does that mean they think the case is already lost or already won? Whichever it means, they are not concentrating and that means they are open to attack.

9.34. When an army feeds its horses with grain and kills its cattle for food and when the men do not hang their cooking-pots over the camp-fires showing that they will not return to their tents, you may know that they are determined to fight to the death.

Again , this should not be taken literally in the context of litigation but there clear indicators for how an opposing advocacy team intends to bring its case to a close.

In a complex trial, when it comes to summing up, the entire team will be present. This is a show of force for the Jury. But for the opposing advocate, this is not a significant indicator. That comes from the condition of their desks.

A team that is over confident will have a clear desk: sure that the Judge or Jury has already taken notice of and accepted the evidence as it has been presented. The advocate will probably remind the Judge or Jury of only a handful of key points.

He will be clear, direct, focussing on those points which he is certain will secure victory.

But a team that is lacking in confidence will also have an almost clear desk: the reason is perverse. The summing up will be based on impressions, on one or two key evidential points, may even be heavy on emotion and / or general scene setting.

It is the style of the closing argument, more than the words used, that will give a clear indication of the level of confidence. An advocate who thinks his case is weak will talk much more, trying to be persuasive. His summing up will not be so clearly focussed.

If both have a clear desk, how can this be a sign? It depends on when the desk is clear: the one who thinks he has won will keep his material to hand during his opponent's summing up and that of the Judge. It will be tidy but ready to be referred to. The one who thinks he has lost will often, even if he considers that he may appeal, pack up his bags and will be less interested in the summing up by his opponent and by the Judge.

Therefore, if the advocate who is to sum up second has a clear desk, his closed briefcase on the table in front of him, he has already, in his mind, left the building.

This is not an infallible guide but it does have some merit.

Someone who is still battling to the end listens carefully to all the summing up, cross-referencing against the evidence and notes, looking for the tiniest anomaly that might be exploited if necessary.

9.35. The sight of men whispering together in small knots or speaking in subdued tones points to disaffection amongst the rank and file.

If the opposing team is holding intra-group discussions excluding the advocate or the team leader, it is very likely to be because they are dissatisfied with progress or the strategy. This principle is perhaps one of Sun Tzu's most incisive. For a litigator identifying this trait in the opposing team, he gains the opportunity for serious advantage.

He needs to apply some of the other principles: to draw in the opposing litigator, along the lines that his support team are not happy with, so as to create still greater division. He needs to find out exactly what the support team are unhappy about and to find a way to irritate that gap. In short, once the leader loses the full support of his team, he is greatly weakened and lost.

Principle 36 gives an indication as to whether the litigator knows he is losing the support of his team:

9.36. Too frequent rewards signify that the enemy is at the end of his resources; too many punishments betray a condition of dire distress.

Although Sun Tzu was speaking of battle, in today's uncertain commercial world, this form of conduct is very common.

For example, many conference companies operate on a business model that works well in the good times but fails completely in the bad. That is why so many conference companies last only a few years, with many failing when the economy enters a downturn. As the downturn develops, they continue their existing business model which relies on a high level of pay and bonuses based on gross income i.e. on sales not profit. As the profits from events goes down, the cost of sales increases as a percentage of income, having a significantly detrimental effect on the P&L account and, ultimately, on the balance sheet.

They also, in order to demonstrate success, run their events in the grandest venues, again increasing the percentage of income that is used in "staging costs."

A business model that pays its staff based a percentage of profits from an event and by using less expensive venues, has a business model that can be sustained in more challenging times.

Many organisations in many industries where the sales are based on numbers not on margin fall into the same trap.

This is exacerbated when there is no provision for clawback of commissions or bonuses paid immediately or very shortly after the sale is made.

And, when the company knows that business is deteriorating, it will often ensure that the same payment model is applied, or even enhanced, so as to demonstrate to staff that the company is not facing difficulty and so keep up morale and to prevent an exodus of talent.

Once the hard times come, the company is then forced to make redundancies which, ultimately creates exactly the circumstances that it had intended to avoid.

Sun Tzu says that, a general knowing he is going to run out of resources, will be extra generous realising that to eke them out is pointless and that his men will be motivated by additional rewards, their confidence boosted and they will fight all the harder. But, when the rewards are almost gone and the battle is not won, he will become distressed and will begin to berate and punish his team. His frustrations and worries at losing will tell in his temperament.

Amazingly, this is seen in Court over and over again as advocates and strategists see their case unravelling.

There is actually a rather odd reason for this: many, many advocates are closet, or part time, performers. Many are in bands, take part in amateur dramatics, in choirs, they are church organists or even Santa Claus at a variety of functions. They like dressing up, they like being the centre of attention, they like being applauded for their efforts. And advocacy is another way of expressing their artistic nature and, like all artists, advocates have an emotional reaction if their efforts are not recognised.

Therefore, like a painter who knows that critics see flaws in his work and dreads them mentioning them out loud, an advocate dreads a judge or jury finding against him.

Good litigators put their heart and soul into the case and good advocates even more so. The one who stands back, uninvolved, does not give a good account of himself because he does not engage with the judge or jury.

And, as we know, much of what has an impact on the arbiters of fact is not *what* is said: it is *how* it is said, including the demeanour of the advocate that makes a big impression.

And so, if a case starts to go wrong, the advocate and the strategists often show signs of distress and that translates into frustration with the support team who will often be subject to demands that would, in other times, be simple requests.

9.37. To begin by bluster, but afterwards to take fright at the enemy's numbers, shows a supreme lack of intelligence.

In the film *Monty Python and the Holy Grail,* The Knights Who Say "Ni" race up to a confrontation, realise their hopeless position and turn tail, all shouting "run away, run away."

We all laugh at them in part because they are so utterly pathetic and weak and in part because they charged in without assessing the risk, only to find that they were doomed to fail.

Sun Tzu a script writer for Monty Python? Well, not really, but the idea remains true.

Sun Tzu isn't talking here about intelligence in the sense of cleverness but about a failure to assess risk and act accordingly.

9.38. When envoys are sent with compliments in their mouths, it is a sign that the enemy wishes for a truce.

It is almost a basic truth that when, during a trial, one party offers the other a deal, it is from a position of weakness. Rarely does someone who knows he has an almost certain win in hand offer to settle for less than he thinks he is going to get at the end of the trial.

It may be that the party making the offer already senses a loss is developing or it may be that he knows that there is a crucial piece of evidence that is going to come up that is going to undermine his case, or that a witness is not going to say what he is expected to say or, even, that a witness is not going to appear at all.

But it is very usual for the party suing for peace (to use old-fashioned diplomatic jargon) is hoping that, by opening negotiations now, he can walk away with something that prevents his case being a total loss.

It follows, then, that to make such an offer during trial is to be seen as an admission of weakness and that such a course of action should be followed rarely and only in extreme circumstances.

9.39. If the enemy's troops march up angrily and remain facing ours for a long time without either joining battle or taking themselves off again, the situation is one that demands great vigilance and circumspection.

When the All Blacks do the Haka, it is a challenge. But it is also a form of defiance, originally written by an Aboriginal Maori who was hiding from a marauding mob. It is used as a ritualistic war dance. But in the context of rugby, it is more than that: it is almost equivalent to a national anthem and is respected as such.

The idea of painted warriors making their presence known is not new: ancient Britons covered themselves in woad and rushed, red mouths and white eyes glaring, towards the enemy lines, stopping short of contact distance.

Sun Tzu says that this, coupled with a stand-off, is a dangerous situation, that a commander is now faced with a new challenge: is the group easily defeated before their support can arrive or is it a trap, that when the defenders make their move, a large force, secreted nearby, will be able to rush the defences?

9.40. If our troops are no more in number than the enemy, that is amply sufficient; it only means that no direct attack can be made. What we can do is simply to concentrate all our available strength, keep a close watch on the enemy and obtain reinforcements.

A draw is not always a bad thing. Sometimes, despite the client's original wishes, circumstances develop which means that each side has a sufficiently good case that litigation risk on both sides makes proceeding to trial an undesirable strategy and an agreement to settle on terms that each side gets some of what they want is the best - even if least popular - solution.

But, says Sun Tzu, if one party thinks that he has the chance to build additional strength, then he may decided not to compromise but instead to hold a stand-off while he ascertains if reinforcements (in litigation additional evidence) can be obtained.

9.41. He who exercises no forethought but makes light of his opponents is sure to be captured by them.

Sun Tzu says, plainly, that one should never underestimate one's opponent, even if the opponent appears weak and under-resourced.

It is a valuable lesson. David and Goliath battles between tiny and large firms are often fought outside the Court's arena for the simple reason that the large firm tries to overwhelm the smaller firm during the litigation process. But once the case is in Court, then the judge moderates the antics of the larger firm - and the theatrics of the advocates. In short, once in Court, there is, in sporting terms, a much more level playing field.

In Court, the litigator's history is (or, at least, should be) irrelevant. All that matters is the current case. But if an advocate is known for his sharp practices, bordering on the disreputable if not actually crossing the line, a judge is likely to keep him under closer control.

And a sole practitioner fighting a team of lawyers is likely to be given - for nothing more than a recognition that he, as an individual, is having a harder time than each of the other team - a little more leeway not in relation to evidence per se but in relation to the way it is presented.

Arguably, it should not be so but it frequently is.

Thus it is a mistake for the big firm to allow a case to reach trial if there is a reason for a technical knock-out or to force a surrender before the case is listed.

There is another reason that the small firm may be under-estimated: small "boutique" firms may be specialists in a highly focussed area which is just one of dozens of areas that the large firm practises in. So a small tight-knit team that specialises in bringing actions in cases of securities fraud has an advantage over a general litigation team in a large firm.

However, special attention must be paid to in-house teams.

I don't know if it's arrogance because they have the name of the company behind them or that they have some kind of chip on their shoulder but my experience is that many in-house lawyers are terrible litigators who think they are highly skilled.

The reasons for this are often that they are defending policies they or their colleagues have created and believe them impenetrable.

Frequently, when external lawyers are consulted to prepare for trial, it is found that in-house lawyers, obstinately and unthinkingly applying those policies, have made statements that they think are protected by those policies in fact act to be admissions if the Court finds that the policies are unreasonable or, even, unenforceable.

For example, a policy to combat bullying may define bullying in terms only of equal opportunities i.e. that if there is insulting behaviour based on age, race, religion or gender, then that would count as bullying but repeated shouting at, swearing at or demeaning an employee without reference to any of those qualifiers falls outside the definition of bullying, regardless of the consequences that flow from it. However, a Court is unlikely to uphold the compnay's narrow definition of bullying, preferring instead to give the term its ordinary and natural meaning.

9.42. If soldiers are punished before they have grown at-tached to you, they will not prove submissive; and, unless submissive, then will be practically useless. If, when the sol-diers have become attached to you, punishments are not en-forced, they will still be useless.

9.43. Therefore soldiers must be treated in the first instance with humanity but kept under control by means of iron dis-cipline. This is a certain road to victory.

Sometimes, it is difficult to know whether Sun Tzu was a pioneer and that over the thousands of years since he posited his views they have become ingrained into homogenised human behaviour or whether he simply reduced to writing some things that are basic common sense.

These two principles are classic examples of how an employer uses psychology to bind his staff to him. Basically, reward them, even with smiles, at the beginning and they will become attached to you and will not want to suffer disap-proval. It is that fear of disapproval, properly exercised, that keeps them in line. Therefore where disapproval is warranted, it must be exercised swiftly and fairly and without fear or favour so that all know that they really do not want to suffer the consequences of disappointing their leader.

In this way, not only is loyalty engendered but so is an enhanced work ethic.

But punishments must not be arbitrary: both the reason for punishment and the punishment itself must be consistent from case to case or else it causes division and dissent amongst the team which leads to lack of concentration and poor perform-ance as well as, ultimately, a breakdown of discipline and, unlike in an army where such action is subject to severe pen-alty, desertion in the form of staff resignations or, worse, defection in the form of joining a rival firm.

9.44. If in training soldiers commands are habitually en-forced, the army will be well-disciplined; if not, its discip-line will be bad.

9.45. If a general shows confidence in his men but always in-sists on his orders being obeyed, the gain will be mutual.

Sun Tzu emphasises that system and controls must be designed, applied, followed and, if they are not, enforced. Dis-cipline is not only imposed by the leaders; it is imposed by the men themselves. A leader should not have to micro-manage: he should be able to define the plan and delegate its performance.

This is not always easy. There is an increasing tendency amongst young graduates to assume they know best and, regardless of how often they are told that they must follow defined processes, they think they can achieve the same ends by some other means.

For example, a clerk in one of my own companies, given eight steps to follow in order to achieve a specific result in one hour had not finished the work after almost two hours. When challenged, she said she had been choosing the items in the order she wished to do them and had not finished. Worse, the work she had done was useless and had to be started again. Done by another clerk according to the instructions, the work was done, properly, in less than one hour.

A recruit into the IT department in another of our companies was given, on his first morning, some simple tasks to do, in part to assess his ability to follow instructions and in part to assess his capability in the basics of more complex tasks. He announced that that was not what he wanted to do, that he wanted to do programming and that therefore he had not commenced the tasks. Instead he had loaded an instant messaging program that all employees were told in their induction course was not permitted and had spent his time chatting on-line to his friends who were also starting new jobs.

In part, this problem is due to a failure in universities to explain to undergraduates that the mere fact of having a degree does not mean that they are equipped for office life nor, frankly, much use initially. Many employers complain that new graduates expect pay that far exceeds their value to the company and benefits that long-term employees have worked for years to earn.

It is not only fresh graduates that create such a difficulty.

It is far too common to hear senior members of staff say "that's not the way we do it here" when new policies and systems are introduced. In fact, change management, despite being greatly in fashion as a management topic in the 1980s, has not moved on very far.

There are many documented reasons why change management is so fraught. One is the simple issue of induction and training: in many businesses, training is by the "sit by Vera" method. What is the "sit by Vera method?" It's simple, some one is told "sit by Vera, watch what she does and learn from her."

In today's complex, processes and compliance driven world, that is not acceptable. Vera probably has dozens of bad habits and/or short cuts. New staff should be taught the current systems and controls and their performance of them should be monitored and deviations rectified.

Another reason that systems and controls are ignored is the "there'll be a different system along in a few weeks" syndrome. Simply, where there is frequent change, staff abandon all hope of keeping up. It's one of the tactics used in communist states: if the people don't know what they are supposed to do, they are always on edge and more easily controlled. In a commercial environment, however, it ends up with staff - often those in key positions - adopting a passive-aggressive attitude, pretending to follow the new systems but in fact barely changing at all. This is not the same as the revision of tactics in the course of litigation: that is, as Sun Tzu has made clear, a necessary part of the management of a campaign. We are here talking about the office's own systems and controls, including case management systems.

People really, really dislike change that they think will remove some of their autonomy. They like to think that they are responsible and will do a good job without being told exactly how to do it. And for many, many tasks, that is true. But consider the person responsible for concocting the recipe for cola: he knows everything's better with coke (which may or may not be some kind of protected mark if used with a capital "C" but here it's not because it denotes an abbreviation for cocaine), but social, medical and legal obligations insisted that it be removed from his recipe. Many employees, especially those who have been doing a job for many years, disagree with the need for change and / or the benefits of change. Certainly, change for the sake of change causes considerable annoyance.

But the most important objection to change - and therefore resistance to systems - for senior employees is the most simple: habit. In many ways, this underpins most of the other objections. Simply, people like familiarity: it gives them comfort, it allows them to focus on the actual task rather than the way it is performed. Telling a production line worker that he has to pick up a gear-knob with his right hand when he has been picking it up safely and efficiently with his left hand for twenty years is forcing him to change his work flow. Telling him that the whole purpose of the change is to introduce uniformity will create resistance and produce an unhappy worker. But if the reason for it is that, due to a changed delivery system the cart will now appear on his right instead of on his left and that the delivery system has been changed so that the car that he is fitting the gear knob to will now arrive in front of him without its doors to make the fitting of internal bits and pieces easier and he can see that changing his habit will actually benefit him.

In a law firm, where there has been no computerised time recording system, to get a senior partner to start filling in a time-sheet is often an uphill struggle. He's used to jotting a note on a piece of paper and it, eventually, finding its way to the file to be costed when the file is next billed.

In litigation, case management systems - computerised or on index cards and a diary - are essential for the good conduct of the case.

Poor litigators will write a letter and simply wait for a response and, if one does not come, the file will remain in the cabinet until someone goes through files one-by-one either looking for files to bill to generate revenue or to see if any-thing has gone to sleep and to make sure that there are no pending negligence actions.

A good litigator is on top of all deadlines and ensures that cases are always making progress. And it is this context that systems and control are most necessary.

But the rules of conduct and the rules of Court are also to be viewed as systems and controls. Therefore they must be integrated within the litigator's internal policies and proced-ures.

At their simplest (and potentially their most dangerous) such systems and controls are simply check-lists. But used properly, they drive the case towards its conclusion.

If senior litigators are not confident that their team will fol-low the systems, then ultimately cases will fail, negligence actions will follow and the firm's reputation will suffer with all the consequences that would bring.

Space is big. You just won't believe
how vastly, hugely, mind-bog-
glingly big it is. I mean, you may
think it's a long way down the road
to the chemist's, but that's just
peanuts to space.

Douglas Adams
Author

10. Terrain

10. Terrain

In Chapter 9, it was said that the battleground is the Courtroom. And so it is. But the detail of the terrain is, as previously noted, inside the heads of the arbiters of fact i.e. the judge and / or jury.

Often, in relation to the combating of terrorism, it is said that it is a battle for the hearts and minds of the people. That is exactly what is happening in a Court. Facts are great: impressions, as we will see, count for much, too.

The first part of this Chapter, principles 1-13 focus on terrain. The remainder have a wider implication. Therefore, in the first part, we will be looking at advocacy, evidence and dealing with witnesses.

10.1. Sun Tzu said: we may distinguish six kinds of terrain, to wit:

(1) accessible ground;

(2) entangling ground;

(3) temporising ground;

(4) narrow passes;

(5) precipitous heights;

(6) positions at a great distance from the enemy.

Where the jury is not receptive, or the subject matter or the language relating to it is complex, then the advocate must take extra care to ensure that his case does not become lost as the jury struggle to understand it. In cases where the subject matter is distasteful, for example in a sexual assault or rape case, then the defence will already have a hurdle to overcome. Similarly, if the defendant is of a class that juries have a natural resentment for e.g. lawyers, bankers, tax inspectors, gang members then it will be necessary to paint the defendant in a positive light.

It is not enough to use the GBAH defence. What is the GBAH defence? It's when things are so desperate that a defendant's mother is called and her best evidence is "he's a good boy at home."

10.2. Ground which can be freely traversed by both sides is said to be "accessible."

10.3. With regard to ground of this nature, be before the enemy in occupying the raised and sunny spots and carefully guard your line of supplies.

Is the jury receptive to the case as presented? If so, then there will be less difficulty in presenting it. The jury must understand the subject matter and the language used, as previously discussed.

10.4. Ground which can be abandoned but is hard to re-occupy is called "entangling."

10.5. From a position of this sort, if the enemy is unprepared, you may sally forth and defeat him. But if the enemy is prepared for your coming and you fail to defeat him, then, return being impossible, disaster will ensue.

Sun Tzu says that it is sometimes thought possible to leave a point unmade, to return to it later and to press it home more forcefully. But to do so is to risk that, when it is pressed, the opposing litigator is better prepared than he had been at the time the point was foregone.

The minds of jurors are mysterious places. It is impossible to accurately predict how they will react to any particular evidence, especially oral evidence. There are simply too many variables from how well the witness answers in examination, through his demeanour to the dreadful prospect that his evidence on the stand will differ from that in his witness statement.

And that is before the juror's own state of mind and prejudices are brought into play.

Even more worrying is the question of a herd instinct in juries.

What is herd instinct? It's when a group moves in the same direction at the same time, often without any obvious sign.

Lemmings, migrating herds of buffalo, shoals of fish all move in such a way.

And so do people.

Herds are made up of leaders and followers. The aim of any good advocate is to work out who amongst a set of jurors falls into which group.

It may prove counter-productive to identify and target an obvious leader: the other jurors may feel left out, assuming that their opinions are not going to be important. And so they may, out of a sense of rebellion, simply decide to do the opposite of what the leader says should happen. Contrary-ism is a long recognised issue in the jury room where one or more jurors hold out not because of any firmly held view of the evidence but because, as he sees it, he has not been afforded sufficient respect.

Of course, an advocate wants to tap into the herd instinct and so he must find a way to get the leader to accept his arguments without alienating the remainder of the jury.

And, of course, the argument applies to any panel of, e.g. magistrates, not only to juries.

The foreman of a jury will, often, be a self-promoting, even self-absorbed person.

Jurors select a foreman from amongst themselves but even before the jury starts formal selection, there are a number of "tells" as to who is likely to be selected.

Those who consider themselves suitable to be a foreman are those who consider themselves natural leaders. Someone from the military or law enforcement at a low- to - middle rank, where a little power goes a long way, will often fit squarely in this box. A neat tie, careful choice of jacket and trousers, polished shoes are all indicators of this type as is physical bearing: he won't march but he will walk upright and sit straight. He will look at whoever is speaking and speak in a clear, firm voice.

Academics also view themselves as suited to be foreman: they consider themselves able to collate and analyse information. Often their clothes will be less well presented and their shoes will not be so polished. They will not have a formal bearing and their voices, while clear, will often not be so forthright or, even, their answers so obviously black or white, right or wrong.

In the USA, for example, jury selection is something of an art, while in other countries, an advocate gets, more or less, what he's given unless he has good cause for objection.

A US advocate will be looking for someone with a recognisable status brought about by his job, someone who is able to rationally and calmly analyse and respond to questions and who demonstrates both decisiveness and a probable ability to persuade (if not cajole) those who do not follow his lead.

It is well established that "blue collar" workers will often follow a managerial or professional worker, such as doctor, nurse or a senior manager in a commercial concern. And, as noted above, several surveys have shown that juries are often made up of as much as 80% blue collar workers - or the unemployed. It follows then, that on the average jury, an advocate is looking for only two or three people as potential foremen.

But there are exceptions: while a senior banker may normally be highly regarded the position will probably be reversed at times of socio-economic pressures e.g. recession: where banks are considered at least partially blameworthy, a banker may be a bad choice because others, perhaps having lost their homes, will not defer to a banker.

Advocates sometimes try to exclude those who appear to be too dominant or forceful or opinionated during selection. Research quoted but not identified in some US sourced material says that a correlation exists between an extrovert foreman and deliberation times: although no explanation is given, it is easy to guess (right or wrong) that the reason for this is that the extrovert is given a platform takes the jury room as a performance.

Other traits that have been identified as tending to lead to an individual being selected are:

a) someone who talks a lot. It appears that, as he tries to "sell" his own benefits, he will simply wear down the other jurors who would rather pick him as foreman than delay a tea break (or something).

b) ego: this is difficult to quantify but basically, it involves using a range of techniques to assess how the individual regards himself and his self-worth. The more self-important, the greater the likelihood that he will try to insist on his own selection.

c) surveys show that more juries select men than select women as foreman. It is said that the difference is especially pronounced in civil trials - in fact only 3% of the time according to Rodney R. Nordstrom, PhD, JD. The same source says that in 95% of criminal trials, the foreman will be white and in 70% of cases he will be male.

d) animated: no, not a cartoon character. It means that jurors appear to think that a person who uses expansive hand movements, obvious facial expressions and other visual cues is more suited to a foreman's role, perhaps as an extension of leadership.

While the US system of empanelling a jury is unusual, in some countries the identity of potential jurors is made available to the parties so that they may "vet" them in order to try to identify those who should be subject to a "peremptory chal-lenge" that is rejected by one or other party without having to give a reason. There are also challenges for cause where, if a specific objection (e.g. a juror knows one of the witnesses or the defendant) a juror may be stood aside from that case.

It is, therefore, the job of the advocate to try to identify the likely foreman and to make sure that he understands each point; but not to the exclusion or irritation of the other jurors.

Jurors have, in many studies, been found to follow a herd instinct. There are some trendy studies that call this the "risky-shift" concept of conformity.

Nuts: let's keep it simple. Often because they don't under-stand, because they are lazy, because they want to get home to the children or for a dinner party or just don't want to be the one who stands out in a crowd, jurors will just play follow-the-leader.

The "Simon Says" school of jury deliberation is a serious problem and that's why identifying and targeting the probable foreman is so important.

The end result is that, as a group, the jury will adopt a stronger position than they would have adopted individually. Few think that one lemming on his own would jump into a raging torrent: but a thousand of them do it without much hes-itation.

It's the same in a jury room.

It's part peer pressure but it's also for all of the reasons out-lined above and more.

It's linked to a long-established psychological phenomenon known as "group think." It's difficult to hold onto an isolated position when all around adopt a common stance. Human nature is to fit in, to harmonise or even sing in unison.

So, if a defence advocate recognises that the prosecutor has made something of a hit with the expected foreman, the defence advocate will look for one or more jurors who might adopt a contrary view and look to create, in effect, a feeling of rapport and support with them, to fight off the effects of group think or even cajoling, even in the face of complaints from other jurors that their lives are being disrupted by a failure (as they will often phrase it "a delay") in coming to the "right" conclusion.

It is therefore important during opening argument and summing up to make eye contact with each juror, so that each juror believes that the advocate is speaking directly to him.

And this is an especially important point because research in the 1970s in England found "There is a natural tendency to disregard what is said about things which the jury cannot understand; nice distinctions over the precise meaning of a rule of law, or the judge's assessment of expert evidence, may thus pass into oblivion " (from "The Jury" - W R Cornish, Professor of English Law, LSE, London).

Jurors are not stupid - but they are human and humans, in general, are not good at retaining and organising information, especially that which is delivered orally. Jurors should, there-fore, be encouraged to take notes. Research shows many do not know they are permitted to do so.

In some jurisdictions, the Judge's summing up and legal directions (which can be complex, convoluted and long) are handed to the jury in writing. Elsewhere, they just have to keep up. And given the appalling standard of summing up by some judges (who, not to put too fine a point on it fluff the law and then wonder why a jury acquitted on an apparently straightforward case), supposedly rogue decisions are not surprising.

So, how much do jurors actually hear, retain and process?

An academic paper (www.nicmadge.co.uk - which see for material cited) summarises some of the issues in summing up: it says:

"Although there is no English or Welsh research into how much jurors remember or understand, there is research by psychologists into memory, recall and understanding. In 1956, George A. Miller concluded that "the span of immediate memory impose[s] severe limitations on the amount of information that we are able to receive, process and remember." His research suggested that there was a limit of seven chunks of information (plus or minus two) which could be retained. More recently and more significantly, Robert H Margolis of the University of Minnesota , has written about how much patients remember from what they have been told by doctors and other health care professionals. According to Margolis, studies indicate that about 50% of information provided is retained. Between 40 and 80% may be forgotten immediately. In one study, patients could not recall 68% of the diagnoses given to them about their own health in a medical visit. Of the information that is recalled, about half is remembered incorrectly. "So about half is forgotten immediately and half of what is remembered is wrong." In other words, patients remember correctly only about a quarter of what they are told.

Intelligence levels have not been shown to affect the proportion of information retained, but elderly patients do tend to remember less than younger patients. Information presented in simple, easy-to-understand format is remembered better than information presented in a more complex manner. The more information presented, the lower the proportion that is recalled by the patient. Written material, when used appropriately during a consultation, can enhance recall of information "

Does Madge know what he's talking about? He does. He's a Judge.

Have you still got your pot of coffee and the biscuit barrel handy? You are going to need it because, now, we are going to enter - literally - a parallel dimension. Remember that we have seen that litigation is not only about that which is before you, but it is also about interpreting things from a much wider viewpoint.

It follows from what has just gone before that prosecutors want to increase the chance of herd instinct and group-think while defence advocates want to reduce it.

And here's how: in order to secure a conviction, prosecutors must bring the jury to a consensus, to secure a unanimous verdict or, if the court will allow it, a verdict by a near-unanimous majority.

In order to secure an acquittal, the defence must bring the jury to a consensus to secure a unanimous verdict or, if the court allows a majority verdict, to ensure that sufficient members remain in dissent that the threshold for an acceptable majority cannot be reached.

The jury is made up of individuals. But, as we have seen, they have a tendency to move in blocks.

Those blocks are made up of alliances that may be real or imagined between jury members based on any number of factors

- attraction to each other based on any one of a multitude of factors from perceived common background, physical attraction, intellectual common ground

- mutual repulsion to another member - the way he speaks, dresses, smells

- follow-the-leader (as discussed above)

- a desire not to stand out ("Simon Says," discussed above).

So, a prosecutor needs to make each juror feel that he is part of the whole and that the whole is moving in the same direction. He wants them to move like those shoals of fish that mill about, seemingly with no order, then suddenly unite, turn and dart away as one.

A defence advocate is faced with a choice: does he try to make that shoal turn and travel towards his objective or does he keep disorder, no one making a decision that unites the shoal or, at least, make sure that there are sufficient independent thinkers that he can rely on not to join the shoal.

In short, can he defeat that herd instinct; or can he use it to his advantage?

A prosecutor is looking to produce a choir singing in unison, a defence advocate is aiming for harmony where everyone is heading in broadly the same direction, all going to end up at broadly the same point but with differences. He aims to make those differences so substantial that individual jurors actually reach a different conclusion while still feeling that they are part of the whole and for the others to respect that point, even if they do not agree with it.

Both a prosecutor and a defence advocate are anxious to avoid disunity: a jazz musician who plays discordant noise and claims that his audience is in some way intellectually beneath him because they do not appreciate his art would make a terrible advocate just as, in the minds of all but those with equal pretensions or those who are so insecure that they accept what he says, he makes a terrible musician.

For a finding of guilt, the jury must unite behind a decision that the defendant is guilty beyond reasonable doubt. But they may not reach that decision on the same basis as each other. It is for this reason that prosecutors introduce nebulous concepts and present them as fact. It is easier to manipulate the emotions of jurors than it is to manipulate their reason, easier to win their hearts than to win their minds.

That is why prosecutors put before the jury arguments of means, motive and opportunity. It is why they put before the jury photographs of gruesome murder scenes which, in fact, do not link the scene to the defendant in any way. They tell the jury that the photographs are upsetting in order to build, like the screeching music in Hitchcock's Phsyco, the tension, to preface the horror they will see. But, in fact, the photographs do not have any impact whatsoever to the central question of whether the defendant did, in fact, kill the deceased unless they show the defendant in the act.

Therefore a defence advocate should seek to exclude photographs of the scene of crime except insofar as they provide direct evidence of the presence of the defendant and / or his involvement in the death.

If the Judge refuses to exclude the photographs and allows a jury to see them, then the usual response of the defence is to get them out of the minds of the jury as quickly as possible. Therefore cross-examination on them is often cursory. But, provided that the photographs do not provide any direct connection between the accused and the deceased and the actual killing, then the defence should in fact focus on them and take control of the evidence and the impact it has on the jury.

It follows, then, that the defence should take cross-examination to considerable depth: the officer who took the photographs is probably not the officer who puts them into evidence - prosecutions are a team effort and it is accepted that it is sufficient for one officer from the scene to give evidence including to enter photographs taken by another. In theory, this looks like breaching the principle against hearsay but it is not because prosecutions are brought in the name of the Crown or the state and therefore agents of the Crown or state stand as one, at least until someone notices a discrepancy which can be exploited.

The fact that the officer who put the photographs into evidence is probably not the officer that took them can, itself, be exploited. The jury is pre-conditioned to expect that witnesses are witnesses as to fact, that is to say that they say what they saw. But the photograph, if taken by someone else, is what someone else saw.

OK, now let's get really, really techie. Remember how I said that we should always keep things simple?

I lied.

You are familiar with Newton's Cradle, that frame with steel balls hanging on strings so that, when one ball is lifted and dropped, the force with which it hits the next ball along is transferred, from ball to ball, until the last ball which, having no ball to transfer its force to, flies up into the air. Then it falls back and the force is transferred in the opposite direction. Eventually, a combination of friction and gravity reduces the force at each fall and equilibrium is restored. Send two balls, and two balls at the other end rise. But at the other end, the other two balls do not rise as one and, therefore, do not fall as one: the outer ball, having only air to push against, rises slightly further than the second ball which had to transfer some of its energy to the outer ball and, as the routine plays out, the difference between the end and second balls becomes more marked until only the end ball rises until it, too, comes to a stop.

Keep that in mind.

Now remember back in school, in those physics classes you hated so much? Remember that the only things that were fun were chasing blobs of mercury around the desk, setting fire to things or even blowing them up and, the simplest and most fun of all especially if you were working alone, playing with iron filings and a magnet, which eventually led to your demands for an Etch-a-Sketch for Christmas?

Imagine making a thin straight line of iron filings. Now, half-way along that line, starting from some distance away, introduce a magnet and draw it slowly closer to the line of iron filings. What happens?

If you move quickly, then a clump of iron filings breaks away from the line and rushes towards the magnet, perhaps losing a few on the way.

But, if you move very, very slowly, then each iron filing itself becomes magnetised, passing its magnetic charge to the filing next to it. Gradually, the centre of the line begins to pull towards the magnet - and those filings next to it begin to move with it. If the magnet is powerful enough and if it is moving strongly enough, then the magnetic charge reaches along the line but the attraction along the line is not directly to the magnet but to the filings next to each other. Therefore, instead of the whole line of filings moving towards the magnet in a clump, the centre of the line moves towards the magnet and the rest of the line pulls in behind it, creating a bell shaped curve which, to be really geeky, demonstrates on a graph (literally, graphically) the level of magnetic force that is being delivered at that point on the curve.

OK, keep that in mind, now let's leave the physics classroom and go outside to play. We are going to play marbles. There are two types of game - the one on a flat surface and the one on a manhole cover with raised sections. We're going to play the one on the flat surface. We know that if our marble hits another marble centre to centre, the second marble shoots off at a straight line. But sometimes we don't want that. For example if it heads off in a straight line it would knock our own position-winning marble away. So we hit it slightly off-centre, knowing that the target marble will shoot one way and our own new marble will shoot off at another, making a shape like a letter V where our position-winning marble is safe in the gap. We are using tangential forces to knock away threats while leaving our own position strong. You didn't realise that playing marbles was really learning the basics of curling, bowls and even shove ha'penny, did you?

Right: remember that, too, and let's go back to Newton's Cradle. Instead of the traditional straight line Cradle, let's imagine a circular cradle. It works differently to the straight line model.

To understand how differently, we're going to head off to the playground where there are some swings. When you sit on the swing and go up and down, you go up and down in a straight line: you are always looking at a series of points that are in a vertical line from that at which you started. Now imagine the position if the frame holding multiple swings was arranged with the swings one behind the other instead of alongside each other (making sure that one swinger cannot connect with another for safety's sake), when all swingers are at rest, they are (except the one in front) all looking at the back of the head of the swinger next in line. That's what the balls in a traditional Newton's Cradle would see if they had eyes.

Jump off that swing and head for the old-fashioned fair-ground ride where you sit in a seat like a swing. The ride moves in a clockwise circle. When the ride is at rest, when you sit, you are sitting around a circle, but now you are looking over the left shoulder of the person in front, not directly at the back of his head.

When the ride starts, you are lifted up, higher and higher as a result of centrifugal force: that's the force that tends to push you out from the centre of a revolving object. Some physicists deny the existence of centrifugal force but to them I say this: take a position on the outside of a corner when a racing car loses grip and stand your ground because, if centrifugal force does not exist, the car won't fly off the track and hit you. Or explain why a washing machine can be crammed so full of laundry that no more will fit when it's dry but, after it's been made wet (and therefore both denser and heavier) and spun at high speed it sticks to the outside of the drum and there is lots of space inside.

We're still with the circular Newton's Cradle. On the fair-ground ride, as centrifugal force pulls you higher, your line of sight moves. No longer are you looking over the shoulder of the person in front but far to his left. This is not only a function of trajectory but also of torsional forces which twist you out-wards. The torsion is created by the fact that you are held into position by two cables, one on your right and one on your left. They twist at different rates, the one on your right, that is nearer the centre, moves less than the one on your left. The cables do not change length but the one on the outside would need to become longer if you were to remain facing in the same direction as before i.e. looking over the shoulder of the person in front. And to compensate for that lack of stretch, the two cables modify their position relative to each other. Because they are connected through the seat you are strapped into, the seat twists and so, therefore, does your view. If you hold your head straight ahead throughout the ride, you will see changes in your view. Those views are the vectors along which the ball travels when it is hit off-centre.

So, in the circular Newton's Cradle, the forces from the dropped ball do not impact on the next ball in a direct line. When it connects, new forces are at play and the second ball flies off at a tangent; its vector. When the balls fall back, they do so in a way that, if we spent a huge amount of time in both experimentation and calculation, we could predict. But there are huge variables not the least of which is exactly how much force is applied (i.e. the height from which the first ball is dropped) to the second ball and how much torsion is effected by the strings. When the balls drop back, their points of impact with other balls result in something that looks very much like chaos even if, mathematically, there can be some order proved.

Breathe a sigh of relief: we're going back to familiar ground - the court room.

If the members of the jury can be considered as being like those steel balls, are they aligned as in a traditional Newton's

Cradle or in our difficult-to-predict circular version with added forces to contend with?

That is something that differs from jury to jury and it's the purpose of jury selection. But it's also something that differs from day to day, from witness to witness even, in some cases, from time of day to time of day. What a juror was convinced of when he left Court one day, he may have re-assessed during the night. Indeed, because jurors are human, that is a very likely event.

Sleep is when the mind does its paperwork: it indexes, tabulates, analyses and files all the stuff that has been accumulated during the day. Things that don't make sense at night, often do in the morning. When people say "sleep on it," they are actually recognising that the conscious thought is not actually very good at sorting stuff out. Depending on whose views you read, it's either unconscious or subconscious thought that does that properly. I don't care which of those two options it is: the fact it happens outside the court-room and therefore out of the advocate's control is the issue at hand.

And so, the advocate's first job of the morning is to try to work out how many of last night's supporters he lost and how many of the other side's, or those that were wavering, he has gained.

He cannot presume that he has a straight line version of Newton's Cradle, even with a carefully chosen jury. He must always assume that he has a circular, difficult to predict version prone to tangential interpretation complicated by torsional movement.

In short, he must always assume that individual jurors will go off in unpredictable directions some of which are complicated by twisted reasoning.

So how can he control those reactions?

Do you remember when school physics got exciting, just before your final exams and you were left hanging, like waiting for the next episode of a melodrama, the heroine dangling over a violent sea crashing against jagged rocks? Do you remember when your teacher started talking about black holes and the space-time continuum and .... and then just left you, knowing that just as it got good, you would leave physics behind because you plan on being Chief Justice some day?

Well, the good news is that you can - indeed should - still study the good stuff. What you probably don't notice is that you already do.

Isaac Newton is often credited with discovering gravity but that's nonsense because if he had, then from the beginning of time until he did, nothing including him and his parents would have remained anchored to Earth: everything would have flown off because of centrifugal force as the Earth spins so, obviously, gravity existed long before Newton. In fact, in the early 21st century, ancient Chinese research was discovered displaying workings similar to those of Newton but from many centuries earlier. I am not going to derogate from Newton's influence because he did a lot to explain gravity and lots more, especially the laws of motion.

Juries work according to Newton's laws.

First : every object remains in the same state unless a force is applied to it. That's "inertia." To make any object move, we must overcome inertia and so it is with each juror: his state of mind will not change unless the advocates, with the aid of evidence, change it.

Second: an object accelerates (i.e. moves at a variable velocity) depending on the force applied. This is qualified by saying (as we saw in the examples of the marbles and balls) that the vector of acceleration is controlled by the vector of force.

Aristotle, note, says the object moves at a constant velocity, he does not take account of acceleration so ignoring friction and gravity.

Third, for every action, there is an equal and opposite reaction.

There is a valid argument for saying that the first law is a subset of the second law.

OK, back to black holes and the revelations they give us. An initial thought of a black hole is that it is empty, that there is nothing there, that its gravitational pull is so strong that not even light can escape. Look at the water in a bathtub as it forms a vortex and pulls down everything in a circular motion, dragging in from the outside first, concentrating it all into a sludge before finally making a gruesome sucking sound as water, other matter and even air is sucked in.

That's what a black hole is: everything that gets close is pulled in but they do not get pulled in in a straight line: they are pulled in bit by bit, they orbit the hole, gradually falling towards it until the pull is so strong that their rate of descent become impossible to halt. The reason that The Moon does not fall into the Earth is not because it is too far away (f that was the case, the tides and dust storms discussed elsewhere would not happen) but because other gravitational forces hold it in tension and therefore re-set its position.

So, far from being empty, a black hole is, in fact, full of everything it can gather. If it could be penetrated and its secrets given up, it is a source of truth.

Therefore, what we are really trying to do in a courtroom is to get the jurors in a circle around the black hole we create to make them believe in our truth and to prevent them being sucked away to an alternate truth created by our opponent.

We can't make a black hole in a court-room but we can replicate the concept. We can, in effect, put a magnet into the middle of the circular Newton's Cradle creating our own form of gravity: that means we can reduce the tangent at which the balls fly away, so reducing their effect when they come back. If the cradle is on a rapidly spinning turntable, our magnet can mitigate the effects of centrifugal force and therefore reduce torsional forces.

And how do we do that? We make our arguments attractive, compelling, difficult to avoid. And we make sure that our opponents' arguments are shown to be lacking in anchors to the truth. Note, that is not the same as proving them false.

In the case of photographs, we prove that the person who is producing them was not present at the time they were taken. For sure, the chain of custody will show what they are but then, when specific questions as to interpretation are raised, the answers can be demonstrated as having been formed at a different time to when the photographs were taken.

Newton showed that reality is actually a perception: we each have different views of reality but each reality is valid. He showed, for example, that an event that occurs in a fast-moving vehicle occurs at a fractionally different time for those engaged in it and those that witness it. That was how he began to explain the space-time continuum. He argued that light is made up of particles that travel at vast speed and that, therefore, what we now see in space and consider current events in fact happened long ago. We know know that to be true (well, the particle bit is still open to debate but the rest of it is accepted): we now know that we can look up to, stare at, fall in love under stars that burned out millions of years ago.

When we look at a photograph, it is the photographer's view. When we look at photographs in evidence, they are someone's view of what should be produced.

The next time you walk down a road, fix your eyes on a lamp post. Which shop is it outside? As you get closer, directly opposite and then further away does it seem to be outside different shops, the butcher, the baker, the candlestick maker? Yes, it does. So while each view presents what you believe to be a fact, it turns out to be an opinion.

(Disclaimer: all persons taking part in this experiment are cautioned to take care not to get run over or bump into something as you walk backwards having passed the lamp post and any and all liability that might arise from performing this experiment is hereby excluded to the fullest extent allowed by law and all allowable damages limited to the price paid for this book.)

Photographs are edited highlights of the room. What was not photographed? Or what was photographed and not put into evidence? Now that the taking of digital images is all-but free, the number of images taken at a crime scene has increased by several factors. Have all those images been disclosed? If not, what not?

And, following Newton's principles of space-time, what is captured on a photograph of a dynamic scene did not happen at precisely the moment it appeared to happen. And it does not necessarily happen in the same place.

A person standing on a railway platform watches a train go by. A passenger jumps into the air and lands on his feet. Without going into really complex analysis of Newton's law, we know that the person who jumped up will land on exactly the same spot on the carpet as he took off from (provided his jump was totally vertical). Note "exactly the same spot on the carpet." While he was in the air, the train moved along the track. Therefore, when he lands, the person looking in sees him land in a place that is different relative to the world outside the train. Who is right, the person inside the train that says he landed on the same spot or the person on the platform who says he landed twenty feet to the right, in front of a red phone box?

Even if we take out the question of space-time (and we should stop this train of thought before we move onto string theory and become totally entangled) the issue of whether the photographs demonstrate the scene at the time of the killing or at some point later is relevant. Therefore, the prosecution should be put to proof of how environmental conditions changed the scene. They will be able to offer only opinions, not facts. They will be able to express only their best guess. And, as discussed elsewhere, an opinion means that there is doubt. The only question, then, is how much doubt is there and how much can be implied if doubt is denied?

Right, let's leave physics for now and look at the jurors as individuals and the advocate's need to either herd them together or to break them apart.

To get a guilty verdict, a prosecutors needs each and every juror to accept his evidence and to reject the defendant's evidence "beyond all reasonable doubt." By definition, then, that means that when any juror that holds out when the others are convinced of guilt must suffer arguments that his doubt is unreasonable. He, on the other hand, argues that their lack of doubt is beyond reason. They may not argue it in those terms but the bottom line is that it is an attack on the intellect or capacity to understand.

As advocates, our job is to maximise how each juror considers the evidence. A prosecutor needs to create a feeling of certainty and security, to take evidence at face vale. A defence advocate needs to make the jury question the evidence. Questions are doubt. By keeping the jury thinking about the evidence, both side's evidence, the defence is ensuring that there is a constant undercurrent of uncertainty. By leveraging that uncertainty, it can be turned into reasonable doubt.

If that uncertainty can be converted into group-think, then so much the better: a unanimous acquittal is a perfect result. But any acquittal is a good result. And that's why the advocate applies tangential forces to the prosecution case, to knock them out of the way and leave his own facts intact; it's why he applies a central force to prevent his opponent spinning the story out of his control, it's why he emphasises that things are not necessarily what even pictorial evidence will show.

Once, you may have considered it ridiculous to say that the central strategies of the courtroom were formed when you were playing with marbles in the school playground. But, with careful explanation, with a removal of cynicism, with careful building of the argument and the application of a little levity from time to time, that idea does not sound so fanciful. You have just learned how to create that magnet or black hole into which the belief and acceptance of ideas is pulled.

10.6. When the position is such that neither side will gain by making the first move, it is called temporising ground.

10.7. In a position of this sort, even though the enemy should offer us an attractive bait, it will be advisable not to stir forth, but rather to retreat, thus enticing the enemy in his turn; then, when part of his army has come out, we may deliver our attack with advantage.

"Temporising" means to buy time. In short, do not rush in just because there looks to be an opening. Indeed, Sun Tzu says that, if an apparent opening is offered by an opponent, it is advisable to pull back and to try to suck him into our own trap. Frankly, that looks like a somewhat dangerous plan in most cases. Perhaps a safer strategy is to wait and see what develops and whether the opening is real.

Gentle questioning is, of course, the essence of cross-examination: to invite answers that appear innocuous but which turn out to be preparatory to the main thrust of argument. It is in this context that we can see Sun Tzu's principle clearly.

10.8. With regard to narrow passes, if you can occupy them first let them be strongly garrisoned and await the advent of the enemy.

10.9. Should the army forestall you in occupying a pass, do not go after him if the pass is fully garrisoned but only if it is weakly garrisoned.

Where there is a strategic advantage to be had, then there are benefits in waiting for the enemy to walk into a place where the territory is controlled by your own forces.

In litigation, this translates into, for example, knowing of a passage in a document that can be used to demonstrate an admission, perhaps inadvertently made but to which no reference, or hint of a reference, is made prior to trial. However, it can be put to the witness at trial with a particular interpretation, therefore in public but equally importantly, with the benefit of privilege attached to the making of the statement in court.

As a result, the statement can be reported, with the interpretation.

Previously, I have argued against the use of the media. However, in this narrow case, it can be used to great effect. A party, concerned with its image, can be greatly embarrassed by a document that implies less than honourable conduct especially when that conduct can be exposed with some carefully chosen editorialising.

And if the implication or even an express statement shows the culture of the company to be open to question, then its implications go beyond the case in hand and can have a direct impact on the business generally.

There are two objectives in this course of conduct: it is diversionary. One's opponent is forced to deal with the fall-out at a critical time in the trial when his resources are already fully deployed in a manner called for by his battle plan and therefore a sudden, unexpected attack from the flanks - which is what a PR crisis is - demands a sudden and unplanned redeployment therefore creating gaps elsewhere in his battle plan.

But there is more: it is also also designed to force them to consider settling because they do not know what else might now become of interest to the media with the consequential reputational risk. This strategy moves some of the conduct of the action from the strict legal position to the public relations / crisis management arena which is something that many businesses are very anxious to avoid.

10.10. With regard to precipitous heights, if you are beforehand with your adversary you should occupy the raised and sunny spots and there wait for him to come up.

10.11. If the enemy has occupied them before you do not follow him but retreat and try to entice him away.

If an advocate can take an unassailable position at the beginning of a trial, or even later as the evidence unfolds, he should take it and simply wait for his opponent to attack. Attacks uphill are always from a position of weakness unless they are sneak attacks by marauders, intent on nibbling away at both defences and confidence. Therefore if one's opponent has taken a strong position, instead of trying a full frontal attack it makes more sense to try to reduce the strength of his position.

It almost always proves counter-productive to ask the question "you said X. Is that the truth?" Even the more law-yerly "I put it to you that when you said X you were lying," elicits a blunt response of "No, I was not."

To provide a Judge or a Jury with the opportunity to hear a witness say, in just two or three words, that he is, indeed, abiding by his oath, is not a very clever idea.

It is far better, then, to leave the statement he made without such a frontal attack. It's better to behave like a shoal of piranha than like a shark, better to undermine the evidence gradually rather than to try to knock it down with one blow.

And so, it is better to approach laterally, as said earlier, to play the man not the ball, to find ways of undermining his credibility rather than to try to undermine his bald statement.

He may be a person who claims that he is a moral person: has he had an extra-marital affair? Has he had an affair with another man's wife? Have there ever been questions over his expense account?

By such a roundabout approach, the apparently unassailable standpoint of a supposedly upright witness is undermined.

This links to the question of how the arbiters of fact might decide that a witness is being truthful. Often, they will, perhaps subconsciously, rely on non-verbal communication, often called "body language."

How much can body language tell?

There is a theory that, when a person is lying, he tends to glance up and to the right, looking towards two o-clock, for example. The theory says that, when a person is telling the truth, he tends to look up and to the left - towards ten o-clock.

The reason, psychologists have long argued, is that a person looking to the right is constructing an answer but a person looking to the left is remembering an answer.

But recent research conducted jointly by the University of Hertfordshire in England and the University of Edinburgh in Scotland has found that there is no strict correlation between the telling of a lie and those specific eye movements. Moreover, when a person was instructed in identifying the eye movements, it made no difference to their perception of whether a person was lying or telling the truth.

The evidence included the study of videos of press conferences which provided long close-ups of speakers. Some later found to be lying, others to be telling the truth.

One of the researchers, Dr Caroline Watt from Edinburgh said "A large percentage of the public believes that certain eye movements are a sign of lying and this idea is even taught in organisational training courses. Our research provides no support for the idea and so suggests that it is time to abandon this approach to detecting deceit."

The theory began as part of the study of neuro-linguistic programming ("NLP"). The new research began when it was discovered that "according to this notion, a person looking up to their right suggests a lie whereas looking up to their left is indicative of truth telling. Despite widespread belief in this claim, no previous research has examined its validity. "

In short, it's pop-pschology and may or may not be a myth. It turns out that it is more likely myth than truth.

And it turns out that it's not the theory that's at fault but a disconnect between the English used in the study and those who have interpreted and popularised it.

The problem with pop-psychology is that it quickly gains a critical mass and, in the Web 2.0 world of social media and Wikis of various sorts, lazy copycats simply perpetuate errors in pursuit of content to fill up the space between the ads they hope will make their on-line fortune.

For example http://www.wikihow.com/Detect-Lies says "You can usually tell if a person is remembering something or making something up based on their eye movements. When someone is remembering details, their eyes move to the right (your right). When someone is making something up, their eyes move to the left. " Aside from confusing us with which left and right the entry is talking about, note the use of the term "making something up."

The full, authoritative, study is at

http://www.plosone.org/article/info:doi/10.1371/journal.-pone.0040259.

Full citation: Wiseman R, Watt C, ten Brinke L, Porter S, Couper S-L, et al. (2012) The Eyes Don't Have It: Lie Detection and Neuro-Linguistic Programming. PLoS ONE 7(7): e40259. doi:10.1371/journal.pone.0040259 . Like many academics, much of the research material they quote is, in fact, their own prior research.

The study also makes it clear that the pop-psych view is not what the original NLP theorists said. When they were talking about "constructing" they did not mean "inventing" or "making something up." They meant that a person was formulating his answer from information in his memory. Hence the fault is in the use of English and the ideas have been passed around in a kind of French Whispers game.

In short,

- to look at two o'clock meant to be finding the components of the answer, perhaps even making a calculation, rather than making something up;

- to look at 10 o'clock was to be trying to find a complete memory, for example an image or a memory of an event seen or a word or phrase said.

In effect, the up-and-right movement displays a series of operations while the up-and-left movement displays someone who is trying to find the equivalent of a photograph or a VCR (etc.) in their memory.

Given that pop-psych has transliterated this into saying that one movement is an indicator of lying while the other is an indicator of telling the truth, the next question is why so many people have fallen into the trap of not only accepting it but of perpetuating it. According to the study "assuming there is no relationship between the proposed patterns of eye-movements and lying, why should people come to believe that such a pattern exists? One possibility is that people are more confident in their lie detection abilities when they believe that they are following a scientific theoretical framework, such as that seemingly provided by NLP. "

The conclusion is startlingly blunt: "The results provide considerable grounds to be sceptical of the notion that the proposed patterns of eye-movements provide a reliable indicator of lying. As such, it would seem irresponsible for such practitioners to continue to encourage people to make important decisions on the basis of such claims. "

There is a great deal of academic study on the subject of reading faces but most of it is held behind paywalls or some other form of subscription. www.plosone.org is one of a new generation of publishers of peer-reviewed academic research which publishes under the open source Creative Commons Attribution licence.

What the research does not say is that the eyes do not provide any form of indicator: it merely disproves the notion that there are fixed and identifiable patterns of the types referred to. It does not, for example, disprove "shifty-eye syndrome" or where a person avoids eye contact.

So, what does it tell an advocate if a witness' eyes dart around the room during examination?

2007 research at Yale University and the University of Delaware, USA, followed up on a 1989 paper by one of the same authors, Helene Intraub. Her research demonstrated two things about "shifty eyes."

The first is that the person is looking around in order to rapidly gather information. Intraub had earlier found that a person focusses on a specific spot for somewhere between one third of a second and two seconds (approx). During that time, the brain receives and processes detailed information.

But between those focussing events (sorry, it's difficult to find a suitable description without sounding pretentious) the eyes do, indeed, dart around. And instead of focussing for at least half a second (which is 500 milliseconds), they alight on subject matter for just 50 milliseconds. There is, therefore, some kind of stop-start motion but it is so quick that the conscious perception of someone watching that movement cannot see it.

According to Intraub's earlier research, much of the information gathered in this way is incomplete: perhaps we can explain it as if the eye is scanning the scene and producing an outline view and the brain then decides what is sufficiently important to be filled in and prioritises those areas. What Intraub found was that the information obtained on the first pass was incomplete. If the same information was picked up again, in the same manner, the brain did not cross-refer the two snap-shots but filed them both as separate and incomplete images.

For our purposes, then, the result demonstrates something in addition to what we originally looked at this topic for: it shows that genuine memory is not reliable where it has been obtained as a part of this rapid-eye-movement based intelligence gathering.

Returning to the original question: do rapidly moving eyes indicate that a person is being dishonest? According to Intraub's findings, the eyes are actually involved in what she terms "boundary extension." In short, assessing the person's surroundings for all manner of information including threats.

Bearing in mind that a witness is under stress and in a position of uncertainty, then (in an entirely unscientific leap by me), it seems logical to say that a person who is looking around the room with quick eye movements is, in fact, reacting naturally to his environment and therefore the specific eye movements under discussion are unlikely to be an indicator of dishonesty.

So, if the eyes do not give away a liar, what about other movements?

Some say that a "jiggly leg" is an indicator of stress. But that seems to be wishful thinking. I, personally, know many people who exhibit jiggly-leg behaviour and in each case the cause is the same: they are very bright people who are being expected to perform far below their intellectual capacity and are very, very bored. The jiggly-leg is a means of absorbing some of the so-called nervous energy and diverting it through physical movement so as to avoid simply getting up and walking away from the tedium.

In extreme cases, they may be regarded as ADHD sufferers and that the jiggly-leg is a tick.

That is not to say that some jiggly-leg behaviour might not arise from the stress of telling lies. It does, however, demonstrate that it is not a good indicator of a liar.

Hand movements are generally held to be a reasonably accurate indicator of lies. Again, the pop-psychology brand of analysis says things like "a liar's physical movements will be limited and stiff [with] little arm and hand movement." Then, often, the writer of that passage goes on to list a dozen or so hand movements most of which involve lifting the full arm. Some claim that a liar will sit with his palms facing down so as to reduce a feeling of vulnerability. Try sitting with your arms on the arms of your chair with your palms held up. Does that feel natural?

Vocal indicators also come into play. First, is the witness playing for time while formulating or remembering an answer? This is characterised in various ways, for example, asking for the question to be repeated or repeating the question before answering. "Spacer words" such as "I'd like to..." or "actually...." are means of delay but have become so commonplace that they are now often just a normal speech pattern for many people. For example "You look beautiful tonight" is not, technically, the same as "you are beautiful." In fact, the former is a kind of back-handed compliment akin to "you scrub up well." But few women would take issue with either comment.

It's the same with the space words "I just wanted to [e.g. thank you]," "I'll just go ahead and.." or "It's a pleasure to be here tonight in, where the hell am I?" to quote some long-forgotten - and much forgetting - rock star on tour.

A witness who is not telling the truth, or the whole truth, may try diversion. He will give a truthful answer but not necessarily an answer to the question that is asked. He hopes that it is close enough to give an impression without his subterfuge being noticed. And if he is challenged, he hopes to get away with "I've already answered that question."

He may try to change the balance of power between himself and the advocate. Ways of doing this are to draw himself up, if seated to sit upright and back in his chair and look down his nose at the advocate, speaking in a belittling tone, as if the advocate is a naughty schoolboy in front of a long-suffering schoolmaster. Or he may fake anger (sometimes not so fake) - in a way that is similar to Sun Tzu's description of an aggressive stance, expecting that it will not be followed up on.

Or he may try to play the victim, shrinking away from questioning, making himself small and looking up at the advocate, speaking meekly or generally pretending to be offended or hurt by the examination.

Often, a liar will use stock phrases that he has learned and practised. If he is asked the same question a few minutes apart, his response will often be identical. Related this is that, if he does in fact vary his words, he will often go back to correct them to fit the learned format.

If he does not use stock phrases, he may try to hard to be believed (although this is also true of someone who is nervous) and over-explain or add in details that he hopes will make his version of events more credible e.g. "what colour coat was he wearing?" "it was black with red stitching and patch pockets. He was carrying a brown briefcase." Of course, it could also be that the witness is anxious to be as helpful as possible.

Are there any sure-fire indicators that a person is lying? No. Shy and / or nervous people exhibit all the same traits as liars. Ironically, the person who exhibits confidence, who does not stumble, who gives his evidence clearly and concisely and without deviation might just trigger suspicions that he is too good to be true. While there are those that would like to say that there is science at play, the reality is that, outside a lab with access to brain-pattern analysis, the science is at best in its infancy and at worst wishful thinking.

The most important lesson to learn, then, is that one should not rely on a single indicator. Use what is termed "clusters" - which means looking for several indicators that point towards the same conclusion.

Equally important is how the witnesses and advocates express themselves: not only the import of what they say but the way in which they say it.

Clarity is vital: for example on 27 June 2012, an Indian newspaper (The Times of India which is unrelated to The Times) carried a headline "TV anchor cuts hair for charity, loses job." The article says "A Muslim TV anchor's decision to support cancer awareness by chopping off her hair has cost the woman her job at a Malaysian TV channel, which wants her to grow back her mane to an "acceptable" length before being allowed to resume work."

So, did she lose her job or was she suspended pending her hair growing back?

A British minister, Vince Cable, responsible for business and industry, a department that supervises The Insolvency Service, told reporters that a company had "gone bankrupt." In the UK, individuals go bankrupt. Companies enter administration or receivership or are wound up. The term "bankrupt" does not apply to companies.

All over the world, politicians are working hard to confuse in the minds of ordinary people "tax evasion" and "tax avoidance," the former being illegal, the latter being entirely legal.

A press release from the USA's FBI was headed "Check Cashiers in Brooklyn, Philadelphia, and Los Angeles Charged for Alleged Violations of Anti-Money Laws." "Cashiers" was supposed to be "Cashers" and does the USA really have "Anti-Money Laws?"

There is a drift towards using the term "unlawful" when what is meant is "illegal." Unlawful is civil harm, illegal relates to criminal conduct. Similarly, there is a drift towards confusing "oversight" (which indicates neglect) with "supervision."

If there is insufficient clarity in the way arguments are presented, jurors stand little or no chance of understanding the case. Indeed, defendants in financial crime cases know that the easiest route to an aquittal is simply to confuse the jury so they cannot honestly say they have no reasonable doubt. Surprisingly, prosecutors are rarely equipped to simplify the case so that jurors are not confused.

Regardless of whether it is in correspondence, in pleadings or in Court, litigators must say what they mean and mean what they say.

In recent years, since the late 1990s in fact, there has been a tendency towards vagueness in official language, including (unforgivably) the drafting of legislation. In countries where there has been a deliberate move towards driving down the average age of the judiciary, Judgments can all too often be seen to include examples of imprecision.

This cannot be good for any system of justice: the practice of law depends on a clear and consistent interpretation of statutes and on precedent. It is these things that allow litigators to advise their clients on litigation risk in the particular circumstances of their case.

Surely, the facts might change but the law should remain the same?

It's easy to see how this has happened, at least in Common Law jurisdictions and, especially, those for whom the UK's Privy Council is or until recently has been the Court of Final Appeal.

The problem arose because England made the decision to appoint Alfred Denning, an extraordinarily gifted lawyer to the bench and he rose through the ranks to become a Law Lord. In 1962, aged 63, he took what he described with characteristic laconic humour as "a step down" to become   Master of the

Rolls - the most senior Judge (after the Lord Chief Justice) in the Queen's Bench Division of the courts of England and Wales. It was not a step down: it put the Lord (as he was by then) Denning in the position where he was able to pick and choose his cases and the bench that sat with him. As a result, his decisions rarely went to the House of Lords, then the Court of Final Appeal in England and Wales.

That was certainly not the case in his earlier career where his cases were frequently appealed and he had a much higher than average rate of having his decisions overturned. And yet, his rate of dissent, according to Edmund Heward, one of several to write biographies of Denning, was only in 16% of cases in the House of Lords, leading to a feeling that his skills in advocacy had not been shelved when he took to the bench: it seems he used them as much in the retiring room as he had from the floor of the Court.

Denning was, at heart, a judge driven by conscience more than strict interpretations of the law. Although he did admit to being an opponent of the rigid principles of precedent and he made what seemed to be contorted reasoning to distinguish the case before him from precedent where it appeared to him to be just to do so.

Unfortunately, after Denning, England saw a rash of lawyers who thought (indeed, still think and many are now at the top of the Profession) that their intellect compares with Denning's. In the 1990s, it became increasingly difficult to predict the outcome of a trial simply because too many judges wanted to emulate Denning.

Some, seeing Denning in a simple, revolutionary, light have taken that unpredictability into the realms of contrariness, actively making findings that undermine both the word and intent of statutes. This has been notably so in my own area of counter-money laundering laws.

Since The Proceeds of Crime Act 2002, those laws have also suffered by a serious lack of precision in the language in which they are drafted with the result that there is considerable scope for Judges to decide on their own interpretation. The idea of dictionary of judicially defined words has all but gone out of the window when laws have been drafted in the UK since the late 1990s.

This tendency has also been seen in other countries: Australia and New Zealand have passed counter-money laundering laws that are written in simple words but have such a complex structure that few have ever really understood them.

It seems contrary to good sense that a piece of legislation supposedly written in "plain English" needs a raft of "explanatory notes" and "guidance." Those things were not needed when certainty of language was in play and those drafting laws had a sufficient command of the language.

In Court, language must be precise. Companies that do business together should not be regarded as "partnered with." We should never hear the term "with our partners" unless there is actually a legal (even if implied) partnership is in place. Suppliers and customers are not partners because there is no shared risk. Just because two groups issue a common report on a particular topic does not make them "partners."

The term "stakeholders" is meaningless, or perhaps has too many possible meanings. Who knows? Certainly not a juror.

Again, in terms of age, jurors of middle age and above like to hear "husband" and "wife." They do not like "partner." Girlfriend or boyfriend is fine, so is cohabittee. The phrase "common-law wife" is in almost all cases not accurate; simply shacking up together does not create a union at common law: there must be some kind of ceremony, with witnesses who can attest to the fact that the parties intended to bestow on each other all the benefits of marriage even though they did not register it as statutes require. Oddly, then, those that are most likely to have a genuine common-law marriage are members of biker gangs who take part in a ceremony over the seat or handlebars of a motorcycle.

Exactly what does the PR dream phrase "going forward" mean? It's been current for about 20 years and I still have no clear idea of what anyone using it is trying to tell me.

Any and all buzzwords are designed for one of a limited number of purposes:

a) shorthand for a group sharing a common interest. It's jargon. Sometimes it is to provide accurate comprehension amongst members of the group, sometimes it is used to exclude non-members from understanding what is being said. It is said (probably falsely) that Cockney Rhyming Slang was developed so the criminals of a small district (Cheapside) in the east of the City London (where true Cockneys come from) could converse without the police being able to follow. And so "stairs" is "apples and pears" which would then be truncated to "apples."

b) to obfuscate, i.e. to confuse the listener. Management-speak is especially prone to this: the idea is to make phrases sound benign so as not to upset markets or lovers of soft-skills.

And so we have a raft of words such as "outplaced," downsized," and so on because no one has the courage to say "made redundant" or even "sacked."

Businesses say they are "operating in a challenging environment" when they mean that business is not going well. They say that sales are "poised to (re)accelerate" which means they have unsold stocks that they about to liquidate at fire-sale prices to generate cash flow.

Jurors understand "percent" but not "basis points," the latter having found its way into financial-speak and adds nothing except uncertainty to what is being said.

"Action" is not properly used when someone says "I gave it to X to action." Just say "do."

"Onboarding" - just call it what it is: signing up a customer and verifying his bona fides.

"Human capital" or even "human resources." It's "personnel," or, even, "staff."

"killer app." (admission: I actually like this one in the real world but not, unless it is explained, in Court.) An "application" that we think is going to make us a market leader because we will be the first to market with this idea or, alternatively, it is so much better than anything else currently available. Also known as "the better mousetrap."

"In the [think of a subject] space" is not only irritating but adds in sound that decreases the juror's ability to gather, retain and use information. Use less words to ensure more comprehension. So, this phrase can be, e.g., "in marketing" instead of "in the marketing space."

And I have no idea what a paradigm shift is and I have not wish to find out despite endless management people using the expression in front of me for a decade. I'm sure that many jurors have exactly the same response to this kind of nonsense.

In a case involving banking or finance, a juror will have to guess (using his own background use of language) when he hears the phrases "discount rate" or "take a haircut." He will think someone is going to get 10% off the price of a new shirt or to go to the barber's (as if!) and, while he tries to work out why he should care, the evidence moves on.

Do not use, and discourage your witnesses from using, TV speak: in the real world, police officers do not walk into a room and say "what you got?" Or any of the other stock phrases that script-writers litter the airwaves with. One of the current crop (2012) is "let's see what pops." It is just a catchy phrase and, again, causes distraction while the juror tries to understand what the speaker is trying to say.

Similarly the use of military expressions in non-military life (especially prevalent on US generated TV programmes) does not impress a jury. They do not want to hear that a company decided to issue proceedings against a competitor in order to "nuke 'em." Regardless of the impression given by so much TV, the truth is that the vast majority of people are repulsed by violence and the language and mannerisms that relate to it. Therefore using language that supports or suggest violence is a way of alienating the jury.

It follows, then, that witnesses should be warned against acting tough, using imprecise or misleading language just as much as they should be warned against the use of foul language. Like it or not, a witness is a salesman for his version of events. He is not a lecturer whose words are likely to be taken at face value.

His evidence will be challenged, often rigorously. The more clearly he states his evidence, the less work the jury has to do to understand and retain it, the more likely he will be believed. And if he can avoid irritating them by posturing, so much the better.

We know that people retain only a small proportion of the information presented to them orally.

Some simple maths gives a hint as to how to increase the chances that the jurors retain and understand what is presented to them.

1,000 words means, according to the research, that only some 100 words will actually be retained and understood. And if they are retained and understood, then they can be used in the decision making process.

Do we know which 100 words will be retained and understood? No, not exactly. But we can do a rough estimate thinking through the triggers that affect people listening to speech.

But there is another thing to add into the mix: some people do hear a lot more, they retain a lot more and they not only understand a lot more but they apply it not just at that moment but they will remember it and use it, or at least recite it, for a long time. Who are these people? They are the people that listen to what has become known as "talk radio." But it's not the hyperactive, offensive, talk radio : it's the staid, informative radio that - ironically - began mass broadcasting in the years between WWI and WWII.

In the UK, Radio Four and the BBC World Service retain a broadly similar approach to on-air speech. It's not about speaking some contorted pronunciations as in "received English" - which has an awful lot to answer for including bad spelling in many countries around the world where phonetics are based on a horrible mangling of English by middle-ranking colonial civil servants.

And its not about "standard English." Accents are fine and, indeed, in some cases have been proved to have a positive (or negative) effect on the way information presented by that person is perceived.

For example, a survey in the UK found that certain regional accents were regarded as inherently trustworthy and others as inherently untrustworthy.

The reason that BBC R4, in particular, delivers information in a way that is retained is because, for most of its programming, it follows a simple rule: any complex subject can be explained so long as the structure of the explanation is simple. Note, that does not mean over-simplification of language. But it does mean staying away from buzzwords and - equally importantly - it means using less words, not more. And it means not making up words - if the correct word can't be found, then either look it up or find a suitable alternative. It means using words correctly, not using another word and then telling the person listening that, if they don't understand, it's their fault. Finally, it means not adding suffixes, prefixes into words nor using nouns as verbs, for example.

It seems counter-intuitive to say that to increase the amount of data retained under the 100/1000 ratio to use less words. It seems logical to say that, if we want someone to retain 200 words, we should give them 2000.

But we are interested not just in numbers, but in quality. Remembering data is only part of the issue: we need a jury to retain the correct data and to apply it accurately.

People hear what they want to hear or what they think they hear. As advocates, then, it's our job to make sure they hear what we say and grasp what we mean.

And it's our job to make sure that they understand witnesses, too.

The simplest way to make sure that a judge or jury hears what we say is to speak clearly. Speaking clearly is not difficult: it is made up of four different aspects - enunciation, pronunciation, projection and speed.

Enunciation is making sure that words are properly formed. Ignoring the possibility that an advocate has a genuine speech defect, a much more serious problem is advocates who are hard to understand because they mumble, they don't open their mouths, don't fully use their lips and tongue when they speak. Muffled speech results in a presumption that the advocate is not confident and if he is not confident, it implies that he does not believe in his client's case.

Worse, there is little that undermines an examination more than when a witness has to ask an advocate to repeat the question.

And if a juror does not hear what the advocate is saying, unlike a Judge, he cannot interrupt and ask for it to be repeated or read back from the transcript.

It is important not to go too far in the opposite direction: hectoring or strident speech alienates jurors, judges and witnesses.

Pronunciation is important because, like emphasis, it aids comprehension. In some cases, pronunciation and emphasis coincide: for example, how should one stress the word "harassment?"

The correct stress is on the first syllable. It's irrelevant why it has become common to stress the second syllable. The end result is simple: it undermines the impact of the word. The force of the word comes from the "h" (which is never, ever, silent and equally should not be in words such as "herbs" or "hotel" - we are speaking English not French).

Foreign words present a challenge: is it "Moscow" or "Moscoh?" The answer is that it is spelt Moscow but pronounced "Moscoh."

And if anyone who uses "Moscow" says "we say it phonetically," show them the word "Arkansas" and ask them to say that.

An advocate should never, ever, use a faux foreign accent when using a foreign word or name. While the French call the region most famous for fizzy wine "Cham-pahn-yu" for the rest of us it's correct to say "sham-pain."

On the question of enunciation and emphasis, it's fine to be conversational. Conversational is engaging for any audience be it in a theatre or a courtroom. And from the advocate's point of view, a conversational style is more natural and keeps his thoughts flowing more smoothly and more logically than a stilted, formal, almost lecturing, presentation.

Projection is where many, many advocates fall down. Projection is not the same as shouting or even raising one's voice above normal speech. In fact, projection is designed to allow a room to be filled with speech at its normal level without resorting to amplification or raising the voice.

When a voice is projected naturally, every person hearing it gets, broadly, the same feeling and it's a feeling of intimacy. A properly projected voice feels almost like someone is speaking directly into one's ear. A shout or raised voice has the opposite effect: it makes people shrink away.

Projecting the voice is not difficult, once the basic techniques are mastered. This is not the place for tuition on how to speak. For those that wish to learn, the simplest thing to do is to find some singing/vocal exercises and to generate the sound from the throat and chest cavity not from the back of the nose.

Moving sound generation from the nose to the mouth is the single biggest step. If you can feel your Adam's Apple vibrating as you speak, you are making the sound from the correct place. Then it's just a matter of making sure you are using the correct "echo chambers" in your head and body for natural amplification and breathing correctly.

This technique has an added advantage: research shows that people (women in particular) respond best to a deep voice. There are lots of reasons posited for this ranging from the sexual to sounding more confident or powerful. Given that the idea of advocacy is a form of seduction (in the sense of persuasion) the deeper voice that this technique generates increases the psychological impact of the advocate's speech beyond the words used.

The final aspect is the speed of speech. If it's too slow, jurors lose interest, if it's too fast, they cannot hear, process and file the information they are being given.

Here we are not looking at how much information is given in a given time (that's coming up in a few moments) but at the actual number of words per minute that are spoken.

There is no right and wrong speed: what works for one witness, judge or jury may not work for another. The advocate must, therefore, constantly check the lie of the land, make sure that the people he is addressing are moving at the same speed. Repeated eye contact will give him an indication as to whether they are, in some cases literally, on the same page.

The next challenge is to make sure we are not overloading the judge or jury with too much to absorb. Amazingly, it's not only a question of simplifying sentence structure nor even the length of sentences although both of those have their place. It's also a question of reducing the number of syllables they have to contend with.

And so, for the vast majority of purposes, the word "transport" should be used instead of "transportation." Adding superfluous syllables to words might impress the intellectually challenged who want to appear clever but it will not impress someone who just wants to know how goods get from A to B.

"What means of transport did you use?" is better than "what means of transportation did you use?" But there's another reason for using the simpler word: remember the importance of inflexion?

The natural stress on the word "transportation" is on the second "a." Think about it: by using that version of the word, you are directing the juror's attention to a part of the sentence that is actually irrelevant. You want the juror (and, the witness) to know that the important part of that sentence is how goods were moved i.e. the transport. And in the word "transport" the natural stress falls on the "trans" part, so focussing the entire sentence on the important point.

There are other benefits: by making the point of the question clear, the witness's response time will be shorter. Studies show that micro-seconds of delay are picked up by listeners and other studies show that listeners interpret delay as structuring an answer and, therefore imply that the answer is less likely to be entirely honest, straightforward and true. Note that this is not the same point as was made in relation to eye movements. There were were talking about "constructing" an answer. Here "structuring" means trying to phrase an answer so as to give or to avoid giving a particular impression or effect.

How many zeros in a "billion?" It depends on age and geography. Even today, people taught English (as distinct from American) know that a billion is a million to the power two. That's why it says "bi." In the 1980s, the UK government apparently officially redefined "billion"to be the same as used in American i.e. 1,000 million. There remains considerable confusion. And that confusion can be found even in US government documents where the US Department of Defense uses the term "billion" in its table headings - but adds a footnote to confirm that in using it it means 1,000 million. Across southeast Asia, it is common for people in business to question the term and ask exactly how much is meant. From the point of view of a user of , for example, pounds, euros or US dollars, one might ask how many people can actually care about a billion, regardless of how many zeros it has. The answer is that, with more than 9.000 Indonesian Rupiahs to one US dollar and, therefore, a million rupiah being worth a little over USD100, the leap to 1,000 million is not very big for many businesses.

Also, there remains uncertainty as to how the term is accepted: listen to almost any TV presenter and there is considerable emphasis on the "b" in "billion." That implies a lack of confidence in the use of the word and whether the audience will understand and / or differentiate from "million." From an advocate's point of view, if he has to emphasise a word to avoid confusion, he should avoid it: out of twelve people, it's very likely that someone will be confused.

There is no doubt that there is divergence between localised forms of English. In Malaysia, for example, "to send" means what the rest of the world means by "to take." So "I'll send you home" means "I'll give you a lift."

In my own world, the USA has pushed through the term "anti-money laundering." The correct term (which was in use in Europe in the late 1980s) is "counter-money laundering." The difference is that "anti" suggests that it is possible, even desirable, to block all money laundering. Neither is true. In fact, contrary to the usual presumption, governments do not want to prevent money laundering: what they want is for criminals to launder their proceeds of crime but for e.g. the financial sector to identify it so that it may be frozen and confiscated. In this way, society is enlisted to "counter" the money laundering that is happening, not to prevent it happening in the first place.

The opposite is true in relation to terrorist financing where the US has driven through the term "counter-terrorist financing." But the aim is to prevent funds entering the financial system in the first place and, if they do, to prevent them leaving the system and getting into the hands of or being made available to terrorists. It is not to track and trace the funds that are moving for the simple reason that terrorist financing rarely looks suspicious and therefore rarely triggers reports. Therefore, it would be correct to speak of "anti-terrorist financing."

In the days after 11 September 2001, US officials created a word that is completely nonsensical. Although it seemed as if use of the term "hawalas" had died out, in late June 2012, the US Treasury issued a media release in which the word appeared repeatedly.

"Hawala" is a payment system. A person who conducts hawala is a "hawaladar." In short terms, we would speak of "using hawala" instead of saying "I'm using a hawala service." It is important to note that because (except in short-hand) the addition of an "s" makes no sense. A to call an individual "a hawala" as some US originated documents do is to completely misuse the term. It's like saying "he's a banking."

Again, made up words affect the credibility of the speaker. They demonstrate that the user does not know his subject and, therefore, what he says is open to question.

Many people see changes in language as dumbing-down for example, referenda v referendums. I would argue that to use the correct (which is often not the same as the more common) version, gives weight to the advocate's presentation. That gravitas adds to the other techniques that strengthen the jury's view of the advocate and the case he presents. In the UK, we have seen, since the late 1990s, a marked deterioration in the standard of English with e.g. "stadiums" and "forums" now being in common use. But, again, this is generational and also affected by education levels and another indication of how close attention must be paid to the make-up of a jury so as to gauge what style of language is likely to be best received.

It's not only words: phrases cause confusion, too.

For example, a person protests his innocence but he protests against injustice. It, therefore, make no sense for someone to say "I was protesting the use of mice in a laboratory" if he is, in fact, trying to prevent such use.

There is always a place for playing with words: it's fun and English is at its best when it's being pulled, twisted and made into shapes it was never designed to make. But the advent of global mass communications has resulted in English being changed from something that could be bent so far out of shape that it seemed to be something different entirely but would bounce back a few moments later, assuming its original form to something that gets bent and stays bent. Now what was often a private play on words between friends gains a permanence through news and social media.

While there is a place for playing with words, Court isn't it. The game only works when all those playing have a common understanding of how the words are being bent and can, therefore, see the true meaning. By extension, therefore, this means that there is no place in advocacy for irony or, generally, for sarcasm.

To ensure that a jury, judge or witness understands exactly what is being said, words should be used in their generally understood context and given their ordinary and natural meaning.

That does not mean that an advocate should try to impress a jury with his command of a large, perhaps even esoteric, vocabulary. A jury member who does not understand a word has no opportunity to discuss it with his neighbours and no opportunity to look it up. He has one or more of several responses: the first is to feel inadequate. The second is to feel anger. Next is surrender.

Inadequacy will often manifest itself in his trying to understand the point which means that the advocate has moved on but the juror is left behind. He therefore misses the first point that he did not understand and one or more points that follow. He will lose track of a line of argument that depended on that first point, and, even if he tries to catch up later, the juror will not understand any of that line of argument or, worse, he will have guessed and got it wrong, negating the line of argument the advocate is putting forward or, worse, finding against it.

If he is angry, his focus will be on the advocate and he will simply stop listening to what is said while he thinks angry thoughts. Again, there will be a period where the juror is, intellectually, absent and all that the advocate says is lost.

If the juror surrenders, he might as well be asleep. This state of affairs is much more common than one might imagine. Jurors, judges even advocates simply space out when they are required to think too much. In the time honoured expression: the lights are on but there's no-one home.

And showing off is plain silly: I was sitting on an aeroplane with two trendy parents directly in front, talking to their three (ish) old daughter who wanted to sleep. They wanted to keep her away. were using full adult language which is fine but every time the mother talked about drinking water, she said "agua" - as in "do you want to drink some agua?" Seriously: how mindbogglingly pretentious? Had she asked the question in a Spanish sentence, it would have been fine. Some advocates make a similar mistake: thinking that they can use a foreign word and sound clever.

It's not just language that has the effect of turning a juror's mind to mush: technical evidence e.g. as to tracing funds in a financial action is often mind-numbing for jurors.

There is a conflict: the Court has to know how the evidence was obtained, that it was obtained properly, so as to allow it. But a Jury really does not care exactly what process was used to obtain an Order giving access to a bank account halfway across the world. It's enough that they know that the Order was obtained.

Too much detail overwhelms people. What advocates, in their role as technicians and tacticians, find fascinating, important, even fun, is actually really rather boring to everyone else. And bored people switch off. And when they switch off, it's very difficult to make them switch back on again.

If a juror has been bored for a full day by an exchange between an advocate and a witness, when the witness enters the witness box the next morning and the advocate stands up, the juror will have a sinking feeling. An attentive advocate can actually see jurors slump in their seats as they realise their position - and that things are going to start exactly where they left off the night before. All the rest and diversion they had overnight disappears.

Ironically, as an advocate, in some respects one wants that recollection of rest and diversion to disappear: one wants the juror or judge to slot right back into the same place in the evidence so as not to have to recap. But one wants the juror to be alert.

So, how does an advocate deal with testimony that lasts overnight or, sometimes for day after day?

There is no hard and fast rule. But if we borrow from the world of entertainment, we can use the expression "always leave them wanting more."

While the chances of building cross-examination to a cliff-hanger are not high, it should always be possible to arrange questioning in such a way that something interesting can be carried over.

For example: "The defendant says that his car just leaped forward while he was sitting at a set of traffic lights. If His Honour thinks it expedient, perhaps we could break for today at this point and then tomorrow morning look at how this might happen?"

It looks like examination, but it's really addressed to the Jury and to the Judge. And so long as the timing for the end of the day is broadly right, most Judges will get the hint that something technical is coming up and that morning-fresh jurors are likely to be more receptive.

10.13. These six are the principles connected with ground.

10.14. Now an army is exposed to six several calamities, not arising from natural causes but from faults for which the general is responsible.

These are:

(1) Flight;

(2) insubordination;

(3) collapse;

(4) ruin;

(5) disorganization;

(6) rout.

10.15. Other conditions being equal, if one force is hurled against another ten times its size the result will be the flight of the former.

The "other conditions being equal" phrase is the key to much of Sun Tzu's strategic thinking.

His ideas are about developing ways to even up the odds in an unbalanced arena, to avoid a competitive disadvantage.

In our terms, we are looking to tip the Scales of Justice in our client's favour, even if we are outnumbered, to allow the small firm to compete on the same level as the larger firm.

We used to have a slogan: choose the brain, not the name.

The truth is that giant consulting firms, be they lawyers, accountants or any other might buy in their staff because of the university or business school they went to. But that's a cop-out: they are presuming that the selection process for academia is the same as the selection process to be a good practitioner.

That is not so. It is arguable that it is not even a good primary filter.

There are those that think that someone who has achieved first class honours in their bachelors' degree is in some way more able than others but in truth, they are often suited to back-room research or are very good at remembering and reciting stuff and at writing opinions but they rarely excel at the cut and thrust of litigation.

A good litigator is good at research and he is good at remembering stuff. But he does not simply record it or recite it: he cross-references, constantly creating links between different data including that which is not immediately and obviously relevant.

Good litigators and good advocates are not pedestrian.

In my work in developing counter money laundering strategies, we have a number of easy to remember phrases. One of them is "criminals don't think in straight lines, they think around corners." We use that in relation to compliance and risk management, to try to encourage those who are supposed to be able to identify criminal activity to realise that they must be as creative as the criminals who are trying to access the bank's services.

The same concept applies in relation to litigation. That creativity is not only to be found in large firms. Indeed, in large firms, creativity is often stifled by overly burdensome management systems and a fear of a possible negligence action if risky strategies go wrong.

A smaller, lighter force can move faster, it can be more inventive, it can change its plans more quickly and behave more radically, its lines of communication are shorter.

It can be seen that, in a pitched battle where neither side has any other advantage, a force ten times larger will inevitably prevail. But it is not inevitable that there will be no other advantage.

10.16. When the common soldiers are too strong and their officers too weak, the result is insubordination. When the officers are too strong and the common soldiers too weak, the result is collapse.

Every campaign must have a leader. He must be able to control his team and to ensure that the team will follow instructions. While they must be allowed some freedom, it must be within acceptable boundaries otherwise indiscipline and insubordination follows and the team will not perform properly. But a leader must also have regard to the needs of his men, ensuring that they have rest, sustenance and that they are well chosen for their abilities. If any of these three are not met, then the team is enfeebled and will collapse.

In litigation, this translates to ensuring that the team is literally fed and rested - far too many litigators, especially advocates, work through the night, or nearly so, under pressure because they are not properly resourced with sufficient or sufficiently competent manpower or time.

As usual, we must remember the basis of a win is always, at its heart, the same: preparation, preparation, preparation.

There is another dimension to this principle: that there is little point in having brilliant leaders if the support staff are inadequate. The leader's grand designs will fail if those who are required to implement them are of insufficient quality to do so.

10.17. When the higher officers are angry and insubordinate and on meeting the enemy give battle on their own account from a feeling of resentment, before the commander-in-chief can tell whether or no he is in a position to fight, the result is ruin.

Sun Tzu says that a where senior staff are frustrated because the litigation partner is holding off from action that they want to take, if they take matters into their own hands and act instead of awaiting instructions, the action will fail.

10.18. When the general is weak and without authority; when his orders are not clear and distinct; when there are no fixed duties assigned to officers and men and the ranks are formed in a slovenly haphazard manner, the result is utter disorganisation.

A weak leader is a liability. The weakness may relate to discipline but in the context of this principle, it relates to a weakness of intellect, plan or will.

The weak leader does not know what to do, he cannot command his forces, such commands as he does give are not clear and there is a general loss of respect with the result that the entire case preparation turns into a muddle as people do, individually, what they think is best.

The result is, in polite terms, said to be disorganisation. Less politely, it's a failure waiting to happen.

To bring such a mess back from chaos to be a properly formed case is not easy and it is not cheap. The costs of fixing it should not fall upon the client but will often do so with nebu-lous billing items.

That is both unfair to the client and, arguably, unprofes-sional. It is also, arguably, fraudulent billing.

Given the serious consequences of such allegations, it is important that firms recognise the limitations of partners and assign them to functions they are competent to perform, even if that means, during the conduct of a case, the are subservient to a more able litigator who holds a more junior position in the firm.

In short, the firm should ensure that each task is assigned to the best man or woman for the job and that ego plays no part in that decision making.

10.19. When a general, unable to estimate the enemy's strength, allows an inferior force to engage a larger one, or hurls a weak detachment against a powerful one and neg-lects to place picked soldiers in the front rank, the result must be rout.

In another example of the "he who fails to plan, plans to fail" mantra, Sun Tzu says that to face down a large force with a small one because of a lack of intelligence, or sends in a weak advocate to against a strong one or even fails to put the best members of the team into the correct roles is to ensure not merely a loss but an epic fail.

Cross refer this to the very first principles: choose the team carefully right at the outset.

10.20. These are the six ways of courting defeat, which must be carefully noted by the general who has attained a responsible post.

10.21. The natural formation of the country is the soldier's best ally; but a power of estimating the adversary, of controlling the forces of victory and of shrewdly calculating difficulties, dangers and distances, constitutes the test of a great general.

Knowing stuff is good but that's ordinary and it's the role of the support team. To win, the leader must be capable of taking a helicopter view of the entire case, including the strengths and weaknesses of the case and team on both sides, of the issues involved in preparing and prosecuting the case because that's his function, not the day to day grunt work which he must, nevertheless supervise and approve.

10.22. He who knows these things and in fighting puts his knowledge into practice will win his battles. He who knows them not, nor practices them, will surely be defeated.

Read, learn and inwardly digest this principle. An absentee leader, one who delegates without maintaining both knowledge and command, should expect to lose.

10.23. If fighting is sure to result in victory, then you must fight, even though the ruler forbid it; if fighting will not result in victory, then you must not fight even at the ruler's bidding.

Once more, Sun Tzu returns to his theme that, once the objectives have been set by the client, the means by which those objectives are reached should be in the discretion of the litigator.

What the litigator should not do is fail to take a point that will secure an advantage only because the client says not to take it; similarly, he should not take a point that will deliver no advantage only because the client says to take it.

The first circumstance is unusual; the second is common where clients wish to cause embarrassment or other harm to the other party beyond the likely result of the case. For example, a client may not be satisfied with being awarded damages: he might insist that the case is presented in such a way that his opponent's reputation is destroyed. This is not a course of action that a litigator should be involved in.

10.24. The general who advances without coveting fame and retreats without fearing disgrace, whose only thought is to protect his country and do good service for his sovereign is the jewel of the kingdom.

A litigator should seek victory for his client, not fame for himself. That is the essence of professionalism.

10.25. Regard your soldiers as your children and they will follow you into the deepest valleys; look upon them as your own beloved sons and they will stand by you even unto death.

Sun Tzu's graphic sentimentality is somewhat out of character for him. But his idea is simple: treat one's team well and that will engender such loyalty that the team will be more supportive than one that feels neglected, used and abused. However, as he says in the next principle, it is possible to treat them too well and that leads to a lack of discipline and, ultimately failure.

10.26. If, however, you are indulgent, but unable to make your authority felt; kind-hearted, but unable to enforce your commands; and incapable, moreover, of quelling disorder: then your soldiers must be likened to spoilt children; they are useless for any practical purpose.

10.27. If we know that our own men are in a condition to attack, but are unaware that the enemy is not open to attack, we have gone only halfway towards victory.

10.28. If we know that the enemy is open to attack, but are unaware that our own men are not in a condition to attack, we have gone only halfway towards victory.

10.29. If we know that the enemy is open to attack and also know that our men are in a condition to attack, but are unaware that the nature of the ground makes fighting impracticable, we have still gone only halfway towards victory.

Sun Tzu argues that there is no point in preparing for battle only to find out that there are no places at which an attack can be mounted.

Similarly, it is a failing to discover that there is a place to attack but that we are not ready.

Finally, knowing we are ready and so is our opponent is insufficient if the battleground is not ready.

As so often, Sun Tzu is labouring the twin points of preparation and intelligence gathering.

In each of principles 27, 28 and 29 he talks of "going halfway towards victory." That means that all the expenses of preparing for battle have been met but that without actual battle ensuing, much of that expense will have been wasted.

10.30. Hence the experienced soldier, once in motion, is never bewildered; once he has broken camp, he is never at a loss.

Once the trial is under way, let nothing hinder it; allow no surprises to derail it.

Expect surprises and be prepared to deal with whatever the other side - or the Court - throws at you.

10.31. Hence the saying: If you know the enemy and know yourself, your victory will not stand in doubt; if you know Heaven and know Earth, you may make your victory complete.

So, know your own case and team, know your opponent's team and his evidence and understand the court. In that way, surprises can be kept to a minimum, your strategy can be made to play out and victory, not only at trial but also in enforcing the orders is more likely.

Liberty lies in the hearts of men
and women; when it dies there,
no constitution, no law, no court
can save it.

Billings Learned Hand
US Judge

11. The Nine Situations

11. The Nine Situations

11.1. Sun Tzu said: The art of war recognizes nine varieties of ground:

(1) dispersive ground;

(2) facile ground;

(3) contentious ground;

(4) open ground;

(5) ground of intersecting highways;

(6) serious ground;

(7) difficult ground;

(8) hemmed-in ground;

(9) desperate ground.

11.2. When a chieftain is fighting in his own territory, it is dispersive ground.

Several commentators have interpreted this principle as saying that a battle fought on home ground may be lost because soldiers retire at the end of each day's battle to see their families or, even, to wander off in the middle of a battle to see to their families' welfare or - at its simplest - for a break or to hide. Some say that, if the soldiers know the ground, they will scatter.

There is some merit in this when a hearing is conducted in a home court: it is easy to become distracted by things happening in the office. It is easy to dash back during breaks or to have documents, etc. delivered to the court and tempting to work on them while a hearing is actually in progress.

The less diligent support staff may head for a favourite restaurant during lunch or a favourite tea shop during a break - and be late back. After court ends, under the pretext of a post-mortem on the day's activity, they may retire to a favourite wine bar. Therefore, even though there are definite "home court" advantages, there are also aspects of it that require attention and discipline to ensure that not only the present case is not compromised but also other cases which members of the team are handling.

11.3. When he has penetrated into hostile territory, but to no great distance, it is facile ground.

Some commentators take the view that Sun Tzu is here saying that a commander should cut of his own lines of retreat once he has entered enemy territory in part to prevent desertion but also to make the point to his men that he has no intention of turning back.

They interpret the term "facile" as meaning somewhere that is still within striking distance of home, both physically and emotionally.

In the context of a trial, I would argue that these interpretations should be modified to say that the move onto hostile ground should be undertaken with a show of force and intent making it clear to all concerned, including one's own team, that battle will be joined, that there will be no surrender and no quarter.

11.4. Ground the possession of which imports great advantage to either side is contentious ground.

Of course, setting out to make a show of force might be nothing more than bravado. Sun Tzu's "contentious ground" relates to where one side is significantly stronger than the other. In our terms, that would be where there is an obvious imbalance of evidence, although one has to wonder why, if there is such an imbalance, the case comes to trial at all. An early settlement would be in everyone's interests.

"Contentious ground" should, perhaps, be read as meaning "ground in contention" i.e. the land that is both being fought over and in.

11.5. Ground on which each side has liberty of movement is open ground.

Open ground is that which allows free ingress and egress: in short, neither side is able to contain the freedom of movement of the other.

In litigation, this is the opening phase of a trial: neither side has, generally, gained any advantage although that is, of course, the point of opening speeches. But, unless and until any pre-trial applications are determined and the first evidence is given, there is almost total flexibility of each side to deliver whatever strategy the litigator has chosen. In short, he may keep his options open until evidence commences.

11.6. Ground which forms the key to three contiguous states, so that he who occupies it first has most of the Empire at his command, is a ground of intersecting highways.

Once the trial starts, the freedom of movement is curtailed and although there may be multiple paths available, once the paths are set, moving between them will be difficult. Therefore, once the in-trial strategy is set and commenced upon, it will be difficult to "change horses midstream."

In part, this is because the development of some strategies will, in fact, involve burning some bridges, preventing a retreat. In short, once given in evidence a statement cannot be unsaid. Therefore the evidence as presented is a step along the highway that that strategy represents.

It is for this reason that the final choice of strategy must be made very carefully.

11.7. When an army has penetrated into the heart of a hostile country, leaving a number of fortified cities in its rear, it is serious ground.

Once moved forward and having defined the last point to which a fall-back is possible, as progress is made, armies will build fortifications to which they can fall back as an interim measure during a march forward if conditions become difficult or attacks too severe.

A fall-back position is not the same as a "plan B" or any other way of describing alternate plans. A fall-back position is a place to which retreat can be made to a point of safety or, at least, strength.

In litigation, this is done by the marking of certain pieces of evidence as key, pieces that cannot be questioned or undone.

For example:

- the body of a person was found in the park.

- Scientific evidence shows that he died somewhere else and was transported to the park.

- The body has a severe injury to the head.

- The conclusion is that he was murdered several hours before being left in the park.

The facts are that the remains of a human were found in the park. Everything else is an opinion. It may be an opinion by a highly respected authority, but it is nevertheless an opinion. It may be supported by scientific information but that information is not "evidence:" it is a probability. It may be a very high probability, but it is nevertheless a probability. He may have an injury to the head which medical opinion says would have rendered him incapable of locomotion, but it is an opinion.

Say, for example, that he was the pillion rider on a motorcycle, riding without a helmet and sitting higher than the rider who went under a tree branch that hit the passenger and knocked him off. Realising his friend was dead and knowing that riding his bike in the park was an offence, the rider simply kept going.

For sure, there are legal aspects to the conduct that would render the rider culpable but those circumstances do not meet the basic tests for murder.

Therefore, the fall-back position - the equivalent of the fortified cities in Sun Tzu's principle for the prosecution is that a body was found at x position and that it had suffered head trauma. Those facts are incontrovertible. Beyond that, it is a matter of satisfying a jury as to whether the opinion of the various experts is enough to knock out the version of events as put forward by a defendant.

11.8. Mountain forests, rugged steeps, marshes and fens – all country that is hard to traverse: this is difficult ground.

It is a long established strategy to take steps to bog down one's opponent. The idea is to make him use time, resources and intellect in trying to wade through information as if his wellington boots are being sucked into the mud as he tries to walk.

This is where Sun Tzu's strategies of diversion are, perhaps, most readily seen at trial: by causing confusion in the mind of one's opponent while creating clarity in the minds of the arbiters of fact is a highly successful approach to a trial. It is also very difficult to pull off.

One's opponent is supposed to be able to work out where the case is going. A Judge should, with his legal training, also have a good idea of what is happening. A jury, on the other hand, is - or at least should be - novices and a strategy that jumps from one point to another is like driving on a highway when cars swing from lane to lane without obvious reason or signals. It can be seen, then, that by creating difficult ground for one's opponent, it can create annoyance and therefore alienation in the jury.

There is another way of looking at this principle: that it is inadvisable to create a path that is difficult to follow for the jury. There is much truth in that, as discussed above.

11.9. Ground which is reached through narrow gorges and from which we can only retire by tortuous paths, so that a small number of the enemy would suffice to crush a large body of our men: this is hemmed in ground.

In financial crime cases, the defendant always has an advantage. This is because he has nothing to prove: he has only to prevent the prosecutor proving his case beyond all reasonable doubt. The ultimate defence is, simply, "prove it."

The more complex the case - and financial crime cases are often presented in a very complex manner - the easier it is for the defendant to say to the jury "Do you understand that? I don't, I didn't and therefore I didn't know I was doing wrong." No mens rea, no criminal intent, no crime. Defence wins.

But he doesn't even need to go that far, he doesn't need to raise questions of intent. All he needs to do is to bury the jury in a morass of numerical data, statistics, movement of money between bank accounts, piles of documents including payment authorities, etc.

Oh, wait, that's not what the defence does: it's what the prosecution does in a financial crime case and, in doing so, makes the defendant's life much easier.

The route presented by the prosecution is tortuous. It is easy for the defence to make skirmish attacks on it, to undermine a small amount of the evidence and thereby to undermine the credibility of the whole case.

In short, the prosecution hems itself in by the presentation of a highly complex case when, in fact, in many financial crime cases, a conviction is more likely to be secured by adopting the "less is more" approach.

There is no rule that says that a prosecutor must charge all possible offences, there is no rule that says that he must proceed with all charges and there is no rule that says he must present evidence that does not aid the progress of the case before the Court. When a witness gives and oath to give the whole truth, it means the whole truth as it relates to the charges. It does not require him to say anything relating to matters not before the Court.

In the American case in which the Holy Land Foundation for Relief and Development, a charity, was prosecuted for support of Palestinian group HAMAS, the trial became so complex that the jury could not follow it and (much to the annoyance of the US government) delivered acquittals on some charges and became deadlocked on others. A second trial followed in which the number of charges was dramatically reduced and on that occasion, the jury came to the decision that the US government wanted, albeit in highly dubious circumstances.

See BankingInsuranceSecurities.com for the full stories:

Trials: confusion reigns in US case

23 October 2007

A copy of the jury's verdict form is at
http://bankinginsurancesecurities.com/content/download/2
4363/214620/file/hlf_ver-1.pdf

Sanctions: new Holy Land Foundation trial ends with predictable results

25 November 2008

For the sake of completeness, it should be noted that the following sentences were handed down:

Ghassan Elashi: 65 years for support of Hamas, money laundering and tax fraud.

Shukri Abu Baker: 65 years for support of Hamas, money laundering and tax fraud.

Mufid Abdulqader: 20 years for conspiracy to provide material support to a foreign terrorist organization; conspiracy to provide funds, goods and services to a specially designated terrorist; and conspiracy to commit money laundering.

Abdulrahman Odeh: 15 years for conspiracy to provide material support to a foreign terrorist organization; conspiracy to provide funds, goods and services to a specially designated terrorist; and conspiracy to commit money laundering.

Mohammad El-Mezain: 15 years for providing material support to Hamas.

All defendants appealed their convictions and on 7 December 2011, all appeals were dismissed. The grounds of appeal were that the use of anonymous witnesses and other issues prevented a fair trial.

Judge Carolyn Dineen King of the Fifth Circuit said ""While no trial is perfect, this one included, we conclude from our review of the record, briefs and oral argument, that the defendants were fairly convicted. For the reasons explained below, therefore, we affirm the district court's judgments of conviction of the individual defendants. We dismiss the appeal of the Holy Land Foundation for Relief and Development."

The full appeals judgment is at www.scribd.com/doc/75019312/Holy-Land-Convictions-Affirmed-by-Fifth-Circuit

A Dallas newspaperhas published the full appeals documents at http://crimeblog.dallasnews.com/2010/11/secret-israeli-witnesses-lack.html/.

Amazingly, the basis of appeals was that the defendants were prejudiced because their lawyer withdrew, leaving them without representation and that the anonymity afforded to the Israeli witnesses did not afford the defendant the opportunity for cross-examination. What was not, it appears, pleaded was that the original jury had found the defendants not guilty but then were exposed to outside influences for a period of time during which a sufficient number changed their minds so as to force a hung jury.

The case demonstrates points made earlier: that there are prejudices that will be applied - and not only by the jury. It also proves that some litigators do not take all points available to them. Finally and specifically relating to this principle, it shows that, in order to increase the prospect of securing convictions in the second trial, the prosecution greatly simplified the issues before the jury.

11.10. Ground on which we can only be saved from destruction by fighting without delay, is desperate ground.

Sun Tzu describes as "desperate ground" that which is all but lost and in which what we, in modern terms, would call desperate measures are needed in order to prevent that loss.

In Sun Tzu's world, this means an all-out assault or a full-blooded defence with no quarter given or expected.

In litigation, this point is reached when the evidence is stacked up against us.

When retreat is cut off, when the fall-back positions cannot be reached and when one's opponent can wound us without a significant chance that we will have sufficient ammunition or even will to fight back, we must muster all our available strength in a do-or-die effort.

It is at this point that we throw caution to the wind and use every tactic and argument we can think of, even those that have little chance of success.

We must take every point, striving to undermine each and every aspect of the other side's case.

In a criminal trial over a small matter, when cases were presented by police officers, I knew that my client's prospects of success were at best slim: his defence was simple - he did not commit the offence. However, there was strong circumstantial evidence against him and although he had not admitted the offence in interview, he had been very unclear in what he had told the investigating officer. He was regarded as evasive when in fact the real problem was that he was not very bright. I had no alternative but for him to give evidence so that he could repeat his denial, knowing that in cross-examination the very experienced police officer would appear to dismantle his denial, in part simply by confusing him and causing him to look untrustworthy.

My strategy was, therefore, simple: I had to disrupt the cross-examination.

I therefore challenged every question, arguing that the question was not clear, that it was not in fact a question, that the question did not seek to elicit facts but was phrased in a way designed to prejudice and any other argument I could think of. After some time, my client had not had to answer even a single question during cross-examination. The officer looked at me, then at the Magistrates. He said, in effect, "I can't do this: if I can't ask questions, I can't cross-examine." And with that he sat down. Defeated, he did not challenge my single question in re-examination: did the defendant do the act complained of? "No, sir," he said.

I won. The simple denial and the failure to elicit any supporting evidence to damn the defendant from his own mouth was sufficient to enable me to demonstrate that the evidence that had been presented was merely circumstantial and that the prosecution had not, therefore, made out its case.

It was brutal, effective and desperate and, had the Court considered my harassment of my opponent to be inappropriate, a high-risk strategy. I was aided by the fact that the Magistrates were not legally trained and therefore unsure as to where the lines were as to what questioning was permissible, sure that because of the way I speak, the way I dress and the confidence I exude would encourage them to lean in favour of my interpretation: the police officer, like many officers of the day, was not so well spoken, dressed like an ageing detective and did not expect such an all-out attack so he was taken by surprise which undermined his own confidence and, therefore, ironically, made his own case look shaky when that had been his intention with regard to my client.

Sun Tzu summaries the above as follows:

11.11. On dispersive ground, therefore, fight not. On facile ground, halt not. On contentious ground, attack not.

11.12. On open ground, do not try to block the enemy's way. On the ground of intersecting highways, join hands with your allies.

11.13. On serious ground, gather in plunder. In difficult ground, keep steadily on the march.

11.14. On hemmed-in ground, resort to stratagem. On desperate ground, fight.

The three principles following are grouped together.

11.15. Those who were called skilful leaders of old knew how
to drive a wedge between the enemy's front and rear; to prevent co-operation between his large and small divisions; to hinder the good troops from rescuing the bad, the officers from rallying their men.

11.16. When the enemy's men were united, they managed to keep them in disorder.

11.17. When it was to their advantage, they made a forward move; when otherwise, they stopped still.

Sun Tzu advocates the long-established principle of divide and conquer. Where forces are disassociated from their commander and divisions from each other, chaos can be engendered. Therefore by preventing the rear-guard supporting the vanguard, or the vanguard returning to aid the rear-guard, or by keeping two flanks busy so that neither can aid the other, an advantage can be gained.

It is not a difficult concept but it can be difficult to execute because, although harassment and skirmishing can be distracting, to fully execute this strategy, there must be a greater strength in the attacker.

After all, if the party under attack has followed the principles in this book, he will know not to be tricked into assuming that a skirmishing group is a precursor to an all out attack and therefore fortify that front and, in doing so, weaken other places which may, in fact, be the real target.

Sun Tzu, advising attackers, says to use skirmishes to distract and taunt the defence.

And so it is in litigation: small applications, before and during the trial, can disrupt the flow of a case and that disruption can, of itself, lead a jury to lose something of the understanding they have built up. It is the challenge of the party holding the centre ground to ensure that such regular, small-scale, attacks do not divert his attention - and therefore that of the jury - from important point that was being made.

11.18. If asked how to cope with a great host of the enemy in orderly array and on the point of marching to the attack, I should say: "Begin by seizing something which your opponent holds dear; then he will be amenable to your will."

Do not kidnap the opposing advocate's wife or steal his laptop from his desk. While Sun Tzu would, no doubt, have considered such tactics not only acceptable but, in appropriate circumstances, actively desirable, they are not so in litigation.

So how can we apply this principle?

Again, we return to playing the man not the ball: if the advocate is proud of his reputation of delivering killer opening speeches, then disrupt it. Ignore convention: it is only by common practice (and the preferences of some judges) that such speeches are not interrupted - there is nothing in the Rules of Court or the Conduct of Advocates that requires one advocate to sit in silence giving his opponent a free run to make statements and to editorialise in a way that would result in the jury starting off with a prejudice. And, once his speech is done, then re-run it in one's own opening speech, gradually knocking down each of the firm statements he had put forward.

While he may not, as Sun Tzu says, become amenable to your will, he will know that, if he is to be successful in his devious behaviour, he is going have to be a lot more subtle and a lot more clever. The danger with that is that the jury don't see the subtlety and, once more, it must be be knocked down.

11.19. Rapidity is the essence of war.

Hit the ground running. Far too many advocates like to break a case in gently. I was once told that, in a magistrate's court, it is necessary to make every point three times: once to introduce it, once to drive it home and once so that even magistrates can understand it.

I never found that necessary. By making each point early and forcefully, I was able to ensure that the magistrates had very little opportunity to form a view that was prejudicial to my case. When appearing before Judges, there was an even more important reason not to waste the Court's time being unduly repetitious: although it is true that not all judges are especially bright, it is true that most are not stupid (I exclude those jurisdictions where the judiciary is an elected, political, position where stupidity does seem rather more common).

Having gained some momentum, it is vital that it is not lost. When a point is clearly made, move on quickly to a point that reinforces it, or that causes additional harm to one's opponent's case.

Think of it like a racing driver overtaking : as soon as he passes, he cuts in front of the car he has just passed, causing the other driver to lose momentum, perhaps because he has to reduce power slightly in order to reduce the risk of collision with a car that is, suddenly, on the piece of track he expected to use. Even in a more powerful car, he will struggle to make up what he has lost, giving the driver that had overtaken not only the place but also some breathing space.

In advocacy, there is a similar argument: once the point is made, move on. That leaves one's opponent struggling to fix the point that has just been made and struggling to catch up with the next point. Don't worry about the jury: they don't know about the drama: they will keep up.

11.20. The following are the principles to be observed by an invading force: the further you penetrate into a country, the greater will be the solidarity of your troops and thus the defenders will not prevail against you.

11.21. Make forays in fertile country in order to supply your army with food.

11.22. Carefully study the well-being of your men and do not overtax them. Concentrate your energy and hoard your strength. Keep your army continually on the move and devise unfathomable plans.

11.23. Throw your soldiers into positions whence there is no escape and they will prefer death to flight. If they will face death, there is nothing they may not achieve. Officers and men alike will put forth their uttermost strength.

11.24. Soldiers when in desperate straits lose the sense of fear. If there is no place of refuge, they will stand firm. If they are in hostile country, they will show a stubborn front. If there is no help for it, they will fight hard.

11.25. Thus, without waiting to be marshalled, the soldiers will be constantly on the qui vive; without waiting to be asked, they will do your will; without restrictions, they will be faithful; without giving orders, they can be trusted. .

Principles 20-25 are repeated from elsewhere and have been commented on there.

11.26. Prohibit the taking of omens and do away with super-stitious doubts. Then, until death itself comes, no calamity need be feared.

Talismans of one kind or another are legion and often secret. Lucky socks or underpants, a special order for putting on one's robes, a particular tie or the way it is knotted, favourite cufflinks, a style, perhaps even a colour, of suit are normal. A quick kiss and "good luck" from a spouse or a hug from the kids are commonplace. Even carrying an old briefcase, battered beyond recognition but a testament to all that has gone before, is often seen being carried into Court. Everyone has something.

Talismans are not only good luck charms: they are symbols of faith and not necessarily faith in a religious sense. A wedding ring might be seen by some as a form of brand but for many others it is seen as a sign that one's spouse is always there, giving support even when far away. The same might be said for someone who always wears a watch given to him by someone special.

Rituals are also important: some may choose to predict the way the day is going by playing the card game patience on their computer. Some may always go to the toilet before going into court, always standing at the last urinal and washing his hands in the middle basin.

These things are all to do with confidence and comfort, they are part of the self. It is noticeable that the best performers in Court are often those who take care over their appearance. They approach advocacy in a holistic way: emotionally, intellectually and physically. When they walk into court, they already believe in their ability to win.

Sun Tzu says to take away all of those things from one's own men. I have to disagree. They are the things, from the "advocate's strut" to the timbre of the voice, that generate the complete advocate.

By definition, then, it follows that to take away some of those things from one's opponent undermines his confidence in himself.

And that is Sun Tzu's point: if something can be taken away, then it is best if it is taken away by one's own side before battle is joined.

But if it is something that cannot be taken away, then I would say leave it alone.

And if anyone tries to steal an advocate's lucky underpants, then that is, really, trying a bit too hard.

But there is one significant aspect to Sun Tzu's principle that is worthy of comment.

In a criminal case that I was watching, not taking part in, a witness who was supposed to be putting up bail for her son, could not evidence how she would fund the bail if he absconded. Her son's legal team had not bothered to ask those questions before she went into the witness box. The magistrate asked where the money would come from. She said "God will provide." Counsel said "Oh, I see," and looked at the Magistrate. Repeated attempts to rephrase the question, to elicit a source of funds or some form of security were met with the same answer from the witness and the same response from counsel. With each of his "Oh, I see"'s, the Magistrate looked at the barrister with increasing bemusement.

He did not see. And worse, he had not foreseen. And after a while, the other advocates in the room (which had filled up because the jungle drums had beat out that something bizarre was happening and those hanging around in the corridors had come to watch) could not contain their laughter. But in the context of this principle, it is the witness's responses that were more important.

She was not prepared for the questions and even less prepared to give answers. And so she relied on a presumption that God (who clearly was not taking especially good care of her son) would come good for them.

She is not the only one who has that approach in Court. Advocates who turn up, trusting in God or some other force to help them present a poorly prepared case or even parties who go to Court thinking that there will be some kind of divine intervention are, generally, doomed to fail.

It's true: crazy, rogue, decisions do happen against the weight of the evidence and despite disparity in the skill of the advocates but it is something of a leap to consider them truly miracles.

I am not decrying anyone's beliefs, nor denying miracles. I am saying that to put one's trust in a "God willing" attitude is misplaced. There's a saying that God helps those who help themselves. That means that God gives support to those who want to address their own problems but he does not solve their problems for them.

By all means, take faith into the Courtroom: but do not rely on it to dig an advocate or a case out of a hole. Take strength from that faith, whatever it is, but remember that the events are shaped by those in the Courtroom.

11.27. If our soldiers are not overburdened with money, it is not because they have a distaste for riches; if their lives are not unduly long, it is not because they are disinclined to longevity.

The commentators adopt an interpretation of this principle that is at odds with my own. They say that if soldiers fling away their money and lives it is through loyalty and a willingness to die for their king, not because they do not value wealth and life.

I interpret this very differently and perhaps more prosaically. I do not read it as a throwing away of that which they have but that they will fight even if the rewards and life are uncertain.

In this way, I see this principle as enshrining the professionalism of the litigator and advocate. It is his duty to work in the best interests of his client, even if there is a financial or reputational cost to him.

11.28. On the day they are ordered out to battle, your soldiers may weep, those sitting up bedewing their garments and those lying down letting the tears run down their cheeks. But let them once be brought to bay and they will display the courage of a Chu or a Kuei.

Stage fright is normal. But it evaporates when the adrenalin of the start of a trial takes over.

We all wonder if we have prepared enough, if there is something we have missed, if there is a hidden ambush, what are the consequences of losing, whether we have left the kettle on. There are a million and one uncertainties that crowd in during the moments before the Judge opens the door to his chambers. But by the time we have stood up and watched him walk to his chair, we enter "work mode."

The outside world is pushed away, the four walls of the Courtroom become our horizon, once the Judge is sitting, we have nowhere to retreat, nowhere to hide.

We must fight.

And that's when we switch and become the warriors that our clients pay us to become, the gladiators they expect us to be, the advocates who will rely on wit like a rapier and facts like a club. That is when we are litigators.

That is when we battle without fear, favour or fatigue and with the courage of combatants of ancient times.

That is when we become legen.....dary.

Maybe.

11.29. The skilful tactician may be likened to the shuai-jan. Now the shuai-jan is a snake that is found in the Ch`ang mountains. Strike at its head and you will be attacked by its tail; strike at its tail and you will be attacked by its head; strike at its middle and you will be attacked by head and tail both.

Shuai-jan is (probably) a mythical snake. Certainly, I and many others have been unable to find a specific reference to it as an actual creature. The word, itself, according to Giles, means "suddenly" or "rapidly" and he suggests that to call a snake by that name was to indicate its attack speed. Giles also argues that the term has become, in Chinese, a kind of short-hand for "military manœuvres".

Whatever the mythical position or its use in parable, the argument is obvious: while the presentation of a case may start at a given time and continue in a linear fashion through time, the case itself is spread in a horizontal fashion. So, if evidence is challenged at the point of presentation, it can be countered by evidence from another part of the case in rebuttal.

And Sun Tzu interpreted this in another way:

11.30. Asked if an army can be made to imitate the shuai-jan, I should answer, "yes." For the men of Wu and the men of Yueh are enemies; yet if they are crossing a river in the same boat and are caught by a storm, they will come to each other's assistance just as the left hand helps the right.

Some have translated this principle as something akin to "the enemy of my enemy is my friend." But that is an over-simplification.

It means that, to coin another phrase, adversity makes strange bedfellows.

There is an aspect of litigation that is common in the USA but rare elsewhere: that of allowing parties who have no direct interest in a case to file representations. It's called an "amicus curiae" or (slightly inaccurately) "amicus brief" and the name originates from the idea that someone, a "friend of the court" might have a valid opinion on certain matters but not on the evidence per se. It is often used by pressure groups to make their views known on matters that interest their members or by the government when it wishes to argue public policy. They are often used in appeals but are admissible only with the consent of all parties or if the Court grants a motion to admit them.

The representations are not evidence, they are not presented by a witness and are, therefore, not subject to cross-examination. They are supposed to be restricted to an opinion on matters that the parties have already raised (hence their use on appeal since at that point the arguments are, supposedly, set).

They are supposed to be independent of the parties and must include a statement that they have not, in whole or in part, been authored by counsel for any party.

The reason they are relevant here is that the pressure groups may often be, generally, in conflict with the party that, on the narrow point of the case, they support.

It is interesting that Sun Tzu used a phrase that has been in common use in English for some long time: when several people are suffering the same difficulty, we say that they are "in the same boat." It would be nice to think that Sun Tzu is the root of this phrase but it's impossible to tell.

11.31. Hence it is not enough to put one's trust in the tethering of horses and the burying of chariot wheels in the ground.

Referring back to the shuai-jan, this principle says, simply, that to stand immobile invites attack from multiple directions at once.

11.32. The principle on which to manage an army is set a level of courage to which all must aspire.

A chain is only as strong as its weakest link and if a member of the team is not pulling his weight, a tug of war is lost.

If you pick your way through my carefully juxtaposed mixed-metaphors, you'll get the point.

11.33. How to make the best of both strong and weak—that is a question involving the proper use of ground.

The tactician's interpretation of this principle is that a weak man in an easily defended position can hold for as long as a strong man on more vulnerable terrain.

How can we use that idea?

I would prefer to use a sideways leap, away from the obvious issue and to the question of the choice of advocate or, even, witness.

It is generally accepted that there is gender bias in the Courtroom. From the point of view of the advocate, in legal systems where robes are not worn, men dress in suits which are distinguished by their cut, colour and state of wear. For women, however the question of dress is a minefield. High shoes with slim heels? A little racy, perhaps?

A skirt and blouse: is a jacket necessary?

A dress: above or below the knee?

Cleavage: to show or not to show? To hint or not to hint?

Should clothes be formal and fitted or designed to fit the season: in short, can a summer dress, in a suitable colour, be acceptable?

Should she wear court (haha) shoes or are open toes or even sandals acceptable?

How would a jury view trousers and a jacket?

And all of this is before we even begin to consider hair and make-up.

Some lady advocates feel the need to power-dress, to show they can compete with the men. They almost ooze testosterone, they become aggressive in their treatment of witnesses and of their opponent.

Others like to appear (falsely, I might add) vulnerable, almost asking a jury to find for them because they are nice.

It is impossible to plan, in advance of the opening of the trial, the perfect approach. In a long trial, there is time to build a rapport with the jury, even with individual members by the judicious use of eye contact and an occasional smile or puzzled expression. In a short trial, there is little opportunity to develop those relationships.

Often, advocacy teams like to have women examine women, coloured advocates to examine coloured witnesses, for older counsel to examine older witnesses, for speeches to be made by someone with a racial, gender or other connection to the majority of the jury.

Whichever course is adopted, it is vital to keep an eye on the reaction of the jury. If a strident advocacy style irritates the jury, it must be ditched, even if it might be considered valuable to bait a witness.

The point of this principle, then, is that the advocate must tailor, or her, physical attributes and style of advocacy to suit the arbiters of fact and to ensure that the judge or jury is not alienated by a wrong choice and that, where multiple advocates are permitted, to use a carefully chosen advocate in different circumstances.

11.34. Thus the skilful general conducts his army just as though he were leading a single man, willy-nilly, by the hand.

A properly ordered team will operate as one, with no divisions and no squabbles, everyone knowing their function and exercising it without constant micro-supervision. The choice, by Giles, of the term "willy-nilly," is imprecise because the expression has two distinct uses which are almost diametrically opposed. The first means "willingly" and denotes full cooperation like a young child will grasp a parent's finger and follow along happily.

The second means in a completely haphazard manner or spontaneously. Clearly, this meaning is at odds with Sun Tzu's basic theory.

11.35. It is the business of a general to be quiet and thus ensure secrecy; upright and just and thus maintain order.

11.36. He must be able to mystify his officers and men by false reports and appearances and thus keep them in total ignorance.

It is difficult to find any application of principles 35 and 36 to the conduct of litigation. Some ancient commentators have said that it means little more than to ensure that there is sufficient information as to strategy revealed even to one's own team to enable the successful prosecution of the campaign but not so much that the plans may be, inadvertently, given away to the enemy.

Taken in that context, it is possible to see some merit in the approach but in general, it seems ill-advised for the team to be kept in the dark.

11.37. By altering his arrangements and changing his plans, he keeps the enemy without definite knowledge. By shifting his camp and taking circuitous routes, he prevents the enemy from anticipating his purpose.

Sun Tzu says that it is important to keep the enemy on the hop, not knowing what will happen next and certainly by using a variety of strategies.

This might include changing advocates, using different advocates for each examination so as to make sure that witnesses cannot be forewarned of the approach that will be taken.

But there is a risk: the jury might become confused by the very things that keep one's opponent uncertain. As with most things, pulling in one direction creates stresses in another, possibly unintended, direction.

11.38. At the critical moment, the leader of an army acts like one who has climbed up a height and then kicks away the ladder behind him. He carries his men deep into hostile territory before he shows his hand.

This is a mix of several previously discussed principles: to take the enemy by surprise, to arrive deep in his territory without warning, even to one's own men and then to cut off one's own lines of retreat so that the body of men fight because they cannot run.

Sun Tzu expands as follows:

11.39. He burns his boats and breaks his cooking-pots; like a shepherd driving a flock of sheep, he drives his men this way and that and nothing knows whither he is going.

In short, the army needs to know only what the objective is: it does not need to know in advance, the plans for achieving that objective. In litigation, in general, that is unsatisfactory.

11.40. To muster his host and bring it into danger:—this may be termed the business of the general.

The leader's job is to get his people ready for battle and put them into the fight.

11.41. The different measures suited to the nine varieties of ground; the expediency of aggressive or defensive tactics; and the fundamental laws of human nature: these are things that must most certainly be studied.

11.42. When invading hostile territory, the general principle is, that penetrating deeply brings cohesion; penetrating but a short way means dispersion.

Sun Tzu says that, once a campaign is started, it should be prosecuted to its end, or at least so far along that everyone knows that abandoning their positions, even temporarily, is not an option. Therefore there should not be pauses shortly after the action starts, much less during a trial. It is not only one's own team that will lose track - more importantly, so will the arbiters of fact.

The Courtroom is not like a Discovery Channel programme, where frequent summaries are made for those whose ability to concentrate is weak, or those programmes where advertising breaks are built into the script and a recap given for those who are challenged in their ability to remember what happened before their potty break.

Even the breaks that are necessary to aid concentration can lead to a juror forgetting or misremembering information and how it links to other things they have heard. There is no opportunity to start the day with a reminder of what happened the previous afternoon.

Where there is a longer break, there is a substantial risk of jurors and judges literally losing the plot.

Therefore, it is inherently undesirable to seek an adjournment, especially in the early stages of a long trial and if it is possible to find a way to fix whatever the adjournment would be needed for without breaking the trial, it should be taken.

11.43. When you leave your own country behind and take your army across neighbourhood territory, you find yourself on critical ground. When there are means of communication on all four sides, the ground is one of intersecting highways.

Note that the Nine Situations did not refer to "critical ground." This, then, is a tenth type of ground, lying before facile ground i.e. territory that is not one's own but which is not hostile. It may not actually be friendly, either.

*11.44. When you penetrate deeply into a country, it is seri-
ous ground. When you penetrate but a little way, it is facile
ground.*

*11.45. When you have the enemy's strongholds on your rear
and narrow passes in front, it is hemmed-in ground. When
there is no place of refuge at all, it is desperate ground.*

Principles 44 and 45 are considered in depth elsewhere.

*11.46. Therefore, on dispersive ground, I would inspire my
men with unity of purpose. On facile ground, I would see
that there is close connection between all parts of my army.*

This principle brings us back to the concept of Group
Think. Can group think be induced in the jury?

There are experiments that have proved that the herd
instinct or group-think can be induced. Indeed, a in popular TV
documentary series, Derren Brown has often demonstrated that
he can hypnotise groups of people. In one episode, Brown
arranged for volunteers to attend a cinema, ostensibly to watch
a free screening of a film. Using simple techniques, some 85%
of the audience fell into a trance and, on waking, believed they
had seen a film when in fact they had not. They all had found
the film hilariously funny but could not remember any detail.

Brown and others have found that extroverts are more sus-
ceptible to this form of control because they have a predisposi-
tion to wanting to immerse themselves in an experience; intro-
verts are less trusting and therefore think harder about what is
going on.

In other experiments, Brown displays that by adopting the techniques of surprise, diversion and confusion, he can very rapidly - within a second or two - hypnotise even those he meets walking down a busy street and that he can then implant thoughts of a course of action which the subject will carry out, either immediately or when some kind of trigger action occurs.

Clearly, one should not even consider such an action in Court, even if one had the skills.

But, regardless of whether you like the concept or the words or find them offensive or, in some cases, frightening, the simple fact is that presenting a case is, in fact, an exercise in controlling the thoughts of others.

In the introduction, I said that litigation is a mind game. We have looked at Sun Tzu's methods of introducing shock, awe and disarray. Elsewhere, I have emphasised that litigation is a battle for the hearts and minds of the arbiters of fact. At various points, I have discussed the ways that jurors, in particular, react to the conduct and speech of advocates. I have driven home the importance of making a connection with the arbiters of fact, to bring them to you.

So, without knowing it, you have already been introduced to the concepts of manipulating the arbiters of fact. And now you know it, you are either shocked or angry. Or confused.

So let's look at this in some more detail. Note, we are not going to look at the kind of mind-control techniques that result in a trance, but we are going to examine susceptibilities and environmental issues some techniques that would result in, metaphorically, the jurors walking across the Court to your side of the room.

First, let's look at the court room itself.

In a formal court, the room is laid out for the precise purpose of maintaining both physical and psychological distance between the protagonists. The number of jurisdictions in which advocates are allowed to wander around the room is tiny. And even in those jurisdictions were it is permitted, individual judges will often instruct advocates to remain in their places, not walk to physically confront a witness, not grandstand in front of the jury. *Boston Legal* is wonderful, but it's not how the vast majority of courts around the world operate; indeed it's not how many in the USA operate. Even in the USA, the "default setting" is that advocates must remain in their place unless they are given permission to walk about. In Texas and some US federal courts, advocates must remain not only in their place but also seated when questioning a witness unless express permission is granted. In some states, instead of remaining in their places, advocates use a common lectern as the place from where witnesses are examined. This is in complete contrast to the popular TV version of trial conduct and, in one of those nice inconsistencies that life throws up, one of the jurisdictions that commonly adopts the lectern is Massachusetts where, of course, *Boston Legal* is set.

The Judge sits on a bench that is elevated. This is for the single and sole purpose of creating a psychological distance between him and everyone else. Both literally and figuratively, everyone must "look up" to the Judge.

The jury, on the other hand, is on the same level as the parties - after all, by definition, they are the peers of the defendant in a criminal trial.

A judge is supposed to be able to be dispassionate, distant. He is supposed to be the embodiment of blind justice. That judges are, in fact, human and have preferences and prejudices detracts from that ideal, as does the fact that they have, even if they try to hide them, emotions.

While it would be nice to imagine that jurors can be equally dispassionate and focus only on the facts as presented in evidence, the reality is that they cannot.

And it's difficult to maintain eye contact with someone who is above you, especially if you have to refer to notes or exhibits: really, we would all look pretty stupid holding such things at shoulder height so as to avoid looking like those little nodding-head toys that were popular additions to the rear parcel shelf of cars in the 1960s, heads bobbing up and down between the Judges' faces and the documents.

Therefore, an attempt to engage a Judge or a panel of Judges on a human level is, by design and by training, much more challenging than to attempt to engage a jury.

But the layout of courtrooms militates against contact between an advocate and a jury. Indeed, in a traditional courtroom, the jury box is placed in such a way that the jury are observers not participants. One advocate will be seated closer to them than the other, obscuring him from the jury's view. The reason is simple: all evidence and speeches are presented to the Court. The jury is, in fact, intended to observe.

They are, in effect, secondary witnesses and they are expected to find in accordance not with what the witnesses saw and believe but what they, themselves see and believe.

In a criminal court, the prosecutor's seat will be set by custom and practice: arriving first does not give an advocate the choice of seat. In a civil action, it is less fixed but often there is a convention that the plaintiff will sit on one side or the other. To make matters worse, different court rooms within the same building may have different conventions.

In civil trials, without a jury, my personal preference was to sit on the right when in open court but on the left when in chambers if we faced the judge but on the right if his room was arranged with a T shape table. I have absolutely no idea why I had those preferences. Perhaps it was nothing more than my equivalent of lucky underpants.

For the advocate who is seated furthest from the jury, he is at a disadvantage simply because he cannot be so intimate with them. He cannot cast quizzical glances, he cannot flash a smile or a twinkling eye to draw attention to some part of the evidence.

So how can he draw the jury into his scheme. In short, how can he induce group think from a distance, especially if he is not able to address the jury directly?

First, whenever he stands, he should look at the Judge first and then look to the jury, making certain to look up and down their ranks, catching as many eyes as possible. He should not look stern. A smile, some kind of welcoming expression is essential.

Whenever he asks a question, the advocate should look at the witness but he should ensure that he speaks slowly and clearly so that the jury hear and understand the question just as well as the witness does. And when the witness answers, the advocate should look at the witness and, when the witness has answered, look at the jury. This has two purposes: first, if a juror is confused, it will usually show on his face immediately the answer is given. Where confusion is visible, a follow-up question should be considered so as to remove the juror's doubt (unless, of course, the purpose of the question was to engender doubt).

Advocates should not repeat a witness' answer. If it needs to be repeated, get the witness to do it. When the advocate does it, it sounds weak, as if the witness needs shoring up. And a weak witness is not believable. Therefore say to the witness "I'm sorry, I didn't catch that. Could you repeat it?" This is not a tactic to use frequently because it irritates Judges who know exactly what the advocate is doing and why.

So, if where the advocate sits or stands prevents the creation of rapport, how can it be achieved?

This is where presentation aids come in because their use can either be used to lecture (in which case they create distance) or to draw in each individual juror so that the advocate become the leader in the group think rather than the foreman.

Of course, gruesome photographs don't work. But to engage a witness in a discussion over a photograph or a document, holding a conversation with him rather than obviously examining him, and drawing the jury in with eye contact at strategic moments creates a sense of community.

The best opportunities for drawing in the jury are, of course, opening and closing speeches. It is here that the use of carefully chosen words and phrases have direct effect.

The most important techniques are suggestion and "anchoring."

Suggestion is where the jury is led to a specific conclusion by the use of words such as "when you heard x, that shows....." Even if a juror formed a different conclusion, the certainty of the words makes him reconsider.

Anchoring is tying that conclusion to the finding one wants. "When it was shown that ...., this leads to the conclusion that....." Again, the certainty of the phrasing creates a feeling in the mind of the juror that any other conclusion is in some way open to question and, in the most suggestible persons, that any other conclusion must be wrong.

Equally importantly, the wording remains buried in the minds of the jurors, waiting to compel his thoughts and even arguments in a particular way in the retiring room.

11.47. On contentious ground, I would hurry up my rear.

This is to combat "the devil take the hindmost." In terms of litigation, the principle means that all the parts of the case must progress together, that no aspect should be left behind. If part of the case is not fully prepared, then that is a weak spot that will, at some point, become open to attack.

11.48. On open ground, I would keep a vigilant eye on my defences On ground of intersecting highways, I would consolidate my alliances.

When there is calm, always be prepared for attack but use the quiet time to make sure that everyone is working together, that alliances with other parties are solid and that any possible divisions are resolved.

11.49. On serious ground, I would try to ensure a continuous stream of supplies. On difficult ground, I would keep pushing on along the road.

It is important to ensure that there are no breaks in the lines of communication. Witnesses should be contacted to make certain that they are prepared and that they remain "on message." And as one gets closer to trial, there should be a focus on preparation and ensuring that, when the trial starts, every aspect of the case reaches the same state of readiness and that there is no delay, in part because a battle-ready force becomes bored and loses interest if such delay arises. By increasing the speed of approach to battle, the team gels and functions as a single unit.

11.50. On hemmed-in ground, I would block any way of retreat. On desperate ground, I would proclaim to my soldiers the hopelessness of saving their lives.

Sun Tzu makes great play at several points of making certain that the team knows that, as one reaches trial, there is no turning back and that the trial is do-or-die. Principle 51 reinforces that message.

11.51. For it is the soldier's disposition to offer an obstinate resistance when surrounded, to fight hard when he cannot help himself and to obey promptly when he has fallen into danger.

11.52. We cannot enter into alliance with neighbouring princes until we are acquainted with their designs. We are not fit to lead an army on the march unless we are familiar with the face of the country—its mountains and forests, its pitfalls and precipices, its marshes and swamps. We shall be unable to turn natural advantages to account unless we make use of local guides.

Again, Sun Tzu repeats that in order to make a safe alliance, we must know the objectives of our partners and the ways they intend to secure them, as well as their ultimate aims. We must also know the hazards of trial and be sure of any local rules, customs and practices that may apply in the courtroom that may be different from those we are used to.

Be familiar with the terrain. When appearing in a Courtroom for the first time, I would go in and look around. I would know where I would be sitting and where the witnesses, other parties and even the press would be. I would do a basic sound test: standing in my own place and, later, in the witness box, I would click my fingers. That would give me an instant feel for the acoustics. Therefore I would have a baseline for how much I would need to project my voice and to make sure that I would be able to assist my witnesses, right at the beginning of their evidence, to pitch their responses so as to be audible to everyone from the Judge, through the Court Reporter to the back of the Court.

Then, so long as the Judge was not in Court, I would repeat the test from my own place when it was full, because people soak up sound and there would be a considerable difference in the room's acoustic values.

Whenever I was speaking, I would listen for the bounce-back from behind the Judge. Many courts built in the second half of the 20th century were designed with acoustic panels behind the Judge specifically to prevent bounce-back. Therefore, those behind me would have more difficulty in hearing what I said than those in front. Given that, in an English courtroom, those behind the advocate include his support team and his clients, it is essential that they can hear clearly.

If they cannot hear clearly, they talk amongst themselves as they try to work out what was said. That means they are not doing the job they are there to do and they cause a distraction to the advocate. And if the judge or a jury sees them chatting, irritation will ensue and irritating the arbiters of fact is not recommended. It is also distracting to witnesses who, in a natural state of mild paranoia, will wonder if they are talking about his evidence and whether he has said the wrong thing.

11.53. To ignore of any one of the following four or five principles does not befit a warlike prince.

11.54. When a warlike prince attacks a powerful state, his generalship shows itself in preventing the concentration of the enemy's forces. He overawes his opponents and their allies are prevented from joining against him.

Again, Sun Tzu says that, in order to secure defeat, it is necessary to divide one's opponents. In the context of litigation, it means to attack those parts of the evidence that can be most easily destroyed and thus to undermine the whole. It is also important to see what alliances the other side may be creating and to remove the co-operation wherever possible to reduce the overall power directed at his own case.

11.55. Hence he does not strive to ally himself with all and sundry, nor does he foster the power of other states. He carries out his own secret designs, keeping his antagonists in awe. Thus he is able to capture their cities and overthrow their kingdoms.

Even though he has alliances, the advocate must follow his own strategy and remain focussed on his own objectives. He must not become diverted by secondary issues that are for the benefit of others. For this reason he must choose his allies carefully and make sure that their objectives are in keeping with his own.

For example, in a case involving pollution of a river, there may be some common interests between fisheries and farmers but general conservationists, while having some objectives in common, may have a different agenda. The fishermen and farmers may want a polluting factory to ensure that no harmful chemicals find their way into the watercourse but a general conservationist may want the plant closed entirely. Where there are local jobs at risk, a court is less likely to order the total closure of the factory if a way can be found to prevent river pollution. Therefore, even though the conservationists' evidence may be supportive, it would reduce the prospects of success to press for their desired outcome.

56. Bestow rewards without regard to rule, issue orders without regard to previous arrangements and you will be able to handle a whole army as though you had to do with but a single man.

Sun Tzu argues for a firm and fair management of the team and its rewards for success in order to promote and maintain unity amongst the team and loyalty to the leader.

11.57. Confront your soldiers with the deed itself; never let them know your design. When the outlook is bright, bring it before their eyes; but tell them nothing when the situation is gloomy.

Sun Tzu says that the team should know the task in hand and what is required of them but not the entire strategy. He also argues for motivating them by delivering good news and concealing bad news.

This is a common management practice but in litigation it is impossible to do because of the need to keep the client

informed of the current risks so that he may review his instructions, including as to costs.

11.58. Place your army in deadly peril and it will survive; plunge it into desperate straits and it will come off in safety.

Sun Tzu uses extreme circumstances to draw attention to the fact that people, especially litigators, do not like losing and that, when defeat seems certain, they will strive even harder to secure a win. This clearly conflicts with principle 57.

11.59. For it is precisely when a force has fallen into harm's way that is capable of striking a blow for victory.

Always have a counter-strike ready. Sometimes this can be used in defence but also it can be used as an attack when an opponent, successful in, for example, an interlocutory application, is complacent or spent.

Some see this Principle as suggesting that desperate people do desperate things. But it is, perhaps, better seen as saying that a good commander, in the face of certain loss, will avoid a total rout and keep something in reserve for a counter-strike.

*11.60. Success in warfare is gained by carefully accommodat-
ing ourselves to the enemy's purpose.*

This principle again relates back to the idea of a feint, of creating a trap by appearing in a hopeless position to draw in the enemy and then to counter-attack with surprise and aggression.

In a trial, this may be accomplished by not taking every point during a cross-examination but rather allowing them to be unchallenged until one's own witnesses are in a position to deliver effective rebuttal evidence.

But there is also another point to be made: an advocate should know when to stop asking questions. It is often said that he should never ask a question if he does not know the answer. But that should be extended to "do not ask a question if you do not know how the witness will answer."

If a conclusion is to be drawn from the witness' answers, it is often not a good idea to put that conclusion to the witness and leave it open for him to undermine the effect of the admissions he has made.

We can demonstrate this with a very old joke:

The Master of Ready Wit and Repartee went to the circus where he was honoured with a ringside seat and pointed out to the audience to whom he gave a dramatic bow in response to their applause.

During the performance a clown came up and asked The Master of Ready Wit and Repartee "Are you the front end of an ass?"

The Master of Ready Wit and Repartee considered his answer carefully, but not for so long as to undermine his reputation for quick and pithy replies. "No," he said. The crowd applauded.

The clown faced him, deep in thought. "Then, Master, I ask you, are you the rear-end of an ass?"

The Master of Ready Wit and Repartee considered his detailed reply. The audience waited with bated breath, knowing that the Master was about to deliver a biting response. "No," he said. The crowd went wild.

The clown did not delay, he did not prepare, he jumped in with his final statement, a conclusion that would for ever demonstrate that he, the clown, had outwitted the pretender before him.

"Then you are no end of an ass," he said, triumphantly, looking around the audience, expecting a roar of approval, holding his arms aloft in a gesture of supreme success, certain that, any moment now, he would be accepted as the true and only Master.

The Master of Ready Wit and Repartee, true to his reputation, replied before the final sibilant had escaped the lips of the clown.

"Piss off," he said.

11.61. By persistently hanging on the enemy's flank, we shall eventually succeed in killing the commander-in-chief.

11.62. This is called ability to accomplish a thing by sheer cunning.

The idea here is never to let one's opponent rest, to always have some kind of surprise or application at hand. By harrying one's opponent, victory can be more readily achieved.

11.63. On the day that you take up your command, block the frontier passes, destroy the official tallies and stop the passage of all emissaries.

As soon as a litigator receives instructions, it must be clear that he is in charge. He must make the client understand that he must not communicate directly with the other side and he must also ensure that there is no unauthorised contact between members of his team and the other side.

As a practitioner, I would regularly find a member of the opposing team and when I needed to discuss something a little out of the ordinary, would use him, finding out information from him or even giving him information that I wanted to filter back. But I would also use him as a conduit for proposals or threats, knowing that, if he believed me, that his faith in his own judgement would act in my favour when he took the proposal to his boss or even his client.

Sun Tzu says that all such lines of communication should be blocked from the outset. But there are always holidays, days when the boss is in Court or other times that secondary lines of communication must be opened in order to prevent the action stagnating or the risk of a negligence action because something was left to await the boss' return to the office.

11.64. Be stern in the council-chamber, so that you may control the situation.

The client is king, remember? But he relies on the advice of the litigator. Even so, the litigator must not act on his own without instructions.

Therefore he must set out the options, explain their relative risks and merits and give clear and strong advice. He must ensure that he has clear, unequivocal instructions before embarking on the campaign or any part of it.

11.65. If the enemy leaves a door open, you must rush in.

Again, Sun Tzu says to prosecute the action with all vigour.

11.66. Forestall your opponent by seizing what he holds dear and subtly contrive to time his arrival on the ground.

11.67. Walk in the path defined by rule and accommodate yourself to the enemy until you can fight a decisive battle.

Avoid dangerous situations and remain in the open until it is time to join battle.

11.68. At first, then, exhibit the coyness of a maiden, until the enemy gives you an opening; afterwards emulate the rapidity of a running hare and it will be too late for the enemy to oppose you.

Ah, how sweet.

I have a very strict gun control policy:
if there's a gun around,
I want to be in control of it.

Clint Eastwood.
Actor, film director, politician.

12. The Attack by Fire

12. The Attack by Fire

12.1. Sun Tzu said: there are five ways of attacking with fire. The first is to burn soldiers in their camp;

the second is to burn stores;

the third is to burn baggage trains;

the fourth is to burn arsenals and magazines;

the fifth is to hurl dropping fire amongst the enemy.

12.2. In order to carry out an attack, we must have means available. The material for raising fire should always be kept in readiness.

Sun Tzu's meaning seems clear but the ancient commentators took a view that seems somewhat contrary, arguing that Sun Tzu means that, to set a fire within a camp, there must be infiltrators ready to act when instructions are received.

This is not so far away from the reality in some cases. It is widely known (and was accidentally confirmed in a conference in England some years ago) that the USA's CIA has placed agents within banks in London to gather intelligence.

The use of a paid - or pressured - informant is also common practice, even if that informant's evidence cannot be used in proceedings due to the rules of evidence or questions of the informant's safety.

And, of course, criminal gangs, newspapers and dodgy lawyers frequently pay policemen and others for information on investigations, criminal records or even information on car number plates, etc.

Each of these can be seen as infiltration and the information obtained can then be used to, in figurative terms, light a fire under one's opponent.

Sun Tzu dedicates a complete chapter to the use of spies. We'll get to that shortly.

12.3. There is a proper season for making attacks with fire and special days for starting a conflagration.

12.4. The proper season is when the weather is very dry; the special days are those when the moon is in the constellations of the Sieve, the Wall, the Wing or the Cross-bar; for these four are all days of rising wind.

It is, perhaps, ironic that Sun Tzu, having in the previous chapter said that all talismans and superstitions must be cast aside, now applies Chinese astrology to argue the ideal time for attack by fire. Remembering that Chinese and "western" astrology are based on the skies in the northern hemisphere, his comments are interesting in themselves.

His argument is based on the notion that there are "28 Mansions" in the constellation. The Wall is part of the northern sky and each of the other named days is in a separate quadrant. They are the days of the full moon.

Pagans believe that the full moon brings wind - especially the April moon.

It is established science that the full moon affects tides. The biggest effect is when the full moon and the sun's proximity combine which is in spring. That is why low-lying land is often flooded by tidal flows in spring and how rivers get seasonal "bores." The reason is simple: the greater gravitational pull created by those circumstances works on everything that isn't nailed down - and the thing that's least nailed down is water because its movement is relatively frictionless.

But what is also not nailed down is dust. In fact, studies on Mars have shown that its two moons create such a pull that there are frequent large dust storms which give the impression of there being wind which, Mars having very little "atmosphere," there is not.

Back on Earth, similar, but less spectacular, gravitational dust storms occur. They are less spectacular because the dust has to combat both air pressure and air density: unlike water moving in water, dust in air has to combat high levels of friction.

Remembering that Sun Tzu was engaged by an Emperor in the North, he would have been familiar with both the weather and the terrain. The far north of China, large parts of Mongolia and nearby is a huge desert: the Gobi. In winter, it is freezing, in summer it is baking. In spring, there are huge dust storms that carry hot dust south and coat large areas with dust. The dust storms are so big that NASA has captured images of thousands of square miles. One, from April 2012, is at http://earthobservatory.nasa.gov/NaturalHazards/view.php?id=77771

And with all of those storms and tidal movements comes wind.

Now I can hear you thinking: WTF is he talking about the moon and tides and wind and weather for?

Ancient religions and superstitions never go away: they just get recycled for a new audience. And the neat thing about ancient religions and superstitions is that, at their heart, they have basic truths.

And it doesn't matter if one talks about paganism, animalism, spiritualism Buddhism, Judaism, Hinduism, Taoism (or any other -ism) or Christianity, Islam or frankly any other belief system no matter if it's classified as a religion or not.

One of the non-religion belief systems is that of Feng Shui (pronounced "fung shoy" as in "troy").

Feng Shui is, in some ways, a branch of Chinese astrology. It interprets events based on the movement of the moon and the stars through the 28 mansions (which for those less disposed to grandiose terms are generally termed "houses").

And it is here that we see what Sun Tzu was really talking about: he was saying that the study of the moon and the stars will predict favourable conditions much more reliably, long term, than the study of the weather. Given that the Chinese publish calendars showing new moons for up to 4,000 years ahead, to plan when winds, rain and dust storms will provide super-dry, perhaps even pre-heated air, would aid a plan to set fire to an settlement built from wood or an encampment under canvas.

In litigation, then, Sun Tzu's principle can be applied to say that there are ideal times for undertaking certain actions and that, with careful study of all the available information, those times can be discerned.

In short, when the signs are favourable, attack with force and without delay; when they are not, prepare to defend or, rarely, wait until the signs become favourable.

12.5. In attacking with fire, one should be prepared to meet five possible developments: (principles 6 - 10)

12.6. When fire breaks out inside to enemy's camp, respond at once with an attack from without.

Attack by fire is designed to rely on our primal fear of fire and to cause panic and confusion, to break down discipline within the opposing force. Remember Sun Tzu's earlier exhortation to attack when the opposing force is in disarray. Here, fire is expected to cause such disarray in such a way that discipline cannot be readily restored.

Regardless of how it is started, a fire is an attack from within. It follows that both physical and emotional responses are to look inwards.

That means that there are unguarded or at least under-guarded points. A commander has a choice: battle the fire and risk the perimeter or assume that an attack will come and risk lives, stores and shelter.

12.7. If there is an outbreak of fire but the enemy's soldiers remain quiet, bide your time and do not attack.

Therefore, if all remains calm, it means that the opposing forces are either so strong that they could afford to deal with the fire and still maintain defences and/or that the opposing general recognised the risk of attack and his men are so well disciplined that the loss of their stores and shelter is less important than their defence of their positions. In either case, it means that a defence is expecting and prepared for an attack and therefore the attacker should hold off.

In litigation terms, if the plan was to cause a distraction by, say, an interrogatory and then to follow it up with an attack based on information secretly - but lawfully - obtained, but the other side is not distracted, then to use the information at that point would be a waste. It is better to keep it back until a more suitable opportunity can be generated or presents itself.

12.8. When the force of the flames has reached its height, follow it up with an attack, if that is practicable; if not, stay where you are.

Avoid premature action.

12.9. If it is possible to make an assault with fire from without, do not wait for it to break out within but deliver your attack at a favourable moment.

The previous principles have focussed on a fire started within the settlement or encampment. But Sun Tzu also considers fires that surround or can be driven towards the enemy.

A careful general will cut or burn away the combustible vegetation around his camp so preventing an opposing force from setting such a fire.

But in litigation, that is not possible. There is always something that is left out, something untidy, a nasty little secret that will undermine one's opponent's case or the advocate's confidence or the concentration of a witness. And it need not have anything to do with the case per se.

For example, a man wearing a wedding ring can be complimented on his cologne, with the comment that his girlfriend must be special because wives don't give that kind of scent.

There is no need to wait for a response: the harm is done by the comment. Either he is guilty and unsettled or not guilty and he's angry and unsettled. In fact, not waiting for a response and denying him the opportunity to deal with it, leaves him seething and therefore increases the effect.

A woman can be unsettled by complimenting her on her cross examination - then sympathising with her that her firm has never appointed a female litigation partner and that perhaps she should consider moving to conveyancing so as to improve her chances of partnership.

Fire can blaze and cause catastrophic results in a short time, but a smouldering fire can do as much harm in its own way.

12.10. When you start a fire, be to windward of it. Do not attack from the leeward.

A fireman is someone who runs into a burning building when everyone else is running away. Sun Tzu says follow the fire, not run into its path. If attackers run towards the fire then the defenders are trapped between the fire and the attack and that makes them desperate; however, if they are chased into defeat, they are demoralised.

In litigation, then, we can see this as a strategy for dealing with vulnerable evidence. If a fire can be started in such a way that the vulnerability is obscured and an opponent chased away from it, instead of back towards it, his defence of it will be weakened. However, push him back towards the vulnerable evidence and he will be forced to confront it. In that, he will stand and fight and he may, by forceful defence, convince the arbiters of fact that the evidence is stronger than it actually is.

But if, knowing it is weak, he is afforded the chance not to focus on it, to avoid drawing too much attention to it he will be grateful and stay away.

And so he will often gladly accept a fight offered on a point that both sides know he can win (that's racing away from the fire) and avoid the fight he knows he might lose (that's the forces chasing behind the flames).

In our terms, then, we should be looking to identify a place to start a fire that will both attract our opponent's attention and draw him away from a weakness in his own case.

Therefore, we may argue that an aircraft that crashed due to a fault in the fuel system with the result and push the evidence on the point of the design flaw. But we may keep in reserve knowledge that he manufacturer has not taken sufficient steps to ensure that it could not happen in the future. We may use that evidence in a surprise attack to raise the question of exemplary damages.

12.11. A wind that rises in the daytime lasts long but a night breeze soon falls.

In his own commentary, Giles admits to being baffled by the relevance of this point. That is surprising given his deep understanding of the history and culture of the work he was translating. In fact, it is quite literal and a logical follow up to the previous comment on the wind. In the North of China, in summer (winter wars were to be avoided whenever possible in the bleak mountainous region with little vegetation and few animals to eat to say nothing of extreme cold), the heat of the day generates hot winds, not unlike the Mistral in France and other parts of southern Europe. At night, as the earth cools, the winds die down.

And so, Sun Tzu is making it plain that, although a night-time fire looks more spectacular than one during the day, the heat of the day and the winds it creates make a daytime attack more effective than one at night.

In litigation the same is true. 15:59 hours, or one minute to four in the afternoon, is the key.

Where a specific number of days is set out in the Rules for service of documents, it is usual for the day of service to be included if service is before 4pm. Therefore, exactly 4pm is late.

As a result service of a three-day notice before 4pm on Monday expires on Thursday; service after 15:59 expires on Friday.

To recalculate in the opposite direction, if a hearing is set for Friday and three days' notice must be given, service at 15:59 on Tuesday is good service; service at 16:01 is not.

Therefore the cut-off time for putting one's opponent under maximum pressure is 15:59. And, in Sun Tzu's terms, that is lighting a fire and making sure that it burns hot, long and bright.

12.12. In every army, the five developments connected with fire must be known, the movements of the stars calculated and a watch kept for the proper days.

It's nice to know that even someone who professes to disapprove of talismans and suspicions nevertheless has some higher power he believes in. And that is said without a hint of sarcasm.

12.13. Hence those who use fire as an aid to the attack show intelligence; those who use water as an aid to the attack gain an accession of strength.

12.14. By means of water, an enemy may be intercepted, but not robbed of all his belongings.

Sun Tzu argues that fire is capable of immediate and significant destruction and disruption. But water, he says, can delay or divert an enemy but not destroy all of his stores, etc.

While that is not entirely true - a watercourse can be diverted so as to flood a low-lying encampment, for example - it is true that, for the most part, creating fire is much quicker, simpler and much less demanding on resources than to turn a large area of land into a water feature.

The creation of a wall of water of such size that it would sweep away a settlement or an encampment would be such a large civil engineering undertaking that it could not be kept secret, would be readily open to attack and afford the opposition time to move to higher ground. And a giant pond takes a long time to fill, also meaning that, in addition to the risk of counter-attack, the strategy might be defeated by the defending force constructing their own watercourse to prevent flooding.

The lesson for us is simple: in fact, it's Keep It Simple....

Complexity in the construction or presentation of a case almost always backfires. Identify the targets and hit them hard and fast then get out, as Sun Tzu repeatedly says, is the surest way to a win.

However, as noted above, for defendants in financial crime or civil fraud cases, their aim is exactly the opposite: it is to introduce as much complexity as possible so as to confuse the arbiters of fact so that they cannot form a strong opinion as to culpability or liability, as the case may be.

12.15. Unhappy is the fate of one who tries to win his battles and succeed in his attacks without cultivating the spirit of enterprise; for the result is waste of time and general stagnation.

12.16. Hence the saying: The enlightened ruler lays his plans well ahead; the good general cultivates his resources.

There are many different interpretations of these two principles by ancient commentators. I beg to differ from most of them: in my view, it means, simply, when a victory is won, convert it to a solid foundation by taking control of the situation, not sitting around eating, drinking and congratulating each other on a job well done.

A battle is like a punch: it must be followed through to have full effect. A punch that stops just as it connects, connects with reduced force.

Therefore, if an order is obtained for the freezing of assets, do not nip to the pub and have a swift half in a mutual back-slapping, high-fiving, fist-bumping display of success.

Get back to the office, get the orders prepared and served and publicised as fast as possible.

A worldwide freezing order is of no value if those holding assets are not aware of it.

What Sun Tzu is saying is that leaving the battlefield having knocked out the other side is a step on the way to victory because but the end result is not yet achieved.

In an action for pecuniary damages, garnishee a bank or other account immediately. In an action for delivery up of goods, have someone standing next to them immediately to ensure there is no waste or damage done out of spite.

A win isn't a win if the profits are not secured.

12.17. Move not unless you see an advantage; use not your troops unless there is something to be gained; fight not unless the position is critical.

12.19. If it is to your advantage, make a forward move; if not, stay where you are.

Principles 17 and 19 are grouped together here because they are the same. Giles says that he is "convinced" that principle 19 has been inserted by someone else later in the history of the document.

Whichever it is the fact is that both of these principles are repeats of things from elsewhere.

Simply, if you can't win, avoid a fight; if you can win, get on with it.

12.18. No ruler should put troops into the field merely to gratify his own spleen; no general should fight a battle simply out of pique.

Sun Tzu says one of the greatest truths of litigation and a great lesson to both litigator and clients.

For clients: just because you are angry or hurt doesn't mean you have a cause of action and, even if you do, it doesn't mean you have a winnable case. This is one of the most difficult things for many clients to accept. A good litigator will advise a client that a case is not worth pursuing.

For a litigator, he must learn not to get involved in squabbles just because he has been out- manoeuvred or irritated by his opponent.

But Sun Tzu goes further.

12.20. Anger may in time change to gladness; vexation may be succeeded by content.

This is almost spiritual, again. Sun Tzu is saying, in effect, to believe in balance, that the universe (or whatever) brings things into order.

But we must remember that he is a warrior, a general for hire at the behest of imperial monarchs who in many cases were themselves little more than warlords.

And so he was dealing with ruthless men who needed to show quick results.

This principle, then, is designed to invite his warlord sponsors to take stock before engaging in a long and costly war unless there were clear and obvious benefits. Revenge comes in many forms and often there is no need for direct intervention.

And a litigator who does not get into verbal fisticuffs over some slight that, in the great scheme of things, was really not very important is likely to live a long and happy life.

12.21. But a kingdom that has once been destroyed can never come again into being; nor can the dead ever be brought back to life.

If a client gambles everything on a win and fails, he can never restore his position. This is a lesson that many corporate managers seem unable or unwilling to learn, preferring to fight than to compromise or to commence litigation rather than see that the loss they wish to pursue is not worth fighting for.

Regrettably, the advent of no-win, no-fee litigation has increased the tendency of clients to become involved in litigation the primary purpose of which appears to be to, in effect, blackmail corporations into settling claims, particularly class action claims, that would never get off the ground if the plaintiffs were required to stump up costs on account prior to starting the action.

That puts defendant companies on the back foot: it's cheaper to settle than fight but the risk of harming their reputation by a public settlement is substantial.

This raises the important question of moral hazard in litigation: consider the propensity of parties to litigate when they have little or limited personal risk e.g. because of insurance, employer or other third party funded litigation or no-win, no-fee arrangements. As noted earlier, such actions undermine justice by compelling defendants to consider settling for purely commercial reasons, even when they have a viable defence.

12.22. Hence the enlightened ruler is heedful and the good general full of caution. This is the way to keep a country at peace and an army intact.

As my pal Chris Hall used to say whenever I got passionate about a case and started storming around the office as I developed a strategy, "take it easy." He was right, the same issues were still there in the morning when clarity had been restored by the lifting of the red mist. And dealing with those issues became not only simpler, but more fun because, as some say, my head was in the game, not focussed on whatever had been irritating me.

If we all worked on the as-
sumption that what is accepted as true is really true,
there would be little hope of
advance.

Orville Wright.
Aviator.

13. The Use of Spies

13. The Use of Spies

13.1. Sun Tzu said: raising a host of a hundred thousand men and marching them great distances entails heavy loss on the people and a drain on the resources of the State. The daily expenditure will amount to a thousand ounces of silver. There will be commotion at home and abroad and men will drop down exhausted on the highways. As many as seven hundred thousand families will be impeded in their labour.

Interestingly, well, not really, is that the costs described by Sun Tzu in this principle are very different from those he quotes earlier.

What is of much more relevance are the points that conducting an action at a distance is more expensive than when it is close to home, that there will be losses of men and equipment during a long campaign to causes other than actual battle and that long-running campaigns cause stresses at home as well as drive members of the team to behave out of character.

Ignore the practicalities of distance for the moment (although they do have their place). Where a case runs for several years, even partners change firms, junior staff more so. Entire firms merge or even disappear - even long established firms. Therefore there must always be a plan for change of personnel.

Long-running litigation can prove to be a drain on the firm's resources: surprisingly few firms adopt a policy of taking sufficient payment on account for at least three months' work of work and even then billing, in full, each month for work done and disbursements made. Therefore firms often run into cash-flow problems. This is especially so in state or insurance funded work.

If a case involves many late nights, especially if it involves trips abroad, staff begin to behave in ways that are not expected. Alliances, even liaisons form among the staff. And hard working, hot headed staff away from home do, sometimes, stray which causes stress in their personal lives, even if their spouse never finds out the reason.

Simply compensating staff with ever more money does not solve these problems.

And if there is a cost to family life, it spreads within the firm as fear begins to take hold that infidelity may be part of the corporate culture. That means that there is pressure at home upon staff not to work late or to make business trips and that has a direct impact on their ability to perform both at work and, potentially, at home.

13.2. Hostile armies may face each other for years, striving for the victory which is decided in a single day. This being so, to remain in ignorance of the enemy's condition simply because one grudges the outlay of a hundred ounces of silver in honours and emoluments, is the height of inhumanity.

Sun Tzu says that it is a duty of the well prepared general to seek information as to the state of the enemy's preparation and that it is false economy to be stingy when it comes to paying someone to provide intelligence as to the other party's state.

He lived in different times. While prosecutors can and do routinely pay bribes or give other benefits for information, it is in most countries illegal for a law firm or its clients to pay, directly or indirectly, any payment that is a bribe or to provide any other benefit. So, regardless of what Sun Tzu says, it is not acceptable unless the payer is acting for a government and records the payments as being paid to an informant.

13.3. One who acts thus is no leader of men, no present help to his sovereign, no master of victory.

Sun Tzu says someone who fails to make such a payment is failing in his duties. In today's climate, better that than end up in jail for corruption related offences.

13.4. Thus, what enables the wise sovereign and the good general to strike and conquer and achieve things beyond the reach of ordinary men, is foreknowledge.

That is true. The difficulty is how to obtain that knowledge legally.

13.5. Now this foreknowledge cannot be elicited from spirits;
it cannot be obtained inductively from experience, nor by any deductive calculation.

13.6. Knowledge of the enemy's dispositions can only be obtained from other men.

That is, then, the gathering of intelligence.

If one cannot pay someone to gather than intelligence and pass it on, how can it be obtained and applied?

Let's start with the idea that it must be gathered legally. By that, I mean that it must not be gathered illegally in order to form the basis of another investigation to disguise its origin and / or to find a way to make it admissible.

It is unacceptable for a lawyer, or anyone acting on his behalf to commit any offence whether it is in evidence gathering or otherwise.

Sun Tzu frequently talks of subterfuge: that's fine, so long as no line is crossed into illegal conduct.

It is also at least arguable that no line should be crossed into unlawful conduct: the very least a lawyer should expect if he does so is to be suspended from practice; he may find himself removed from the Roll or disbarred. "I did it for my client" is not an acceptable argument.

Putting an agent (not in the enforcement / security agency sense of the word) into a rival law firm to gather and pass on information exposes that agent to a range of threats from criminal prosecution through civil action to regulatory proceedings. For example, the Law Society of England and Wales has on many occasions issued notices that no law firm in the jurisdiction may employ a clerk who has been found to have acted in a way inconsistent with the profession, even though the clerk was not, in fact, admitted to practise.

Sun Tzu's ideas are, generally, unacceptable but there are some suggestions as to how it may be achieved and there are some interpretations that may (no guarantees) be just on the right side of what is permissible. Just. Only just.

13.7. Hence the use of spies, of whom there are five classes:

(1) Local spies;

(2) inward spies;

(3) converted spies;

(4) doomed spies;

(5) surviving spies.

13.8. When these five kinds of spy are all at work, none can discover the secret system. This is called "divine manipulation of the threads." It is the sovereign's most precious faculty.

This should be read as saying that one should gather any and all intelligence that might be legally and professionally obtained.

13.9. Having local spies means employing the services of the inhabitants of a district.

This is eminently doable without breaking any law or professional rules. For example, when conducting a case against an out of district litigator, there is nothing at all wrong with consulting his local rivals to enquire as to the way he conducts litigation. Pay them, then they are on retainer and cannot disclose to the one's opponent that the enquiries have been made.

Enquiries would also reveal if the firm has had a recruitment drive - and why: was it because they had had mass defections? Or because they took on a large new client but did not have the resources to handle the work?

13.10. Having inward spies, making use of officials of the enemy.

This, according to ancient commentators, means locating and making use of those who are disaffected, those who have no loyalty to an employer they have left, those who might have an axe to grind with a colleague in order to climb over him and, even "favourite concubines that are greedy for gold."

This latter is clearly not permitted as it involves bribery but there is an exception: if a person who was employed by one's opponent is engaged then the salary paid is not a bribe. It is important that no conflict of interest arises but remember that the conflict of interest relates to the client's affairs not to those of the firm he left. However, it is not acceptable to solicit or receive commercially sensitive information such as which clients one's opponent is pitching for. Nor it is acceptable to create a fake job for the purposes of funnelling payment to someone.

But there are other forms of "inward spies" which do not rely on inviting anyone to do anything to prejudice their own position nor involves any form of benefit. It is perfectly acceptable to build working relationships with clerks in the Courts. While they are precluded from giving information on cases, they can be very helpful in relation to securing hearings in a tight list or for something as simple as opening the Court doors a few minutes early to allow the issue of an emergency application to be heard at the start of the list. This is extremely valuable in the case of injunctions or freezing orders, for example.

My experience is that Court clerks are rarely treated well by lawyers and that simply affording them courtesy and dealing with them with a smile - and not being demanding for the sake of it or as some kind of power play - pays great dividends.

13.11. Having converted spies, getting hold of the enemy's spies and using them for our own purposes.

It is here that Sun Tzu and the commentators are most at odds with what we are able to do: they talk of "heavy bribes and liberal promises."

A converted spy is, in effect, a double agent who has been turned to act for the target.

But a spy may be converted without his knowing it, simply by identifying him (that's not the simple bit) and feeding him dis- or mis-information to carry back to his principal.

The most common way in which this happens is when someone from one's opposing team seeks to socialise but the conversation turns to either the case or the relationships, etc. within one's firm. Usually, the approach will be made to a junior member of the team, perhaps when bumping into them at Court on an unrelated matter, at a sporting or social event or in a favourite watering hole near both offices.

Therefore it is important that all junior members of the team are aware of this risk. A strategy should be developed for dealing with it, the most obvious one is that the junior team member should, as soon as the ploy begins, excuse himself and call the litigator for guidance on what to say.

13.12. Having doomed spies, doing certain things openly for purposes of deception and allowing our spies to know of them and report them to the enemy.

The plan is simple: give one's own team false information and then let them be, in effect, captured and questioned so as to put false information into the hands of the other side and lead them on some kind of wild goose chase.

For example, send a team member to a foreign city to interview someone who is apparently a witness but whose "evidence" is really planted mis- or dis-information.

Then let the team member, believing it to be true, talk freely (but not in such a way that breaches confidences) to someone from the other side, leading them to expend time and resources trying to identify the "witness" and to try to find evidence to neutralise his testimony.

In the incestuous world of lawyers within a city, it is not difficult to find one of one's own team who has a friend - or better still a drinking buddy - in the opposing team.

The reason that the team member is "doomed" is that he must be disciplined for the leak, even though it was a set up. To fail to do so would mean that the trick could never be used again. Obviously, the fact that it was a trick must never be disclosed.

13. Surviving spies, finally, are those who bring back news from the enemy's camp.

This is what one normally describes as a spy: someone who gathers intelligence and brings it back. He must act covertly but he, himself must be visible. He is the opposite of the doomed spy and exercises the opposing function.

But he is also the one who, unless careful, is most likely to cross the line into unprofessional or even illegal conduct, especially if that is a matter of soliciting privileged information.

Finally, a word of caution: bugging and similar activities are not acceptable although surveillance in a public place is, generally, fine and, in some cases (e.g. personal injury cases where video or photographs of a supposedly disabled plaintiff digging his garden) are standard fare.

In some jurisdictions, it is illegal to record a telephone conversation to which the person making the recording is a party without the other party's express consent. More often, it is unprofessional conduct for a lawyer to do the same.

13.14. Hence it is that which none in the whole army are more
intimate relations to be maintained than with spies. None should be more liberally rewarded. In no other business should greater secrecy be preserved.

This relates to the means of communication with spies: it should be direct between the team leader and the spy, not passed through any form of filter. Therefore a spy reports direct to the litigator having conduct of the case, not to his assistants. In part this is so that, if a professional boundary has been crossed, the litigator in charge can ensure that the intelligence obtained does not find its way to the team and therefore colour their conduct of the case.

13.15. Spies cannot be usefully employed without a certain intuitive sagacity.

Spies are, by definition devious. Therefore when engaging someone to gather intelligence, it is vital to be assured of his integrity.

That is, of course, a contradiction: he is being hired for his ability to use tricks and subterfuge which are, of course, acts of dishonesty and dubious morality.

13.16. They cannot be properly managed without benevolence and straightforwardness.

Sun Tzu says that in order to ensure loyalty, those who are put into a position where they are acting out a lie, must be well treated. Even though they are not part of the team and most of the team will never know of their existence, they must be made to feel welcome and cared for by those that engage them. Of course, money is part of that but respect is even more important. And part of that respect is to be "straightforward" with them which, in this context means being clear as to their objectives and being honest. It does not, of course, mean taking them into one's full confidence.

13.17. Without subtle ingenuity of mind, one cannot make certain of the truth of their reports.

There is, of course, the risk that one's own spies might be turned or fed mis- or dis-information. Or they might be so anxious to please that the information they report is tainted in order to produce the result that the spy thinks you want to receive. For example, the supposed intelligence relating to weapons of mass destruction in Iraq.

Therefore the intelligence gathered must be tested before it is acted upon.

13.18. Be subtle! Be subtle! And use your spies for every kind of business.

Sun Tzu says to make liberal use of intelligence gathering which, in a somewhat convenient fashion, links back to the beginning of this work: do not commence litigation until you have all the facts to hand and have formed an overall strategy.

13.19. If a secret piece of news is divulged by a spy before the time is ripe, he must be put to death together with the man to whom the secret was told.

A spy is not only a gatherer of secrets, he is the keeper of them, too. If he breaks that seal, then he and any person to whom the secret was revealed must be dealt with. That does not, include, obviously Sun Tzu's solution of killing them both.

13.20. Whether the object be to crush an army, to storm a city or to assassinate an individual, it is always necessary to begin by finding out the names of the attendants, the aides-de-camp and door-keepers and sentries of the general in command. Our spies must be commissioned to ascertain these.

The examples described by Sun Tzu of tasks that spies should be set are exactly transferable to litigation. It is essential to the idea that one should always know one's enemy and his strengths and weaknesses.

13.21. The enemy's spies who have come to spy on us must be sought out, tempted with bribes, led away and comfortably housed. Thus they will become converted spies and available for our service.

Admitting one's opponent to one's office might seem a strange thing to do but it is common in the stage of discovery known as "inspection."

I used to hold inspections in an off-site conference room rented for as long as required. In that way, my opponents were not wandering around my office under the guise of finding the toilets, getting a cup of coffee or trying to locate the front door so they could go for lunch.

Once, in the offices of a very large London law firm, it amused me to see how far around the office I could get: it was easy because there were frequent doors with key-card slots but many of the locks were turned off and of those that were not, I simply hung around chatting to someone in a cubicle nearby and tagged along behind someone who used a card to open the door.

I was not on a spying mission and I did it for no reason except my own fun. I had finished a meeting and the partner I saw said he had a phone call to make and was I able to find my own way out. What was interesting to me was that no one challenged me. The firm's size gave me total anonymity and simply tripping over and bumping into a cubicle wall gave me a simple conversation starter to let me hang around near a door. And no, I'm not going to tell you which Golden Circle firm it was.

Even now, just because I can, I almost always gain access to buildings that require some form of identification by the production of something other (and of much lower security and more readily forged although I do not use forged documents) than that which they desk has been ordered to obtain.

Therefore, rather than Sun Tzu's idea that the enemy's spies might be turned, I would argue that of much greater importance is security and to prevent the other side gaining access to anywhere that any form of information, even as to the apparent working relationships between members of the team, might be gleaned.

13.22. It is through the information brought by the converted spy that we are able to acquire and employ local and inward spies.

13.23. It is owing to his information, again, that we can cause the doomed spy to carry false tidings to the enemy.

13.24. Lastly, it is by his information that the surviving spy can be used on appointed occasions.

13.25. The end and aim of spying in all its five varieties is knowledge of the enemy; and this knowledge can only be derived, in the first instance, from the converted spy. Hence it is essential that the converted spy be treated with the utmost liberality.

It is instructive that Sun Tzu believes that the best intelligence comes from within the opposing camp.

So let's consider one last example, not from the opposing team but from the opposing client.

Can we identify and secure the services of a whistle-blower who is prepared to give evidence against his employer.

Note that it is illegal to pay a whistle-blower for his evidence although in some countries statutory provisions allow for compensation from public funds, especially where a penalty is applied. Whistleblowers generally do very badly: Nelson Piquet Jr, a driver for the Renault F1 team, blew the whistle on an illegal strategy to ensure that his team leader, Fernando Alonso, won the Singapore Grand Prix. Alonso moved to Ferrari. Nelson Piquet Jr is now racing pickups in the USA.

Finally, a reminder: it is illegal to try to find out what is happening in jury room. So trying to recruit a juror to give updates on the way the jury is moving is not permitted, even in a social environment.

13.26. Of old, the rise of the Yin dynasty was due to I Chih who had served under the Hsia. Likewise, the rise of the Chou dynasty was due to Lu Ya who had served under the Shang Dynasty.

Basically, Sun Tzu is storytelling with a bullet point analysis of the tale of converted spies.

13.27. Hence it is only the enlightened ruler and the wise general who will use the highest intelligence of the army for purposes of spying and thereby they achieve great results. Spies are a most important element in war, because on them depends an army's ability to move.

And so, Sun Tzu wraps up with the point we started with. Litigation is not bluff and bluster, although they have their place. Everything, right from the drafting of the Letter Before Action, to the closing argument at the end of a final appeal must be based upon a full and detailed analysis of all relevant facts, opinion and law.

Because, both in opening and in conclusion, it has to be said again: litigation is a blood sport. It is also an intellectual challenge of the highest order and, always, a matter of honour.

"There's nothing to winning, really.

That is, if you happen to be blessed with a keen eye, an agile mind...

and no scruples whatsoever."

Alfred Hitchcock

Postscript

Among the lessons banged home in this book there are several that are, perhaps, more important than any others.

First: prepare fully, even if you think you've got an easily won case

Secondly, be ruthless where necessary and magnanimous where appropriate

Third, never over-complicate things. You and the arbiters of fact will become tired and confused

Fourthly, be aware of your own and your opponent's limitations and circumstances and how changes can affect your strategy

Fifth, pay great attention to detail, including not only the detail put in front of you but also the detail that's missing. About which: now you've read this whole book, what is not in it?

Answer overleaf

What isn't in this book?

Sun Tzu did not say

"keep your friends close and
your enemies closer."

*Contact Nigel Morris-Cotterill at
www.antimoneylaundering.net*

Printed in Great Britain
by Amazon.co.uk, Ltd.,
Marston Gate.